Weighing Goods

Working Guide

WEIGHING GOODS

Equality, Uncertainty and Time

John Broome

Basil Blackwell

Copyright © John Broome 1991, 1995

First published 1991
First published in paperback 1995

Blackwell Publishers Ltd
108 Cowley Road, Oxford OX4 1JF, UK

Blackwell Publishers Inc.
238 Main Street
Cambridge, Massachusetts 02142, USA

British Library Cataloguing in Publication Data

A CIP catalogue record for this book is available from the British Library.

Library of Congress Cataloging in Publication Data

Broome, John.
  Weighing goods/John Broome.
    p.   cm.—(Economics and philosophy)
  Includes bibliographical references and index.
  ISBN 0–631–17199–1 (Hbk) — ISBN 0–631–19972–1 (Pbk)
  1. Economics—Moral and ethical aspects.   I. Title.   II. Series:
    Economics and philosophy (Cambridge, Mass.)
HB72.B76   1991
330′.01—dc20   90–26662   CIP

Typeset by John Broome using WordPerfect, DrawPerfect and PostScript.
Photosetting by the University of Bristol Printing Unit.
Printed in Great Britain by T. J. Press Ltd, Padstow, Cornwall.

This book is printed on acid-free paper.

Contents

Preface

This is a book about ethics, which uses some of the methods of economics. I think it is already widely recognized that formal methods derived from economics can contribute to ethics. This book is concerned with some features of the structure of good, and in that area I believe these methods are especially fruitful.

Not only do many of my methods come from economics, but many of my conclusions have economic applications, too. I shall, for instance, be investigating the value of equality. I hope, therefore, that this book may attract readers from both economics and philosophy. Inevitably, each group will encounter some difficulties. For philosophers, many of the techniques may be unfamiliar, and perhaps in places daunting. I ask them to be patient with the symbols. Nowhere in the entire book is there any mathematics beyond elementary algebra, and I have done my best to explain the algebraic arguments carefully. (I have twice mentioned logarithms, but only in examples that may be skipped.) The Appendix to Chapter 4 and Section 10.1 may also be skipped. They contain informal proofs, where some readers may find the elementary algebra clusters too densely on the page.

Economists, on the other hand, will find much of the algebra tediously slow. I ask them to be patient too. What, I think, they may find difficult to understand is my focus on good rather than preferences. My techniques come from utility theory, which was developed for preferences, but I have redirected them towards the structure of good. Even to separate a person's good from her preferences will make many economists uneasy; it will suggest to them a worrying paternalism. Chapter 7, particularly Section 7.3, is addressed to this concern. It explains why my argument cannot be built around preferences. I hope these economists will be willing to recognize that there is such a thing as a person's good, which may or may not be determined by her preferences. In working with good rather than preferences I am being more general. I am allowing for cases where good is determined by preferences, and also for cases, which do exist, where it is not. It is not paternalistic simply to speak of a person's good.

This book began life as a long paper I wrote while I was a Visiting Fellow at All Souls College, Oxford, in 1982–83. I thank the college for its kind hospitality, and also the Social Science Research Council, which supported me for that year. I developed various parts of the argument in articles during the succeeding years. They began to come together as a book during a course of seminars I gave at Princeton University in 1988. I am grateful to Princeton for this opportunity. Finally, the Economics Department at Bristol University, where I work, allowed me a term of study leave in 1989 to complete the writing. I am very grateful to the members of the department.

Over the years, I have been very fortunate in the many valuable comments I have received on parts of the book, and on earlier versions of the arguments. I am sure I have forgotten some of the people who have helped me, and to them I offer both apologies and thanks. Those I particularly remember include Jonathan Dancy, Nicholas Denyer, Peter Hammond, Sally Haslanger, Susan Hurley, Daniel Hausman, Donald Hubin, Richard Jeffrey, Douglas MacLean, Amartya Sen, John Skorupski, and Brian Skyrms. My thanks to all of them. I want to express my especial gratitude to John Harsanyi, Shelly Kagan, James Mirrlees, Adam Morton, Derek Parfit and Larry Temkin for the exceptionally helpful and detailed comments I received from them on sections of the book. Besides all these, Duncan Foley, Alan Hamlin, Frank Jackson, Philip Pettit and Paul Seabright were all generous enough to read drafts of the entire book. I am sure the finished product has benefited greatly from their excellent advice. I am very grateful to them.

Parts of Chapter 1 also appear in my contribution to *Foundations of Decision Theory: Issues and Advances*, edited by Michael Bacharach and Susan Hurley and published by Blackwell in 1991. Parts of Chapter 11 also appear in my contribution to *Interpersonal Comparisons of Well-Being*, edited by Jon Elster and John Roemer and published by Cambridge University Press in 1991.

I should also like to acknowledge the help of WordPerfect UK.

Chapter 1

Introduction I:
The Structure of Good

One part of ethics is concerned with good. This book is about that part. Specifically, it is about the structure of good.

More exactly, it is about betterness. Some things are better than others, so that a relation of betterness holds between them. This book is about the structure of this relation. Though I shall use the word 'good' as well as 'better', I am not referring to some metaphysically mysterious entity, but only to the homely matter of which things are better or worse than others.

I shall be particularly concerned with just one aspect of the structure of good. Good occurs, as I shall put it, at different 'locations'. For instance, good comes to different people: there is your good and my good, and the publisher's good. People, then, are locations for good. They constitute one 'dimension' of locations, as I shall say. Good comes at different times, too, so times are locations for good, and constitute a second dimension. The fact of uncertainty gives us a third dimension. We do not know whether our behaviour will cause temperatures to rise globally by one degree Celsius, or two, or five. Each of these possibilities is an example of a 'state of nature'. What happens in one state of nature will be good to some degree, and may be better or worse than what happens in another. So we can think of states of nature as locations of good, forming a third dimension. This book investigates how good occurring at different locations goes together to make up overall good. How is good aggregated? When aggregated across the dimension of people, for instance, is overall good simply the total of people's good, so that the better of two societies is always the one with the larger total? Or alternatively, might a society with a smaller total of good, evenly distributed across the population,

1

sometimes be better than a less equal society with a larger total? I shall be concerned with questions like this.

The methods of economics can help with this project in ethics. I shall be making use of some formal theorems from economics and decision theory. In their original home, these theorems were intended to say something about the structure of preferences. But they can be redirected towards the structure of good instead. Specifically, they link together the different dimensions of good. For instance, they link the way good is aggregated across people with the way it is aggregated across states of nature. So they make a connection between the value of equality and the value of avoiding risk. This book explores connections of this sort.

But before coming to my more detailed argument, I need to talk generally about the idea of the structure of good. Moral philosophy these days is more often centred on rationality rather than good, so my interest in good needs explaining. That is the purpose of this first introductory chapter.

According to some ethical theories, the concern for good amounts to the whole of ethics, not just a part. How we should live our lives, these theories say, and how we should act on each particular occasion, are determined entirely by the pursuit of good. Once we know what is good, or more exactly what is better than what, we shall know the right way to live and the right way to act. Let us call a theory that says this *teleological*. A *nonteleological* ethical theory, on the other hand, gives a role in ethics to other consider-ations besides good. Most nonteleological theories, nevertheless, give some role to good too.[1] So this book will have something to contribute to nonteleological theories too.

But what exactly is this distinction I am drawing when I pick out one part of ethics as concerned with good or betterness? What really distinguishes an ethical theory concerned only with good from any other ethical theory? How, indeed, could an ethical theory be concerned with anything other than good? Is not what an ethical theory is concerned with necessarily what the theory considers good? If a theory says we should live in such-and-such a way, or act in such-and-such a way, does that not mean it considers these ways of living and acting to be good? John Rawls defined an ethical theory as teleological if 'the good is defined independently from the right, and then the right is defined as that which maximizes the good'.[2] This is much the same as the definition I gave. But what distinction is Rawls making? If a theory claims that such-and-such is the right way to live or act, is it not also implying that it is a good way to live or act?

Evidently some work is needed to draw a line between the part of ethics that is concerned with good and other parts. That is the first object of this chapter. This book leaves the other parts aside, and I want first to separate them out clearly. Since teleology is concerned only with good, and with all of good, the boundaries of teleology coincide with the boundaries of good. So I shall proceed by asking what, exactly, distinguishes teleological from nonteleological ethics. This is a useful method for delimiting the concept of good. But it does not mean that the arguments of this book are relevant to teleologists only. As I say, good is important in nonteleological ethics too.

To start with, Section 1.1 describes two ways of making the distinction between teleological and nonteleological ethics, and explains why I think they are unsatisfactory. Sections 1.2 and 1.3 then describe the way I favour. Section 1.4 discusses what type of priority the concept of good has in ethics.

1.1 Acts versus consequences, and agent relativity

How, then, are we to draw the line between teleological and nonteleological ethics? The contrast between good and right suggests one answer. Rightness is commonly thought of as a property of acts, and goodness as a property of states of affairs. So we might make the distinction like this: teleological ethics first evaluates states of affairs, and then determines the value of an act from the value of the state of affairs it leads to – of its consequences, that is; nonteleological ethics, on the other hand, assigns intrinsic value to some acts, independently of their consequences. For instance, the view that breaking a promise is wrong in itself, quite apart from its consequences, would be nonteleological.

The idea is, then, that teleology insists acts are to be valued by their consequences alone, and that this is how it should be distinguished from other theories. This is the source of the term 'consequentialism'. 'Consequentialism' is these days used more often than 'teleology', but it means the same, except that some authors narrow its meaning in a way I shall be explaining. I prefer the older term for two reasons that will soon appear.[3]

However, this way of making the distinction between teleological and nonteleological ethics turns out to fail. It relies on a division between an act and its consequences that cannot be maintained. It is not clear where an act leaves off and its consequences begin. If you perform an act, one consequence will be that you have performed it. If you break a promise, one consequence will be that you have broken a promise, and the wrongness of promise breaking can be taken as a bad feature of this consequence. Teleology, in evaluating the consequences of promise breaking, can therefore take account of the wrongness of promise breaking itself. In this way, the intrinsic values of acts can be absorbed into teleology.

This fact is generally recognized. In all the recent debate about teleology, nothing has been made to depend on separating the value of an act from the value of its consequences. The fact that an act has been done is generally counted amongst the consequences of that act, and the intrinsic value of an act is counted as a teleological consideration in the act's favour. Samuel Scheffler, for instance, says:

> When I speak of the act-consequentialist as requiring agents to produce the best overall outcomes or states of affairs, I do not mean that the act-consequentialist divides what happens into the act and the outcome, and evaluates only the latter with his overall ranking principle. Rather, the act itself is initially evaluated as part of the overall outcome or state of affairs. The act-consequentialist first ranks overall outcomes, which are understood, in this broad way, to include the acts necessary to produce them, and then directs the agent to produce the best available outcome so construed.[4]

I shall follow this practice. I shall not try to distinguish between the value of an act and the value of its consequences. I shall apply the notion of goodness to acts as well as to their consequences, and identify the goodness of an act with the goodness of its consequences. I shall take both to include any intrinsic value the act may have, as well as any good that may result from the act. Teleological ethics, then, in its pursuit of good, will take account of the intrinsic values of acts.

This is one reason I find the term 'consequentialism' unsatisfactory: whatever distinguishes teleological from nonteleological ethics, it is not that the former values only consequences, whereas the latter allows acts to possess intrinsic value.

Now teleology is interpreted so widely, it may seem to leave no room for a nonteleological ethics. Certainly, many values that have traditionally been classed as nonteleological can be brought under the umbrella of teleology taken this way. Of course, it means recognizing many sorts of good and bad besides the sorts recognized by the most traditional teleological theories – particularly by traditional utilitarianism. Breaking a promise must be taken as a bad thing in itself, quite apart from what anyone feels about it, and apart from the happiness, pleasure or pain that may result. Another example: the value of fairness can be recognized by teleology, provided unfairness is taken as a bad thing in itself, whether or not it makes the victim unhappy.[5]

Nevertheless, there are views that are incompatible with even this widely conceived teleology. A famous example is this.[6] Suppose that by breaking a promise I can bring it about that in the future five promises are kept that otherwise would have been broken. Some people would think I ought to keep my promise nevertheless, unless the circumstances are exceptional. This opinion, however, seems inconsistent with teleology. If breaking promises is bad, then the breaking of five promises must be worse than the breaking of one. Other things being equal, then, keeping my promise will have worse consequences than breaking it, even taking account of the intrinsic badness of promise breaking. So teleology, it seems, must be in favour of breaking it.

How might one defend the view that I ought to keep my promise even at the expense of five broken promises? Here is one defence. In this moral dilemma, goes the defence, it is wrong for me to take up a neutral, impersonal point of view, from which everybody's promise keeping counts the same. My own special position in the affair makes a difference to what I ought to do. Keeping *my* promise has a special value for *me*. It may count for me more than the keeping of five promises by other people. My valuations should be 'agent relative', as it is generally put. And why should that be? One possible answer is that I have a greater responsibility for my own acts than I do for the acts of other people, even if those acts are brought about by me.[7] In this case, the five people who break their promises bear the responsibility for this wrongdoing of theirs more than I do, even though it is brought about by my act of promise keeping.

A lesson commonly drawn from this example and others like it is that nonteleological ethics must be agent relative in some way: if it is right for me sometimes to do something that will not have the best possible consequences, that must be because of my particular position as an agent. Conversely, agent neutrality is often included within the *definition* of consequentialism.[8] Consequentialism has come to be distinguished by agent neutrality, and nonconsequentialism by agent relativity. Most of the recent discussion of consequentialism has really been a discussion of agent neutrality.[9]

But I think the debate between agent relativity and agent

neutrality has distracted attention from other important questions. The issue between teleological and nonteleological ethics should be separated from the issue between agent-neutral and agent-relative ethics.[10] It would be a mistake, therefore, to tie teleology down to agent neutrality. This is my second reason for using the term 'teleology' instead of 'consequentialism': to escape from the definition of consequentialism as agent neutral. There is a more natural way of characterizing teleological ethics, which allows for nonteleological theories that are agent neutral,[11] and also teleological theories that are agent relative.[12]

1.2 The working of ethical considerations

When there is a decision to be made, there will often be ethical considerations on both sides. Against breaking my promise in the example is that this would be an intrinsically wrong act. In favour is that it will prevent five wrongs of promise breaking. The considerations must somehow come together to determine which act is right, all things considered. How do they do that? Teleological and nonteleological theories, as I prefer to distinguish them, give different answers to this question.

The answer of teleology is that each consideration contributes to the goodness or badness of the alternative acts. All the considerations together determine how good or bad the acts are. And which act is right is determined by the goodness of the alternatives. For instance, teleology takes the intrinsic wrongness of breaking a promise to be a bad feature of the act of promise breaking, which goes together with other good and bad features to determine the overall goodness of the act. The nonteleological answer, on the other hand, is that ethical considerations do not always work in this particular way. They may determine what ought to be done, not through determining the goodness of acts, but in some other way.

For the moment, I shall use this difference to define teleology informally: a teleological theory is one in which the rightness of acts is determined by their goodness. I shall tighten up the definition in Section 1.3.

A teleological theory will have to specify exactly how goodness determines rightness; it will have to supply a mapping from goodness to rightness. The standard sort of teleology is *maximizing*. The main elements of a maximizing mapping are these. If one act, out of those available, is better than the others, then that act ought to be done; only that act is right, and the others are wrong.

If several acts are equally good, and all of them better than any of the others available, then one of them ought to be done and it does not matter which. Any other act is wrong. *Satisficing* teleology has a different mapping.[13] It says that any action is permissible – not wrong – provided it is 'good enough', even if a better act is available. So when Rawls says that in teleology 'the right is defined as that which maximizes the good',[14] he is being a little too specific. He is referring to standard teleology only. My formula, that in teleology goodness determines rightness, is intended to be more general. But if we set aside nonstandard teleology including satisficing theory, Rawls's formula is correct. In standard teleology, the right act is the best.

The metaphor of *weighing* often fits teleology. Each consideration for or against an act is a good or bad feature of the act. The act's overall goodness is determined by putting together the goodness and badness of these features. This process is often analogous to weighing: good and bad features are weighed against each other.

Not all teleological judgement need be much like weighing, though. It is consistent with teleology to think that some considerations dominate others lexically. You might think, for instance, that any unjust act is worse than any just one, whatever other features the acts possess. There is nothing in literal weighing analogous to this, but your view is teleological because it is about the badness of acts.

You might also think that some considerations are incommensurable with others in a different way. Suppose some proposed social policy will make a community more affluent, but at a cost in social conflict. There is an alternative policy that will better promote harmony, but lead to less affluence. You might think that the benefits of these policies cannot be weighed against each other. You might think that neither policy is definitely better than the other, but that they are not equally good either. If they were equally good, you would be indifferent about which was chosen, but actually you think it matters very much. Your view is teleological. It takes the ethical considerations to be good or bad features of the alternative policies: affluence is good and so is harmony. But it supposes that some sorts of good cannot be weighed against others. Now, incommensurability may be a problem for teleology.[15] In order to accommodate it, teleology will have to show how its mapping from goodness to rightness can cover cases like the one I described, where none of the alternative acts is better than the others, and yet the acts are not equally good either. Are all of these acts permissible, say? If so, what makes the case different from one where they are simply all equally good? But however teleology copes with them, goods that cannot be weighed against each other seem a genuine possibility. They cannot be ruled out at the start.

Furthermore, there may be complicated interactions amongst considerations, which also strain the metaphor of weighing. Chapter 2 contains some examples. In sum, weighing is typical but not definitive of teleology. This book concentrates on weighing, though, and examines in detail one aspect of it.

On page 5, I mentioned one opinion about the promising example: that I ought to keep my promise because my promise breaking counts more for me than other people's. This is an agent-relative opinion. It is also teleological, as I have now defined teleology. It treats the wrongness of promise breaking as a bad feature of an act. It weighs the badness of my promise breaking against the badness of other people's, to determine the overall badness of the alternative acts. For me, my promise breaking weighs more than other people's. In the end, for me, breaking my promise comes out worse overall. Therefore I ought not to do it. This is a teleological argument – an agent-relative one.

One might doubt the validity of this argument, though. It claims that breaking my promise is worse *for me* than keeping it, and one might doubt that such a claim makes good sense. Certainly, there is one clear sense it could have. It could mean that breaking my promise is against my interest: that it would make me less well off than I would otherwise have been. But that is not what it is supposed to mean in the argument. The good in question is not my private wellbeing, and the argument is not appealing to my own self-interest. The good is general good, not mine; but general good evaluated from my own special position as an agent. And one might doubt that good can really be agent relative in this way. Agent-relative teleology appeals to agent-relative good, and one might be dubious of such a concept.

Not many authors have been willing to adopt explicitly an agent-relative concept of good; Amartya Sen is an exception.[16] But anyone who uses an argument of the form I described is implicitly committed to one. On page 13 I shall specify more exactly what I mean by this form.

Now an example of a nonteleological opinion. It, too, is in favour of my keeping my promise in the example, but for a different reason. It also takes breaking a promise to be intrinsically wrong. But it does not treat this intrinsic wrongness as a consideration to be weighed against others in determining the overall goodness of the alternative acts. Instead, the wrongness of promise breaking simply determines that I ought not to do it. It is what Robert Nozick calls a 'side constraint'.[17] So the argument goes directly to what I ought or ought not to do, without first estimating the goodness of the alternatives.

I do not insist that the ethics of side constraints cannot, in the end, be reduced to a form of teleology. Perhaps it can, and Section 1.3 specifies exactly what would be required to make the reduction successful. But certainly, on the face of it, and as Nozick presents it, it is expressly nonteleological according to my definition. Compare, for instance, the view that promise keeping is a side constraint with the view that promise keeping is a good that dominates others lexically. The latter says that, whenever promise keeping is in conflict with any other consideration, promise keeping wins. This view is teleological. It says that breaking a promise is a very, very bad thing, so bad that its badness outweighs all other badness. In the example, it would imply that I ought to *break* my promise. Doing so will lead to only one instance of the great bad of promise breaking, whereas keeping the promise will lead to five. The side-constraint view, on the other hand, does not necessarily insist that promise breaking is very bad. It says only, and simply, that I ought not to do it.

Compare the side-constraint view, too, with the agent-relative teleological view that my promise keeping is a good that, for me, dominates others lexically. Imagine the five other promises in the example are actually mine: by breaking a promise now I can bring it about that I shall, in the future, keep five promises that otherwise I would have broken. Suppose, say, that if I break a promise now, the experience of guilt at my present tender age will stiffen my resolve in future life. In this case, the agent-relative teleological view would imply that I should break my promise now, since that would lead to five of my promise keepings instead of one. Yet a thoroughgoing side-constraint view about promises would say I ought to keep my present promise.

It is commonly believed that the ethics of side constraints is necessarily agent relative. But this is not so. Consider the view that whenever a miner is in mortal danger trapped in a mine, all available resources should be devoted to rescuing him. This will reduce the resources devoted to safety measures in mines, and so lead to the deaths of more miners in the future. Nevertheless, it is what ought to be done. This is a side-constraint view. But it is agent neutral. It says that all of us, equally, should contribute to saving the miner as far as we can.

Since side-constraint theory is an important example of nonteleological ethics, the popular belief that it is necessarily agent relative helps to sustain the popular association between nonteleological ethics and agent-relative ethics. But what makes side-constraint theory nonteleological is not agent relativity. It is the way it takes ethical considerations to work: side constraints determine what ought or ought not to be done directly, and not by determining goodness.

However, side-constraint theory might, perhaps, be called *moment* relative. Take the mining example. (The point is plausible in the promising example too.) At present we have a reason to rescue the miner who is now trapped, and this reason fully determines what we should do now. When the next miner is trapped, we shall then have a reason to rescue him. That reason will fully determine what we should do then. But at present it does not count at all; it gives us no reason to save resources for the future rescue. The reason, then, applies at one time but not at another. So it might be called a moment-relative reason.

It even seems possible to me that, with some work, side-constraint theory might be reduced to a moment-relative teleology, in which certain present reasons dominate other reasons lexically. Perhaps this is a way it might be brought within the fold of teleology. But at least until the work has been done, side-constraint theory stands as an example of nonteleological ethics that is not necessarily agent relative. I shall mention another example on page 15, and another later in the book, on page 159.

1.3 Teleological structure

I defined teleology as the theory that rightness is determined by goodness. In standard teleology, the right act is the best.

But, once again, the question arises: how does this simple definition exclude anything? How could any ethical theory deny that, when faced with a choice between acts, you should choose the best? I have already offered the ethics of side constraints as an example of a nonteleological theory, on the grounds that it does not work by assessing the goodness of the alternative acts. But whatever a theory says about the working of ethical considerations, once it has decided which act ought to be done, one might think there is nothing to stop it just calling this act the best. And surely this would be a very natural thing to do. So any theory could be made teleological in arrears.

Now, I did say that side-constraint theory might perhaps be reducible to teleology. But it would at least take some work, and it is certainly not true that any theory is automatically teleological according to the definition. That rightness is determined by goodness is genuinely a constraint on teleology. It means that teleology is constrained by the *structure of good*, as I shall put it. A teleological theory implies that between acts there is a *betterness relation*:

__ is at least as good as __

(where the blanks are to be filled in with acts), and that this relation determines the rightness of acts. A betterness relation necessarily has a particular structure. When I speak of the structure of good, I mean more exactly the structure of this relation.

I can immediately say one thing about this structure: it is an *ordering*. Acts are ordered by their goodness. That is to say, the relation is transitive and reflexive. For the betterness relation to be transitive means that, for any acts *A*, *B* and *C*, if *A* is at least as good as *B*, and *B* at least as good as *C*, then *A* is at least as good as *C*. For it to be reflexive means that for any act *A*, *A* is at least as good as *A*. These are both necessary truths.

Indeed, I take them to be truths of logic. The schema

__ is at least as *F* as __

denotes a transitive and reflexive relation, when the name of any property is substituted for '*F*'. Things are ordered by their *F*ness.[18] The best way to make this clear is to examine an apparent counterexample. The relation

__ is at least as westerly as __

seems at first to be intransitive, because the corresponding strict comparative relation

__ is more westerly than __

seems to be intransitive. As you become more and more westerly, surely, you end up not westerly at all but easterly. But precisely what property is 'more westerly than' meant to be the comparative of? It might be the property of being to the west of somewhere else. In that case every place on earth has it equally, and nowhere on earth is more westerly than anywhere else. Alternatively, it might be some property of local westerliness, such as westerliness in Ireland. The comparative relation of local westerliness, however, is plainly transitive; think about the relation of being more westerly in Ireland. Or perhaps it might be the property of being to the west of here (Bath, that is). Does this property have an intransitive comparative? Boston is more to the west of Bath than Dublin is, and Papeete more than Boston is. Therefore, Papeete is more to the west of Bath than Dublin is. Is Sydney more to the west of Bath than Papeete is? We have a decision to make about this. We might decide that, being to the east of Bath, Sydney is not to the west of Bath at all. It is not, therefore, more to the west of Bath than Papeete is. No intransitivity here. Or we might decide that Sydney is indeed to the west of Bath, and more so than Papeete. We shall presumably draw the conclusion, eventually, that London is more to the west of Bath than Dublin is. Bath, presumably, is not to the west of Bath, and therefore not more to the west of Bath than London is. No intransitivity here either. Possibly we might decide that Bath *is* to the west of Bath. If we do, we shall be forced to conclude that everywhere on earth is equally as much to the west of Bath as everywhere else, and that I was wrong to say Boston is more to the west of Bath than Dublin is. This discussion shows that, whatever decisions we make, we shall always be guided by logic to preserve the transitivity of the comparative.

Strictly, a transitive and reflexive relation is only a *partial* ordering, or more strictly still a *quasi*-ordering.[19] An ordering strictly needs also to be *complete*. For the betterness relation to be complete would mean that, for any acts A and B, either A is at least as good as B, or B at least as good as A. That is to say, of any pair of alternatives, one is better than the other, or the other than the one, or the two are equally good. But I see no reason to assume the betterness relation is complete; there may be different goods that are incommensurable. I mentioned an example on page 7. In this chapter I shall use the term 'ordering' loosely. When I say the betterness relation is an ordering, I do not mean to imply it is complete. I mean only that it is transitive and reflexive.

Teleological ethics, then, says there is an ordering of acts that determines the acts' rightness. And this is actually enough to *define* teleological ethics. Any ethical theory with this implication is teleological. I am defining teleology, then, by its *structure*.

Standard teleology has a *maximizing structure*: it says there is an ordering of acts such that, if one act out of those available comes higher in the ordering than the others, then that act ought to be done. My more general formula – that teleology says there is an ordering of acts that determines their rightness – is intended to allow for nonstandard theories such as satisficing. If a theory satisfies this condition, let us say it has a *teleological structure*.

Up to now, I have been defining teleology as the view that the rightness of acts is determined by their goodness. I am not now changing this definition; I am spelling out what it means. The reference to 'goodness' in the original definition simply indicates that rightness is determined by an ordering. It does not imply that teleology is defined in terms of a prior notion of good. Each teleological theory determines its own notion of good, constrained by the fact that betterness has to be an ordering. Each implies the existence of an ordering that determines rightness. The ordering is what the theory takes to be the betterness relation.* It defines the theory's notion of good. Any ethical theory with a maximizing structure is teleological, and what it aims to maximize is what it takes to be good.

Look back to one of the opinions I mentioned about the promising example: the opinion that my promise breaking outweighs, for me, the promise breaking of others. This is agent relative. But I described it on page 8 as teleological also, because it takes the ethical consideration that breaking a promise is wrong to work in a particular way. It works by helping to determine the relative goodness of my alternative acts. Now I can say more precisely what this means. It is a matter of structure. It means that this ethical consideration goes, with others, to determine an ordering of the alternatives, which in turn determines what I ought to do. The ordering is a betterness relation, and it defines a notion of good. In this case, it will be an agent-relative notion. I said one might be dubious about agent-relative goodness. But to object to it, one would have to object to the whole ethical theory. The objection cannot simply be that one does not like to use the term 'good' in an agent-relative way. Any agent-relative theory with a teleological structure implies an agent-relative good.

---

* This is not perfectly accurate. A teleological theory implies, actually, that there are *two* orderings that determine the rightness of acts, one the exact opposite of the other. One is the theory's betterness relation, the other its worseness relation.

I have by now departed from Rawls's way of characterizing teleology. Rawls wishes to distinguish a moral theory as teleological, not simply by the structure of the judgements it makes, but also partly by the ground of its judgements. Even if a theory says the right act is the best, he would not count it as teleological unless it also says that this act is right *because* it is the best. As he puts it, teleology gives good priority over right. But once we have picked out theories that say the right act is the best, I doubt if there is really this extra distinction to be made. Suppose a theory identifies a particular act as right on the basis of some principles. And suppose these principles are such as to determine an ordering of acts, so that the right act may fairly be called the best according to the principles. How would we then decide whether or not the theory says the right act is right *because* it is best? Ultimately what makes it right is the principles. But these principles determine the goodness of acts as well as their rightness, and who is to say whether or not they determine rightness directly or by means of their determination of goodness? If someone says, 'The right act is right because it is the best according to the principles', surely it would be odd to disagree.

When it comes down to it, to make his distinction workable Rawls has to rely on a prior intuition about what principles are matters of right rather than good. He himself thinks of good as an impersonal or suprapersonal object for morality, so that the particular duties we owe to individuals count as principles of right. Here is an example of Rawls's intuition at work:

> If the distribution of goods is . . . counted as a good . . ., and the theory directs us to produce the most good (including the good of distribution among others), we no longer have a teleological view in the classical sense. The problem of distribution falls under the concept of right as one intuitively understands it, and so the theory lacks an independent definition of good.[20]

But this sort of intuition does not seem to me secure enough to found a definition on. I, for one, have no intuitive grasp of why the problem of distribution should fall under the concept of right. In Chapter 9 I shall be examining several alternative ways of treating equality of distribution as a good.[21] Furthermore, Will Kymlicka points out that even utilitarianism can be derived in a natural fashion from something Rawls would count as a principle of right: that each person's interest be given equal respect.[22] So on Rawls's intuitive distinction, utilitarianism, arrived at this way, would come out nonteleological. But if it has this result, the distinction is pointless, and certainly not what Rawls has in mind. I think the only way to make a clear distinction is by structure, as I have made it.

That the betterness relation is an ordering is a serious constraint on teleological ethics. I said earlier that it may be possible to recast side-constraint theory as a moment-relative lexical teleology. We can now see what this job would entail. The theory must be given a transitive structure. I do not know whether that would be possible.

   And consider this example. It is a cut-down version of Derek Parfit's 'Mere Addition Paradox'.[23] A couple have a child, and are wondering whether to have another. If they do, they may either spread their resources evenly between the children, or concentrate

Table 1

Children	Children		Children	
First	First	Second	First	Second
11	7	7	12	1

Alternative *A*   Alternative *B*   Alternative *C*

them on the first. The alternatives are shown in Table 1; the numbers in the table stand for the children's degrees of wellbeing.

   The couple might reason like this. In the comparison between *A* and *B*, *A* is better for the first child. And there is nobody for whom *A* is worse than *B*. Whom could it be worse for? – in *A* only the first child exists, and it is not worse for her. So *A* is better than *B*. Or at the very least, *A* is at least as good as *B*. In the comparison between *C* and *A*, *C* is better for the first child and no worse for the second. So *C* is better than *A*. Or at the very least, *C* is at least as good as *A*. But also, *B* is better than *C*, because *B* has a greater total of wellbeing, and has it equally distributed. So it is not true that *C* is at least as good as *B*. Transitivity, however, requires that it should be. This couple, then, might come to the conclusion that there is an intransitivity in the betterness relation. Larry Temkin has used examples like this, taken from

Parfit, to argue powerfully that the betterness relation is indeed intransitive.[24]

But, despite its attractions, this is a conclusion that cannot logically be drawn. If there are intransitivities, they cannot be in the betterness relation. The situation must be described in other terms, however tempting it may be to use the terms of betterness. (It may seem puzzling that it should be so tempting to deny a law of logic. But any paradox is like that: it tempts one to assert both a proposition and its negation.) What Parfit's examples show, I think, is the strong hold teleology has on us. We are strongly drawn to organize our moral thinking around the concept of good. But using that concept imposes a structure – a transitive one – on our thinking. If our thinking does not fit the structure, we shall have to give up teleology, or else restructure our thinking. Certainly, we must not fall into logical inconsistency.

That the betterness relation is an ordering is, by itself, a serious constraint on teleology. But there is much more to the structure of good than just that; there are many other structural conditions that a betterness relation must conform to. Any ethical theory is teleological if it implies the existence of an ordering that determines the rightness of acts. This one structural condition is enough to identify the theory as teleological; the ordering is the theory's betterness relation; it fixes its notion of good. But a teleological theory cannot be *correct* unless its notion of good conforms to all the other structural conditions as well.

The purpose of this book is to examine in detail some of these other conditions. I shall mention just two examples now. First: I shall argue in Chapter 6 that the betterness relation must satisfy the axioms of expected utility theory. And second: this book is very much concerned with the way general good is made up of the good of individuals. I shall particularly be testing out the truth of this popular view about it:

The utilitarian principle of distribution. One alternative is at least as good as another if and only if it has at least as great a total of people's good.

The utilitarian principle says it is best for good to be distributed in such a way as to maximize the total of people's good. It values the total of good only, and not equality in the distribution of good. If the total would be maximized by making the society very unequal, then it says that is what should be done. Chapters 3, 9, 10 and 11 all discuss this principle.

1.4 Does good exist?

An ethical theory is teleological if it says one ought always to do the act that is best. A nonteleological theory must therefore on some occasions say one ought to do an act that is not the best. This may sound paradoxical, and may give nonteleological ethics a paradoxical air from the start. To counter this impression, Philippa Foot in her article 'Utilitarianism and the virtues' takes the radical step of denying that there is such a thing as 'the goodness of states of affairs'. Since I am proposing in this book to examine the structure of the goodness of states of affairs, I need to respond to Foot's denial.

What Foot really objects to is a notion of good that 'stands *outside* morality as its foundation and arbiter'. She is happy with a notion that 'appears *within* morality as the end of one of the virtues' (namely benevolence).[25] And she does not object to notions of good that are constructed within particular ethical theories.[26] What she denies, if I understand her, is that there is such a thing as good existing in advance of ethical thinking, which ethical thinking takes as its object but does not itself determine. She argues that we simply do not have such a notion of good. She might have added, like J. L. Mackie,[27] that this sort of good would be metaphysically mysterious. Let us, at least for the sake of argument, accept Foot's objections to good conceived this way. Teleological ethics, she believes, sees good like this. Is she right?

This chapter suggests a different possibility. Certainly, teleology aims at good. But this need not mean it takes good as an externally determined objective. The pursuit of good may give to ethics, not an objective, but a structure. It may fix the way in which ethical considerations work and how they combine together. It may provide, not a foundation or an objective, but an organizing principle for ethics.

So far, this is only a suggestion. I have argued that teleology should be identified by its structure, but that is not enough to show that this new suggestion is correct. What matters is not how teleology is identified but how it is justified. How might one show that ethics does, indeed, have the structure teleology imputes to it? It needs to be shown, first, that rightness is determined by an ordering. But this is only the beginning of the task of justification. The structure of good, as I have said, includes many other conditions besides simply that betterness is an ordering. Some are described in this book. All of them will need to be justified too.

How? Roughly speaking, there are two styles of argument
available. One is to say there is an object, good, that ethics aims
at. This object determines what ought to be done. Acts will
therefore be ordered by their goodness, and this ordering will
determine their rightness. That would be the first part of the task
of justification accomplished. It may also be possible to accomplish
the other parts too – justify the other structural conditions – by
arguments in this style. These arguments will appeal to a prior
notion of good that stands outside ethics and gives it its object. If
teleology is defended like this, it is indeed as Foot conceives it.

The alternative is to justify each of the structural requirements
individually on other grounds. The most plausible are grounds of
consistency or coherence.[28] This second style of argument will
almost certainly appeal to the idea of rationality. If an act is right,
it must be rational, so the structure of rationality must tell us
something about the structure of ethics. Rationality is constrained
by structural conditions, which have been thoroughly examined
and debated. These conditions are often defended on grounds of
internal consistency rather than by an external object. For
example, a commonly accepted structural condition is that a
rational person must have preferences that constitute an ordering.
That is to say, her preference relation

$$\_\ \text{is preferred or indifferent to}\ \_$$

must be transitive and reflexive. If this condition could be
established on grounds of internal consistency, then one might be
able to argue from it to a conclusion about the structure of ethics:
that rightness must also be determined by an ordering. If this
argument was successful, the conclusion would have been derived
from internal consistency rather than from an external object. And
one might be able to do the same for all the other structural
conditions of teleology.

Once the teleological structure of ethics had been justified in
this second style, the notion of good would then be determined by
the structure. It would arise out of ethical thinking, therefore. It
would not stand outside morality as its foundation and arbiter. If
teleology is defended by arguments in this second style, Foot
should have no quarrel with it.

This book defends various claims about the structure of good.
Does it use the external or the internal style of defence? Neither
purely; both play a part. There is certainly a large proportion of
the internal style. I shall explain in Chapter 6 that in one area it
turns out to be unavoidable. Chapter 6 deals with acts whose

results are uncertain. The goodness of such an act is a tricky notion. Take an act that is likely to have a good result, but suppose it turns out unluckily to have a bad one. It is hard to know whether this should count as a good or a bad act. We cannot expect to find a reliable notion of goodness here, prior to ethical examination, from which one might argue to structural conclusions. At that point in the book (particularly in Section 6.3), my arguments about the structure of good will be derived entirely from the structure of rationality. And that in turn will be derived partly from internal considerations of consistency. The argument in this book, then, is certainly not founded on a complete, prior, external, notion of good.

On the other hand, the notion of good cannot be determined entirely by structural conditions, either. A complete description of the structure of good does not constitute a complete analysis of the meaning of 'good'. An ethical theory may have all the right structure, and so be teleological and possess a conception of good that meets all the structural conditions; yet nevertheless its conception of good may be wrong. An example is the theory that, when faced with a choice, one should always pick the act likely to produce the greatest total of pain. This is a teleological theory, with all the right structure, and its conception of good is pain. But good does not actually consist in pain. So this theory is wrong. It follows that teleological ethics cannot be *fully* justified on grounds of internal coherence. If it could, the theory I have just described would be fully justified. But it cannot be, because it is wrong.

It also follows that there are, actually, external criteria available for assessing the goodness of acts. The theory I mentioned is wrong because it recommends acts that are, actually, bad. It is therefore legitimate to appeal sometimes to external criteria in arguments about the structure of good, as I shall do. For instance: some things, such as happiness, are good, and others, such as pain, are bad. These are external facts about goodness. Foot may be right to doubt the existence of a complete conception of good, prior to ethics, on which ethics is founded. But there are certainly prior elements of a conception. Foot herself, indeed, recognizes enough of a prior conception of good for the virtue of benevolence to take it as its object.[29] Furthermore, I shall argue on page 106 that internal conditions of consistency actually rely on external facts about goodness to give them a determinate meaning. I think our notion of good is formed out of external and internal conditions woven together.

I think the notion of good provides, not an object for ethics to aim at, but a valuable organizing principle in ethical argument. It is an accommodating principle: many ethical views can be made consistent with it. It can accommodate the value of fairness. According to Amartya Sen,[30] it can accommodate the value of respecting people's rights. I have suggested it can accommodate certain agent-relative views. It can accommodate the lexical domination of some values over others. But there are limits. Some limits are structural: there are ethical views that do not fit the structure of good; I have mentioned some in this chapter. Some limits are substantive: the view that one should maximize pain is excluded by a substantive limit. This book is concerned with the structural limits. There may be excellent ethical theories beyond the limits, which cannot be fitted within the structure of good. But even if there are, I think the organizing work done by the notion of good, and the discipline it imposes on ethical argument, is valuable.

Notes

1. Indeed, in 'Consequentialism', Philip Pettit argues that all ethical theories must rely on a concept of good. Where teleological and nonteleological theories differ, he says, is over how people should give recognition to good in their actions.

2. *A Theory of Justice*, p. 24.

3. Susan Hurley first pointed out to me that 'teleology' is a better term than 'consequentialism'. Another matter of terminology: Rawls uses 'deontological' for 'nonteleological'. But I prefer 'nonteleological' because 'deontological' is traditionally connected specifically with obligation.

4. 'The Rejection of Consequentialism', pp. 1–2, note. See also Williams, 'A critique of utilitarianism', p. 24.

5. See Scanlon, 'Rights, goals and fairness'.

6. Williams, 'A critique of utilitarianism', p. 26.

7. See Williams, 'A critique of utilitarianism', pp. 30–1.

8. For instance by Scheffler, 'Introduction', *Consequentialism and Its Critics*, p. 1. Scheffler's own moral theory (in *The Rejection of Consequentialism*), which allows an agent to give special weight to her own concerns, he therefore takes to be a rejection of consequentialism.

9. See, for instance, many of the papers collected in Scheffler, *Consequentialism and Its Critics*.

10. Jonathan Bennett also makes this point in 'Two departures from consequentialism'.

11. Examples are mentioned on pp. 9, 15 and 159.

12. An example is mentioned on p. 8 and p. 13.

13. See, for instance, Slote, 'Satisficing consequentialism' and *Beyond Optimizing*, and Stocker, *Plural and Conflicting Values*, pp. 311–16. It was Nicholas Denyer who pointed out to me that satisficing theories should be included

under teleology.

14. *A Theory of Justice*, p. 24.

15. In *Moral Reasons*, Chapter 6, Jonathan Dancy argues that teleology and incommensurability are incompatible.

16. 'Rights and agency'. A response to Sen, expressing the doubts I mentioned, is Regan, 'Against evaluator relativity'.

17. *Anarchy, State and Utopia*, p. 29.

18. For an analysis of degrees of Fness, see Morton, 'Hypercomparatives'.

19. See Suppes, *Axiomatic Set Theory*, p. 72.

20. *A Theory of Justice*, p. 25.

21. I must be one of those economists whom T. M. Scanlon was once inclined to regard as crass, but now finds some sympathy for. See his 'Rights, goals and fairness'. p. 82.

22. 'Rawls on teleology and deontology'. These two paragraphs of mine about Rawls have largely been inspired by Kymlicka's paper, which explains Rawls's intentions much more effectively than I have. Kymlicka cites R. M. Hare's 'Rights, utility, and universalization', p. 107, as a clear example of the derivation of utilitarianism from the principle of equal respect. Another example is James Griffin's *Well-Being*.

23. *Reasons and Persons*, pp. 419–41.

24. 'Intransitivity and the mere addition paradox'.

25. 'Utilitarianism and the virtues', p. 238.

26. pp. 233–4.

27. *Ethics*, pp. 38–42.

28. The coherentist view of ethics is defended with great thoroughness by Susan Hurley in *Natural Reasons*. On the question of transitivity in particular, see pp. 260–1.

29. pp. 237–8.

30. 'Rights and agency'.

Chapter 2

Introduction II:
Weighing Goods

The weighing up of goods is one aspect of the structure of good, and the principal subject of this book. Sections 2.1 and 2.2 of this chapter describe the general problem of weighing goods, and illustrate it with examples. Sections 2.3 and 2.4 mention some related problems that are not covered in the book, in order to set them aside. Section 2.5 outlines the book's argument.

2.1 Locations of good, and separability

Suppose that this weekend you might either make a trip to London or take your sailboard down to the sea. The results will depend on the weather. Suppose there are two possible 'states of nature': fine sailing weather and bad sailing weather. The prospects are shown in Table 2. In deciding which is the better thing to do, you have to

Table 2

States of nature		States of nature	
Fine weather	Bad weather	Fine weather	Bad weather
Enjoyable trip	Enjoyable trip	Thrills and achievement	Boredom

Alternative *A* (London)   Alternative *B* (sailing)

22

weigh one difference in good if the weather is fine – thrills and achievement rather than an enjoyable trip – against another if the weather is bad – an enjoyable trip rather than boredom. You are weighing against each other two differences in good, each *located*, as I shall put it, in one of the states of nature. The states of nature are *locations* of good.

Another way of describing your problem is that you have to compare the *aggregate* value of the goods that each alternative offers. Alternative *B* offers either thrills and achievement, or else boredom. You have to put those two possibilities together in order to compare *B* with the goods offered by *A*. So you have to put together or aggregate the goods located in each of the two states of nature. As it happens *A* offers the certainty of an enjoyable trip, so there is no problem of aggregation for *A*. But in general your problem in a case of this sort is aggregation across states of nature.

And actually, this second way of looking at the problem is more general than the first. The first way – weighing – already has an important presupposition built into it. In describing it, I said that what counts in favour of taking out your sailboard is what happens in the state fine weather. What counts in favour of London is what happens in the state bad weather. So I was taking the states separately as generators of reasons in favour of one alternative or the other. But in some circumstances you might think this sort of separation between states unjustified. I cannot give a very good example of that now; there are several in Chapter 5. But even in this example, you might doubt the separation of states. At least if you go to London, you *know* what is going to happen. That choice leads to certainty, and you may like to be certain. If so, that gives you a reason in favour of going to London that does not appear if you compare the alternatives one state at a time, as I first suggested. The fact of certainty only appears when you take the states together. So state-by-state comparison is inadequate if you like to be certain. In general, it is inadequate if the value of what happens in one state depends on what happens in another.

To assume that state-by-state comparison is adequate is to assume *separability* between states. Roughly, separability says that the value of what happens in one location is independent of what happens in other locations. Chapter 4 defines it precisely. The assumption of separability, not just in the context of states of nature but in other contexts too, is one of the main subjects of this book. I shall be asking when, and how far, it is legitimate to assume separability. When it is, the metaphor of weighing goods is appropriate; otherwise it is not. When the locations are states of nature, the leading theory about how good should be aggregated across them is *expected utility theory*, and separability is the key assumption of this theory. Chapter 5 examines separability in this particular context.

Now another example. There is a population of people, and we have to compare two possible distributions of income amongst them. The alternatives are shown in Table 3: y_3, for instance, is

Table 3

People					People				
1	2	3	...	h	1	2	3	...	h
y_1	y_2	y_3	...	y_h	y_1'	y_2'	y_3'	...	y_h'

Distribution y Distribution y'

the income of the third person in distribution y. To compare the goodness of these distributions, we have to do a more complicated, many element, weighing operation. We have to weigh the difference in the good of person 1 between the distributions – the difference, that is to say, between how good y_1 is for her and how good y_1' is for her – against the difference in the good of person 2 – the difference between how good y_2 is for her and how good y_2' is for her – and the difference in the good of person 3, and so on. Unless the problem is trivial, some of these differences will be positive and some negative; one distribution will be better for some people, the other for others. So we are once again weighing up differences in good at different locations. The locations now are people rather than states of nature.

Again, the problem could be seen as one of aggregation rather than weighing. To compare the distributions, you could aggregate the good of all the people in one distribution, to arrive at an assessment of the total goodness of the distribution, and then aggregate the good of all the people in the other, and finally compare the two aggregates. And again, the second way of putting it is more general. The first way presupposes that the distributions can be compared one person at a time; it makes an assumption of separability between people. And in our present context, this is a dubious assumption. It assumes that the value attached to one person's income is independent of everyone else's. But if equality is valuable, this may not be so. It may matter, not just how much income a person has, but how much she has compared with other people. So incomes cannot be evaluated one at a time. Separability between people needs careful examining, therefore. This is the subject of Chapters 8 and 9. Notice that what is in question in the example is separability of *income* between people. Separability of something else, such as their total good, might be more plausible. Chapter 9 argues that, indeed, it is.

A third example. You are going to Italy next summer, and you are wondering whether to spend time now learning Italian. The alternatives are shown in Table 4. Obviously this a problem of the same sort. Here the locations of goods are times. There is a

Table 4

Times		Times	
Now	Summer	Now	Summer
Spend time on learning	Get along with Italians	Have more free time	Feel isolated

| Alternative *A* | Alternative *B* |

question, once again, of separability: can goods can be weighed separately time by time, or are there interactions between times that make this impossible? Chapter 11 examines separability between times.

2.2 Three dimensions of locations

The examples in Section 2.1 show how locations of good are spread across three *dimensions*: states of nature, people and times. These are the dimensions I shall be dealing with in this book. Perhaps there are other dimensions that could usefully be treated similarly, but I cannot think of any.

One suggestion is that different *sorts* of good might be treated as locations on a dimension. It is, of course, an important question how different sorts of good – fame and comfort, say – are to be compared or weighed against each other. But that question is not considered in this book. The reason is that I do not see how to achieve any plausible separability in the dimension of sorts of good.[1] I doubt that one sort could be judged independently from others. By contrast, I hope to show there is at least an arguable case for separability in each of my three dimensions, provided everything is properly set up. And separability gives access to interesting connections between the dimensions, which I shall be outlining in this section. These connections are the real point of the book. So I have no place for a dimension without separability.

The examples in Section 2.1 are especially simple because they each have good distributed along only one dimension. Many of the important and interesting cases involve more than one dimension. Here is an example based on one of Peter Diamond's.[2] A kidney is available for transplant. Two people need it; each, without a kidney, will die. The choice is between tossing a coin to decide who is to get the kidney, and giving it directly to person Q. The

Table 5

| People | | States of nature | | People | | States of nature | |
		Heads	Tails			Heads	Tails
	P	Lives	Dies		P	Dies	Dies
	Q	Dies	Lives		Q	Lives	Lives

Alternative A Alternative B

alternatives are shown in Table 5. Each cell in the table is a location for good; a location in this case is a particular person in a particular state of nature.

Diamond originally offered this example as a counterexample to separability between states of nature. If the states were separable, we would be able to compare the alternatives acts one state at a time. So look at the states one by one. In state Tails, the two alternatives are equally good, because in that state they both have the same result. In state Heads, both are equally good, because they have symmetrical results. (Assume there is no reason to favour either person above the other.) The two acts are equally good in both states, then. Separability would therefore imply they are equally good acts. Yet Diamond thinks A is actually better than B because he thinks it is fairer. I shall say more about this example, and Diamond's argument against separability, in Section 5.7.

In the most general case, goods are strung out on a three-dimensional grid of locations. Each location is a person, at a time, in a state of nature. When we compare alternatives, each alternative will distribute good across this grid. Different alternatives will distribute it differently. To compare them, we shall have to put together the goods they produce at different locations, so as to determine the overall goodness of each alternative.

This is the most general form of the question this book examines: how does good distributed across the three dimensions go to make up overall good? It is a question about the structure of good. It encompasses questions about particular dimensions: how does the good of individuals go to make up general good? how does the good that comes to a person at times in her life go to make up the overall goodness of her life? and so on. And one part of the question is: how far is good separable along the dimensions, so that comparing alternatives can be treated as weighing up?

Another part of the question is whether overall good *is* made up entirely of good at locations. Is good entirely made up of the good of people, for instance? Or is there, perhaps, a communal good that is separate from the good of individuals? Is the good of a person entirely constituted by the good that comes to her at particular times in her life? Or are there goods that cannot be tied down to any particular time? In describing my question as I have, I certainly do not mean to take it for granted that good is composed entirely of good at individual locations. Whether it is or not is one of the main questions I shall be asking.

In practice, I shall generally only have to consider two dimensions at once. So I shall not need to draw up three-dimensional tables to display my examples. But taking one dimension at a time is not usually enough. To explain why not, let me say something about the point of setting up this three-dimensional scheme.

My examples show a formal similarity between different problems. There are problems to do with time, with distribution between people and with uncertainty, but they are all problems in which goods distributed across a range of locations have to be put together. A number of authors have exploited the similarity between dimensions in investigating the aggregation of good. They have used our ways of thinking about one dimension to help illuminate another. I shall discuss some examples of this method in Chapter 3.

The argument of this book, however, does not work by similarity.

It does not take aggregation in one dimension and compare it with aggregation in another. Instead, it looks at the aggregation of good in two or more dimensions simultaneously. It turns out, when two dimensions are taken together, that consistency may require them to be treated in connected ways. There are strict, logical connections between dimensions. If goods are aggregated in a particular manner across one, they may have to be aggregated in the same manner across the other; there are mathematical theorems, proved by Gérard Debreu and W. M. Gorman, that suggest this.[3] I say 'may' because the theorems require some preconditions, principally separability in both dimensions. If the problem can be set up in such a way that both dimensions are separable, then the conclusion of the theorems follows. The conclusion, as I say, links together the way good is aggregated in the two dimensions. I cannot spell it out exactly yet, but I can give a rough example, to suggest how powerful the method of argument can be.

Take the two dimensions of states of nature and people. And suppose there is separability in each. Then the theorems say that good has to be aggregated in the same manner in each dimension. This implies, very roughly, that inequality will be a bad thing in the distribution of good between people if and only if risk is a bad thing when facing uncertainty about good. (I cannot yet explain why, or even exactly what this means; that will have to wait till Section 10.2.) So a link is made between the value of avoiding risk and the value of avoiding inequality. This link was discovered by John Harsanyi.[4] It is a consequence of Gorman's theorem, but Harsanyi actually anticipated the theorem in this particular application. I find it remarkable that a connection can be made by a formal theorem between such apparently unrelated topics as the value of equality and the value of safety.

Separability is a crucial precondition for any formal argument in this style. That is why I shall spend so much time on separability in this book. I have already raised doubts about it for the dimensions of people and states of nature. But the doubts are only the beginning. It may be possible to frame the argument in such a way as to overcome them. For instance, between people, separability of income is implausible, but I think separability of good turns out to be an acceptable assumption. That is why my argument is conducted in terms of good rather than income. At places in this book the framework of the argument may seem contrived. But if some artifice is required to gain access to the theorems, it is worthwhile. It will reveal features of the structure of good that would otherwise remain hidden.

Particularly in his later writings,[5] Harsanyi goes further than I have described so far, and claims his formal argument as support for utilitarianism. More exactly, he claims it as support for just one part of utilitarianism: the utilitarian principle of distribution set out on page 16 above, that the goodness of an alternative is determined by the simple total of people's good. A major aim of this book is to examine just how successfully the utilitarian principle of distribution can be defended by arguments based on separability, like Harsanyi's. I shall be making out the best case I can for the principle. But I think, myself, that the case is ultimately inconclusive. The argument contains gaps, which I shall point out as I come to them. Its most serious weakness is that it needs in the end to appeal to separability of good in the dimension of time, and this seems to me implausible.

There is not the least reason to think that separability in one dimension implies separability in another. Each dimension needs to be examined independently. I am myself willing to argue for separability of good in the dimensions of people and states of nature, but not of time. In Chapter 11, I shall describe one possible defence of separability across time, but it relies on a particular metaphysical theory of personhood that I find unattractive: a *disuniting* theory, which denies the full unity of a person through time.

So this book is not to be understood as a defence of the utilitarian principle of distribution. It is an exploration of the logical connections between this principle and principles of separability. These connections are interesting in themselves, and tell us a lot about utilitarianism. The association between utilitarianism and a disuniting metaphysics is especially significant. Consequently, when I come to gaps in the argument, I shall not hold myself responsible for trying to fill them all. Nevertheless, though I do not find the final conclusion convincing, I am convinced by many of the individual steps in the argument. I shall defend those steps as well as I can.

2.3 *Dimensions with varying lengths*

In this section I am going to mention two more examples of weighing goods, not because the problems they raise are dealt with in this book, but because they are not. I want to suggest that my account of weighing goods has potential that is still unexplored and worth exploring.

The general problem of weighing goods is to compare alternatives. Each alternative distributes good across a three-dimensional grid. But the grids need not always have a nice rectangular shape, and the grids for different alternatives need not be the same size. In one alternative, for instance, a person might live longer than she does in another, so the time dimension for her will have a different length in each alternative. Or more people may get born in one alternative than in another. The dimension of people will then have a different length in each of these alternatives.

I have already mentioned one example of this sort on page 15. It was a problem for a couple, wondering whether to have a second child. I shall repeat the table here as Table 6. In this case we are

Table 6

Children	Children		Children	
First	First	Second	First	Second
11	7	7	12	1

    Alternative *A*   Alternative *B*   Alternative *C*

dealing only with the single dimension of people, but the dimension does not have the same length in all the alternatives. It contains just one location in one alternative, and two in the others. The numbers shown in each location in the table are the children's degrees of wellbeing.

My next example is a schematic version of a major problem in the allocation of economic resources, in medicine and elsewhere. Should resources be concentrated on extending people's lives or on improving them? Imagine a person has a decade of life ahead of her. She can use the resources available to her in various ways. She can if she chooses prolong her life by a further decade, and so give herself two more decades to live in total. If she does, she will then have a choice between using up resources evenly over the time, or unevenly. Alternatively, she can choose not to prolong her life. Her alternatives are as shown in Table 7. The numbers represent her degrees of wellbeing during the decades. The locations here are times, and the length of the time dimension is variable. The numbers are the same as those in Table 6.

Table 7

Decades of life	Decades of life		Decades of life	
First	First	Second	First	Second
11	7	7	12	1

Alternative *A*   Alternative *B*   Alternative *C*

These two examples reveal an analogy between the dimensions of people and times, and also a disanalogy. On page 15 I described some reasoning the couple of Table 6 might go through. In comparing alternatives *A* and *B*, I said they might argue like this. *A* is better than *B* for the first child, and there is no one for whom *A* is worse than *B*. The absence of the second child in *A* does not in any way make *A* worse than *B*. Nothing, that is to say, counts against *A*, and something counts in its favour. So they might well conclude that *A* is better than *B*. In the example of Table 7, though, analogous reasoning would be more dubious. In the first decade, *A* is better than *B* for the person. This counts in favour of *A*. But the absence of the second decade in *A* seems, plausibly, to count against it. In this case there is someone for whom this absence is a bad thing, namely the person. So here is a disanalogy.

Nevertheless, in the example of Table 7, it still seems plausible that the person might conclude *A* is better than *B*. She might think a short exciting life better than a long ordinary one, even if the latter contains more good in total. This, though, may put her in the same paradoxical position as the couple of Table 6 found themselves in on page 15. She might find an apparent intransitivity in the betterness relation. And that is disallowed by logic.

Obviously, there are awkward problems here. I am not going to try to sort them out in this book.[6] I mention them to make it plain that, when it comes to dimensions of variable length, new difficulties will arise. But it will still be valuable to compare the dimensions. It will show up analogies and disanalogies. And, more important, it will yield logical connections, and theorems extending Debreu's and Gorman's, that will help to clarify the problems.[7]

2.4 *What things are good?*

This book is about the structure of good, not the content of good.
It is not about what things are good, but about how good things
go together to make up overall good.

I shall not, that is to say, be concerned with what good consists
in. At least, I obviously shall to some extent: I shall be concerned
with whether general good consists in the good of people, and
whether a person's good consists in the good that comes to her at
particular times. But I shall not go further than that: I shall not
be concerned with what a person's good at a particular time
consists in. There are many rival theories about that.[8] Some
people, for instance, believe that a person's good at a time consists
in feeling good; others that it consists in having her desires or
preferences satisfied. And there are many theories besides these.

In principle I want to remain neutral between such theories. I
am interested in the aggregation of good, whatever good may
happen to be. But I cannot stick quite firmly to this principle. A
major part of my argument turns on the relationship between
good and preferences. Chapters 5, 6 and 7 all comment on this
relationship. Nevertheless, I shall retain a neutral stance as far
as possible.

2.5 *An outline of the argument*

Figures 1 and 2 on pages 34 and 35 show a map of this book's
argument. This map is printed here chiefly for future reference;
much of it will not be comprehensible until I have defined more
terminology. Italic type in the map indicates where in the book
the various propositions and inferences are supported. My
argument will not always proceed straightforwardly in the
direction of the arrows; sometimes I shall add support to a
proposition by showing that, perhaps contrary to first appearances, its implications are acceptable. For instance, I wish to
support the claim that general good is coherent. (It does not
matter for now just what this means.) This claim, together with
others, turns out to imply that the Pareto principle is false. Since
the Pareto principle is widely accepted as true, I need to argue for
its falsity independently. I shall do so in Section 7.2, and thereby
add support to the claim that general good is coherent. When a
box on the map contains an italic reference, that means the
proposition receives independent support in the place indicated.

The crux of the book's argument is a theorem I call *the interpersonal addition theorem*. Chapters 5 to 9 are all devoted to establishing the premises of this theorem as securely as possible. The theorem is proved in Section 10.1. The rest of Chapter 10 and Chapter 11 are devoted to interpreting its conclusion.

The interpersonal addition theorem rests on three premises. The first is that each person's betterness relation

__ is at least as good for the person as __

conforms to the axioms of expected utility theory. It is, as I shall put it, *coherent*. Chapters 5 and 6 support this premise.

Expected utility theory is concerned with uncertainty – with aggregation across the dimension of states of nature. It is normally interpreted as a theory about, not betterness, but rational *preferences* in the face of uncertainty. It claims that, amongst uncertain prospects, rationality requires a person to have preferences that conform to a number of axioms. Chapter 5 explains what the axioms are, and defends them as conditions on rational preferences. The principal axiom, commonly known as the *sure-thing principle*, is an assumption of separability across states of nature. Expected utility theory has often been doubted; many authors doubt that rationality really requires a person's preferences to conform to the theory's axioms. The sure-thing principle is the axiom most commonly criticized, and my argument concentrates on that. Indeed, there is one axiom – completeness – that I shall not be defending at all, because I find it dubious myself; this is one of the gaps in the argument that I shall not try to close. But I think the sure-thing principle is genuinely a requirement of rationality. Chapter 5 argues that point.

Chapter 5 is about rationality, but the subject of this book is not rationality but good. Chapter 5 is simply groundwork for what comes next. Chapter 6 sets out from the argument of Chapter 5, and extends it to people's betterness relation. It concludes that these betterness relations are coherent.

But before it can do that, it needs to deal with a preliminary problem. To apply expected utility theory to a betterness relation is to apply notions of betterness and goodness to uncertain prospects. And it may be argued that these notions can properly be applied only to what actually happens, not to prospects of what might happen. Chapter 6, though, describes a probability-relative notion of good that can legitimately be applied to prospects.

The second premise of the interpersonal addition theorem is that the general betterness relation is coherent. I shall use very

34 *Weighing Goods*

Figure 1

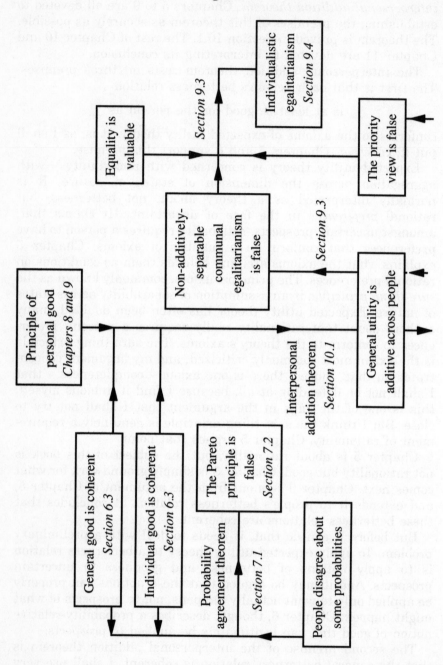

Figure 2

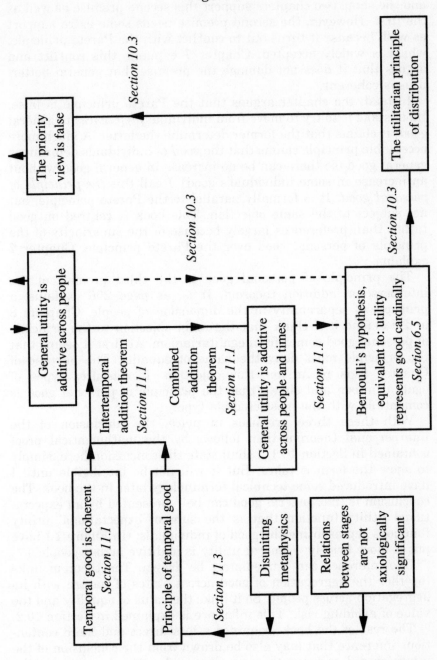

much the same arguments for general as for individual betterness, and the same two chapters support this second premise as well as the first. However, the second premise needs some extra support as well, because it turns out to conflict with the Pareto principle, which is widely accepted. Chapter 7 explains this conflict and argues that it does not damage the premise that general betterness is coherent.

Instead, the chapter argues that the Pareto principle is false. Its mistake is to try to move from individual *preferences* to general *good*; it claims that the former determine the latter. A much more acceptable principle claims that the *good* of individuals determines general good (so there can be no increase in general good without an increase in some individual's good). I call this *the principle of personal good*. It is formally parallel to the Pareto principle, but not subject to the same objection. This book is centred on good rather than preferences largely because of the superiority of the principle of personal good over the Pareto principle. Chapter 7 explains.

The principle of personal good is the third premise of the interpersonal addition theorem. It is, as page 206 explains, a principle of separability in the dimension of people. Chapters 8 and 9 defend it. I think that the main objection to the principle of personal good comes from egalitarianism. At first it seems that the principle must deny the value of equality. The purpose of Chapter 9 is to answer this objection. It classifies types of egalitarianism and shows that the principle of personal good is compatible with the most credible type.

With these three premises in place, the conclusion of the interpersonal theorem then follows by the mathematical proof contained in Section 10.1. I shall state the conclusion here, simply to show the form it takes. But it will not be intelligible until I have introduced some technical terminology later in the book. The conclusion is that general good can be represented by an expectational utility function that is the sum of expectational utility functions representing the good of individuals. (In Figure 1 I have put it more briefly: 'General utility is additive across people'.)

One inference can immediately be drawn. The theorem links together the aggregation of good across states of nature with its aggregation across people. So it links the value of equality and the value of avoiding risk. This inference is explained in Section 10.2.

The rest of the book examines a less direct and more contentious inference that may also be drawn from the conclusion of the interpersonal addition theorem. It may be thought to imply the utilitarian principle of distribution. Section 10.3 shows that the utilitarian principle can indeed be inferred, but only if we add an extra premise: that one uncertain prospect is at least as good for a person as another if and only if it gives her at least as great an expectation* of her good.

I call this *Bernoulli's hypothesis*. It is introduced and discussed in Section 6.5. Like the premise that a person's betterness relation is coherent, it is a claim about the aggregation of good across the dimension of states of nature. Indeed, Bernoulli's hypothesis implies, but is not implied by, this premise. Section 6.5 offers some inconclusive grounds for believing Bernoulli's hypothesis. Section 10.3 shows that the interpersonal addition theorem provides stronger grounds. But again they are not conclusive. That is why they are indicated by a dotted line in Figure 2. So the interpersonal addition theorem gives some support to Bernoulli's hypothesis, and then it combines with Bernoulli's hypothesis to imply the utilitarian principle of distribution.

Still, since the grounds of Bernoulli's hypothesis remain inconclusive, the utilitarian principle remains insecure. Chapter 11 describes a final attempt to secure it. The attempt is launched from the basis of a principle analogous to the principle of personal good: that a person's good is determined by the good that comes to her at particular times in her life. I call this *the principle of temporal good*. It is a principle of separability in the time dimension. Let us add to it one other new premise, which is defended in Section 11.1: that the betterness relation of a person at a particular time is, like the general betterness relation and the betterness relation of a person as a whole, coherent. These premises can be fed into a theorem analogous to the interpersonal addition theorem, which I call *the intertemporal addition theorem*. I shall not spell out this theorem's conclusion here. But Chapter 11 explains that, if true, it would give further strong support to Bernoulli's hypothesis. It would still not prove the hypothesis conclusively, but it would make it hard to doubt. Consequently, it would give a solid grounding to the utilitarian principle of distribution.

But all this depends on the truth of the principle of temporal good. Chapter 11 explains that this principle is, on the face of it, not very plausible. But the chapter shows how it could be defended on the basis of a disuniting metaphysics of personhood.

---

* The expectation of a quantity is defined in the footnote on page 53.

Thus, by a tortuous route, a disuniting metaphysics could give support to the utilitarian principle.

That completes my outline of the book's main argument. But, before I reach the argument itself, there are two more preliminary chapters yet. Chapter 3 examines two other arguments, different from mine, that work by comparing the distribution of good in more than one dimension. These arguments do not use the logical connections between dimensions that I described in Section 2.2. I mention them for contrast with my own argument, which does use these connections.

Chapter 4 sets out the formal theorems that make the connections between the dimensions, on the basis of separability. The appendix to Chapter 4 contains elementary proofs of these theorems.

Notes

1. Susan Hurley considers the separability of different sorts of goods in *Natural Reasons*, pp. 69–76. In 'The additive fallacy', Shelly Kagan denies that different sorts of good are generally separable. But his denial goes further. He denies that the 'factors' that go into moral calculations are generally separable. 'Factors' seems to include, not just goods of different sorts, but goods of the same sort belonging to different people. So he seems to be denying separability of good between people. On the other hand, with qualifications, I shall be affirming it.

2. 'Cardinal welfare, individualistic ethics and interpersonal comparisons of utility'.

3. Debreu, 'Topological methods in cardinal utility theory'; Gorman, 'The structure of utility functions'.

4. 'Cardinal welfare, individualistic ethics and interpersonal comparisons of utility'.

5. For instance, 'Morality and the theory of rational behavior'.

6. I have said something more about them in 'The economic value of life', and in 'Some principles of population'.

7. Such theorems appear in Blackorby and Donaldson, 'Social criteria for evaluating population change', and in Hammond, 'Consequentialist demographic norms and parenting rights'.

8. A thorough recent discussion is James Griffin's *Well-Being*.

Chapter 3

Similarity Arguments

In Chapter 2, I mentioned some similarities between the three dimensions of time, people and states of nature. Several authors have exploited these similarities in their arguments. In this chapter I shall discuss two examples. I do so chiefly for contrast. My own argument has a different method, and I want to show the difference. These similarity arguments take two dimensions separately, and compare the aggregation of good across one with its aggregation across the other. They transfer conclusions previously reached about one to the other. My argument considers the simultaneous aggregation of good across two dimensions, and consequently arrives simultaneously at conclusions about both.

Both the examples in this chapter are concerned with distributive justice: with how good should be distributed across the dimension of people. This puts them squarely within the subject matter of weighing goods; they are concerned with how goods coming to different people should be weighed against each other. Derek Parfit's argument, described in Sections 3.1 and 3.2, aims to cast light on distributive justice by comparing it with the distribution of good across time; John Harsanyi's, described in Section 3.3, by comparing it with the distribution of good across states of nature.

More particularly, both arguments are intended to offer some support to the utilitarian principle of distribution set out on page 16. The utilitarian principle of distribution is one of the main concerns of this book, and that is one reason why I have selected these two particular examples for this chapter.

39

3.1 Parfit, Section 1

Parfit considers distributive justice in Chapter 15 of *Reasons and Persons*. He describes a way in which the utilitarian principle of distribution might be defended. Parfit's defence issues from a particular metaphysical theory of personhood. In Chapter 11 below, I shall describe a different way of defending the utilitarian principle, which derives from a similar theory of personhood. So the comparison with Parfit is particularly useful. My argument deploys the forces of the formal theorems I mentioned in Section 2.2. Parfit's does not. I hope to show that, without the theorems, Parfit's argument cannot successfully reach its goal.

To speak of 'Parfit's defence' of the utilitarian principle is inaccurate. Parfit actually aims at less than a defence. He certainly does not try to *derive* the utilitarian principle from his theory of personhood. Instead, in his Chapter 15, he describes ways of thinking that make the principle more plausible than it may seem at first, and might in practice lead one to accept it. My own project in Chapter 11 is more ambitious. I shall attempt an actual derivation (which will, admittedly, be incomplete in several places). So what follows in this section and the next is not really a description of Parfit's own argument. For the sake of comparison with my own, I have tried to push Parfit's arguments as far as I can in the direction of an actual derivation. Parfit, therefore, cannot be held responsible for my lack of success. Indeed, my interpretation of his work is a very free one, which Parfit cannot really be held responsible for at all.

The utilitarian principle is about the distribution of good across the dimension of people. Parfit's defence compares this distribution with the distribution of good across the dimension of time, within the life of a single person. It has two steps.

The first is to show that distribution in the two dimensions should be regarded similarly: the principles that apply to one apply to both. Many people, for instance, think it unfair to impose a burden on one person for the sake of benefiting someone else, even if the benefit is greater than the burden.[1] This is a principle of distribution across the dimension of people. If it is true, Parfit aims to show, the same principle will be true of distribution across the dimension of time. It will also be unfair to impose a burden on a child, say, for the sake of benefiting her in later life, even if the benefit is greater than the burden. Or, to take another example, if some value should be attached to equality in the distribution of good between people, then some value should be attached to evenness in the distribution of good through a person's life.

The second step of the defence is to show, given that the same principles apply across both dimensions, that actually the utilitarian principle applies to both. So only the total of good matters, not its distribution across either dimension.

This section considers the first step; Section 3.2 the second.

Parfit aims to achieve the first step by establishing an analogy between the two dimensions of people and time. There are, of course, many disanalogies between the dimensions. What needs to be shown is that none of them is enough to justify applying different distributive principles: that none is 'distributionally significant', as I shall put it. There is an issue here about the burden of proof. Someone who does apply different principles in the two dimensions might equally well be asked to show that the disanalogies *are* distributionally significant. Parfit himself does not need to shoulder the full burden of showing they are not, since his aim is only to make the utilitarian principle plausible. But if our aim is actually to prove the principle, we shall have to take the full burden on ourselves.

Parfit says: 'If we are Reductionists, we regard the rough subdivisions within lives as, in certain ways, like the divisions between lives. We may therefore come to treat alike the two kinds of distribution: within lives and between lives.'[2] 'Reductionism' is Parfit's name for his theory of personhood, which I shall be describing. According to reductionism, the rough subdivisions within lives are like the divisions between lives in some ways, but not in others. It needs to be shown that the ways in which they are alike include all the distributionally significant ones. Let us survey some of the ways in which they are different, to see whether any of them might be distributionally significant.

On the face of it, there is this disanalogy between dimensions to start off with. At all the times in her life – at all the locations along the time dimension – a person is the same person. That is to say, there is one thing, the person, that is the same at all these locations. There is no parallel to this fact across the dimension of people. There is nothing that is the same at all locations in that dimension. Across the dimension of people, there are a number of separate things, all people. To be sure, the people occupying the locations may be *members* of the same society, but common membership is not identity. The dimension of time is united by identity; the dimension of people is not. I shall call this the 'identity disanalogy'; it might alternatively be called the 'separate-ness disanalogy'.

Parfit deals with the identity disanalogy by denying its exist-ence. His ground is his metaphysical theory of personhood, which is the foundation of his whole discussion of distributive justice. It is a *disuniting* theory. What I mean by this is broad and imprecise. I shall say more about it in Chapter 11, but a rough explanation will serve here. A disuniting theory of personhood takes a person to be, in some way, *made up* of temporal stages. There is me-last-year, me-today, me-tomorrow and so on. Each of these person-stages is a thing on its own, and together they all go to make up me. In this room at the moment, sitting at the computer, is a person-stage of me. It is not the whole of me, because I am made up out of person-stages, and many of them are not here at the moment. A uniting theory of personhood, by contrast, says that what is sitting in this chair is me, the very same thing as was sitting in it yesterday. It is the whole of me, not a stage.[3]

A disuniting metaphysics eliminates the identity disanalogy. In the two-dimensional grid of people and times, each location is

Table 8

		Times			
		1	2	...	t	...
People	1	s_{11}	s_{12}	...	s_{1t}	...
	2	s_{21}	s_{22}	...	s_{2t}	...
	.	.	.	...	.	...
	.	.	.	...	.	...
	h	s_{h1}	s_{h2}	...	s_{ht}	...
	.	.	.	...	.	...
	.	.	.	...	.	...

occupied by a separate entity, a person-stage. Table 8 shows the grid. Along a horizontal row in the table, lie stages that together make up a person. Along a vertical column, lie stages that together make up a society at a particular time. Neither dimension is united by identity; none of the entities at any location is identical to any other.

I do not wish to argue about the truth of disuniting metaphysics. Let us take it for granted as a premise of our argument. Parfit's disuniting metaphysics, then, removes the identity disanalogy between the dimensions.

Other disanalogies remain. There is this, for one. At locations along the time dimension are a series of stages of one *person*. This is true within any plausible metaphysical theory. Even if a person is made up out of stages, it would be foolish to deny that she is a person. Across the dimension of people, on the other hand, are many different people. The dimension of time is intrapersonal; the dimension of people interpersonal. Call this the 'personhood' disanalogy. Might not this be enough to justify applying different distributive principles in the two dimensions, whatever the metaphysical facts?

John Rawls cautions against relying on analogy between the dimensions of people and time. Utilitarianism, he claims, does so, and that is where it goes wrong. It treats people together as like a single person. It adopts 'for society as a whole the principle of rational choice for one man'.[4] What, precisely, is Rawls's complaint? Is it that utilitarianism ignores the identity disanalogy: the fact that one dimension is united by identity and the other is not? That complaint would be answered by a disuniting metaphysics. Or is the complaint that utilitarianism ignores the personhood disanalogy: the fact that one dimension is intrapersonal and the other interpersonal? A disuniting metaphysics does not deny that.

I do not know which complaint Rawls has in mind. One of his expressions perhaps suggests the former: 'Utilitarianism', he says, 'does not take seriously the distinction between persons'.[5] And a lot of discussion has centred around the separateness of persons.[6] If it is the distinction and the separateness that is seen as important, that points to the identity disanalogy. So the first complaint seems to have been a focus of discussion. Nevertheless, the second complaint seems reasonable enough too. On the face of it, whatever may be the metaphysical truth about personhood, the difference between an intrapersonal dimension and an interpersonal dimension seems enough to justify a different attitude to distribution across the two. It seems plausible that the personhood disanalogy is distributionally significant.

But Parfit denies that. As a extension of his disuniting metaphysics, he has a theory of 'what matters',[7] which he directs against it. We are taking the disuniting metaphysics for granted, so a person is made up of stages. These stages will be related together in various ways. For one thing, the fact that they are all components of one person is a relation between them. Each will be spatio-temporally contiguous to the next, and that is another relation. A third is that they will have some physical resemblances. They will generally speak the same language. And so on. Parfit asks, of these relations between stages: which ones *matter*? For the moment (until page 46) let us take him to mean: which are ethically significant in any way? Since distributional significance is a sort of ethical significance, relations that do not matter are not distributionally significant.

The fact that the stages are all components of one person is not what matters, Parfit argues. Instead, what matters is certain particular psychological relations between the stages. The most important of these relations is memory: one stage will remember the acts and experiences of previous stages. Another is intention: one stage will carry out the intentions formed by previous ones. And there are others too. As a general rule, the stages of a single person are linked by these psychological relations. It is these relations between stages that matter, and not the bare fact that they are stages of a single person. I do not want to pursue the argument about what matters. So let us grant Parfit all this. Let us add his account of what matters to the disuniting metaphysics, as a premise of our argument.

The personhood disanalogy is that, along the time dimension, stages make up a person, whereas across the dimension of people they do not. But we are now assuming that the fact that the stages along the time dimension make up a person does not matter. Therefore, it is not distributionally significant. So the personhood disanalogy is not distributionally significant.

But what about this next disanalogy, though? Along the time dimension, the stages of a person bear to each other the psychological relations that *do* matter, according to Parfit. One stage in a row of Table 8 will remember doing what earlier stages in the row do, and so on. On the other hand, stages in a column, across the dimension of people, do not bear these psychological relations to each other. Call this the 'psychological disanalogy'. According to Parfit, the psychological relations matter; he has already conceded that. It seems that they might easily be distributionally significant, therefore. They might justify us in taking a different attitude to distribution in the two dimensions.

I do not think Parfit would disagree. I think he would allow that the psychological disanalogy might, indeed, justify some different

treatment of distribution across the two dimensions. But nevertheless, he would point out two responses that might be made.

One is what Parfit calls an 'extreme' response. We are assuming
that, between the stages that make up a person, the only relations
that can matter are the psychological ones. Now, independently,
one might have reason to think that, actually, the psychological
relations cannot matter. Parfit refers to many authors who take
this view, or one like it.[8] It implies that the psychological relations
between the stages of a person are not distributionally significant.
So the psychological disanalogy is not distributionally significant.
Though Parfit thinks this response extreme, he also thinks it
defensible.[9]

The second response is this. Let us take the stages of a person
to be longish spans: childhood, maturity, old age and so on. The
psychological connections between stages of this sort may be weak.
Memory fades; people change their values and life plans; and so
on. So the psychological disanalogy may be a weak one. In so far
as it exists, it may be distributionally significant: in so far as
stages along the time dimension are psychologically linked, it may
be right to apply to them different distributional principles from
the ones we apply across separate people. But actually the
psychological links between widely separated stages are weak. So
there are only weak grounds for applying different principles.
Parfit does not think this response extreme. Indeed, it seems to be
his own.[10]

That deals with the psychological disanalogy. It diminishes its
importance, at least. But there are other disanalogies yet. Take
this one. Along a row of Table 8, all the stages have the same
genes, but this is not true across a column. Call this the 'genetic
disanalogy'. Might it not be distributionally significant? Might not
a reasonable principle of distribution take account of this fact of
genetics? In the past, people seem to have found it reasonable for
the sins of the father to be visited upon the sons. Perhaps
American blacks have special claims because of the suffering of
their ancestors. And if genetics is distributionally significant
between generations, surely it must be so within a generation. In
any case, whether or not this idea is initially plausible, we shall
need an argument against it if we are to show that distribution
across people and across times should be treated similarly. We
shall need to show that the genetic disanalogy is not distributionally significant.

So far I have been assuming that, when Parfit says only certain particular psychological relations 'matter', he means that, amongst the relations between person-stages, these are the only ones that have any sort of ethical significance.* This would imply that the genetic disanalogy is not distributionally significant.

But actually I doubt that Parfit does mean this, and his arguments would not sustain it. His notion of what matters arises originally in a fairly narrow context. When we look forward in time, say ten years, most of us take a special interest in a particular one of the person-stages that will be living at that time. I take a special interest in the one that is a later stage of me; you take a similar interest in the one that is a later stage of you. Call this particular type of interest 'egoistic interest'. Parfit's original discussion of what matters is about egoistic interest. When we attach egoistic interest to later stages of ourselves, he asks, what reason have we to do so? Is it just that they are stages of ourselves? His answer is that this is not a good reason. What matters, or should matter to us is that these stages are psychologically related to us, now, by memory and the other relations I mentioned. The fact that they are stages of ourselves is not what matters. As it happens, it is almost invariably the later stages of ourselves that are related to us, now, in this way. So it is right for us to attach our egoistic interest to those stages. But the reason why we should do so is the psychological relations, not the fact that they are stages of ourselves.

Because Parfit's arguments about what matters are developed in this narrow context of egoistic interest, I do not think he would expect them to justify the sweeping conclusion that only these psychological relations are ethically significant *in any way*. For one thing, because of their context, his arguments pay no attention at all to many types of relation. Parfit is initially concerned with the relations in virtue of which a collection of person-stages make up a single person. Some collections of stages make up a single person; others do not because they include stages from more than one person. What determines whether a collection makes up a single person or not? It must be something to do with the relations between the members of the collection. Collections related in particular ways will make up a person; collections not so related

---

* No one would deny that relations such as sameness or difference of genes might be ethically significant in a causal way; they might cause effects that are ethically significant. But I am not talking about causal significance. See my explanation of 'axiological significance' on page 234.

will not. The question is: what ways are those? What are the relations – call them the 'unifying relations' – in virtue of which a collection will make up one person? Do they include spatio-temporal continuity, psychological relations, or what? Parfit first answers this questions, and only later does he go on to ask which relations matter. This leads him to consider, as relations that might matter, only relations that are candidates for unifying relations, or at least for being in some way necessarily connected with the fact that a collection makes up a person. But many of the relations that hold between stages of the same person do so only contingently. This includes many relations that always, though contingently, hold between stages of the same person. The relation of having the same genes is an example. Contingent relations do not enter Parfit's arguments. But I can see no general reason why they should not be ethically significant.

I think, therefore, that Parfit's arguments cannot be expected to show that none of the disanalogies between the dimensions of people and time are distributionally significant.

There are very many disanalogies between the dimensions of time and people. There are very many relations that hold between stages along the rows of Table 8 but not down the columns. Some hold necessarily, some contingently. I think it would be very hard to come up with an argument wide-ranging enough to show that none of them are distributionally significant. This, I believe, is a serious and inevitable problem for an argument by analogy like Parfit's. Such an argument calls for a blanket demonstration that all the disanalogies are distributionally insignificant. And that will be very hard to produce. By contrast, this book describes a defence of the utilitarian principle of distribution that does not require an extensive analogy to be established. It requires only one clearly defined condition, separability, to be satisfied in each dimension.

I do not mean to say that Parfit's arguments are inadequate for his own purposes. It may well be the identity disanalogy that makes it seem reasonable to many people for distribution to be treated differently in the two dimensions. In a later paper,[11] Parfit aruges that different treatment of the two dimensions seems reasonable to many people because of the idea of *compensation*. If a person suffers a harm, she may be compensated for it by a benefit that comes to her at another time. But she cannot be compensated by a benefit that comes to someone else. So compensation is possible in one dimension and not the other. This difference depends on the identity disanalogy. Eliminating the

identity disanalogy may therefore be enough to bring many people
to accept that the dimensions should be treated similarly. And
Parfit aims, not at a conclusive demonstration, but only to make
his conclusions generally acceptable.

3.2 Parfit, Section 2

Parfit's defence of the utilitarian principle of distribution, I said on
page 40, has two steps. The first was to show that the same
principles of distribution must apply both across people and across
time within a single person's life. I cast doubt on that demonstration, but for the sake of argument let us suppose it is successful.
Another way of putting the conclusion is that principles of
distribution should apply to smaller units than people. They should
apply to person-stages. If, for instance, we should value equality
both between people and between the stages within a single
person's life, then we should value equality between all person-
stages, within a life and across lives.

The next step is to show that the principle that does apply,
across both dimensions and across all person-stages, is the
utilitarian one. It needs to be shown, that is to say, that only the
total of good is valuable, and not equality in its distribution. This
section considers that step.

Parfit believes that his disuniting metaphysics helps to make this
step, by making the utilitarian principle more plausible than it
would otherwise have been. Not only does the metaphysics make
the two dimensions similar; it also suggests it is wrong to value
equality in either.[12]

Here is part of his argument:

> Consider the relief of suffering. Suppose that we can help only one
> of two people. We shall achieve more if we help the first; but it is
> the second who, in the past, suffered more. Those who believe in
> equality may decide to help the second person. This will be less
> effective; so the amount of suffering in the two people's lives will, in
> sum, be greater; but the amounts in each life will be made more
> equal. If we accept the Reductionist View, we may decide otherwise.
> We may decide to do the most we can to relieve suffering. To
> suggest why, we can vary the example. Suppose that we can help
> only one of two nations. The one that we can help the most is the
> one whose history was, in earlier centuries, more fortunate. Most of
> us would not believe that it could be right to allow mankind to

suffer more, so that the suffering is more equally divided between the histories of different nations. In trying to relieve suffering, we do not regard nations as the morally significant unit. On the Reductionist View, we compare the lives of people to the histories of nations. We may therefore think the same about them. We may believe that, when we are trying to relieve suffering, neither persons nor lives are the morally significant unit. We may again decide to aim for the least possible suffering, whatever its distribution.[13]

It does not seem to me, however, that this has moved us forward. We have already granted that we should take the same attitude to distribution across time within a life as we take to distribution across lives. This is because the relations between person-stages within a life are not different, in distributionally significant ways, from the relations between stages of different people. So we do not regard people as the morally significant units. This only means that, if we are concerned with equality at all, we shall be concerned with equality between what *are* the morally significant units, namely person-stages. So certainly the fact that a person has suffered more in the *past* will not make us give extra weight to relieving her suffering now. But if she is suffering more *now*, we may give extra weight to it. We could be concerned to equalize the distribution of good between person-stages. All this argument does, then, is remind us that we have changed the units of distribution. It does not suggest that we should be less interested in distribution between them.

Parfit also says that, given reductionism 'it becomes more plausible to focus less upon the person, the subject of experiences, and instead to focus more upon the experiences themselves. It becomes more plausible to claim that . . . we are right to ignore whether experiences come within the same or different lives.'[14] Once again I can make the same answer. Focusing on experiences is not the same thing as aiming to maximize the total goodness of experiences. Suppose an experience is 'the morally significant unit'. So the unit has shrunk to something even smaller than the person-stage, or perhaps to a very short person-stage. We still might be interested in distribution between units. We might be interested in equalizing the goodness of experiences.

I suspect it simply seems natural to Parfit that, as the units shrink, there is less reason to be concerned with distribution between them. Parfit uses the term 'distributive principle' differently from me. A distributive principle, for him, is a principle that gives some value to equality in the distribution of good between people. My 'utilitarian principle of distribution', which gives value only to the total of good regardless of its distribution, is not included. We are naturally inclined to apply distributive principles between people, says Parfit. Now, as the units shrink, we will come to apply them within the lives of single people too. The principles acquire wider 'scope', as Parfit puts it. And it seems natural to him that this may simultaneously give them less 'weight'. Parfit evidently thinks of the utilitarian principle as a neutral basis, on which distributive principles may be overlaid. Consequently, as his arguments remove weight from the distributive principles, we fall back towards the utilitarian starting point. But it needs to be explained why the utilitarian principle is the natural fallback position, and also why increasing the scope of distributive principles should reduce their weight.

Points like these were made by Thomas Nagel, commenting on earlier writings of Parfit's.[15] In *Reasons and Persons*, Parfit responds to Nagel. He argues that if the morally significant unit is shrunk so small as to be just an experience, then it become less plausible to value equality. He offers this argument.[16] If we apply distributive principles with experiences as the units, we shall give the greatest importance to reducing the badness of the worst experiences: to reducing the greatest suffering, that is. Parfit asks how plausible this is. What is so bad about great suffering that it should require such particular attention? Well, he says, suffering strikes us intuitively as *really* bad when it is the same person who is constantly suffering. But once we have shrunk our morally significant unit, the fact that it is the same person constantly suffering cannot actually count for anything. So we have removed this reason for thinking that great suffering is particularly bad.

I think this argument is inadequate. The question at issue is: should we value equality between experiences? If we can reduce the badness of an experience to some particular degree, is that a better thing to do if the experience is originally a very bad one than if it is originally less bad? This is a subtle quantitative question, and you cannot answer it without having some metric of badness for experiences. Parfit's argument just does not have the necessary quantitative precision. In Chapters 10 and 11, I shall be concerned a lot with a question like this one. And the answer will turn on how one sets up a metric of badness. So I am unwilling to accept an argument that is not clear about this.

I conclude that the second step of Parfit's argument by analogy is unsuccessful. Even granted the first step, that distribution across time and across people should be treated similarly, there is no good argument that takes us from there to the conclusion that equality has no value. I hope to develop a different and more successful argument in this book.

3.3 Harsanyi

My second example of a similarity argument is one of John Harsanyi's. It exploits the similarity between the dimensions of people and states of nature. But it does not argue on the basis of similarity alone. Whereas the basis of Parfit's argument is the negative one that we should treat two dimensions in the same way unless there is a reason to treat them differently, Harsanyi offers a positive reason for treating the dimensions of people and states of nature in the same way.

Harsanyi first propounded this argument in a brief article published in 1953,[17] and he has elaborated it in later writings. The account below is drawn mostly from Chapter 4 of his *Rational Behavior and Bargaining Equilibrium*.

Harsanyi is interested in evaluating 'social situations'. A pair of social situations is shown in Table 9. Each entry in the table, such as b_2, stands for the whole of a person's circumstances: her income,

Table 9

People					People				
1	2	3	. . .	h	1	2	3	. . .	h
a_1	a_2	a_3	. . .	a_h	b_1	b_2	b_3	. . .	b_h

Social situation A Social situation B

way of life, education, personal characteristics, and so on. Let us call it a 'life'. Each social situation distributes lives across people. Harsanyi is interested in evaluating social situations like this. At least, he is interested in *people's* evaluations of them. As he puts it, he is interested in people's 'value judgements' about social situations.

Harsanyi takes these value judgements to be preferences of a sort. He calls them 'moral preferences'. They are distinguished from ordinary preferences, he says, by being impartial and impersonal. And he says:

> Individual i's choice among alternative social situations would certainly satisfy this requirement of impartiality and impersonality, if he simply *did not know in advance* what his own social position would be in each social situation . . . More specifically this requirement would be satisfied if he thought that he would have an *equal probability* of being *put in the place* of any one among the n individual members of society.[18]

Harsanyi hopes to discover your moral preferences, then, by the following device. Take a range of alternative social situations. Imagine you are offered a choice between them. You can pick one, and will then find yourself living in this situation. But your position within the society will be random. You will have an equal chance of being in any one of the positions – leading any one of the lives. Suppose, under these conditions of choice, you form preferences between the alternatives. Since you do not know your final position, these preferences will be impartial and impersonal. And preferences that are impartial and impersonal, Harsanyi takes to be moral preferences. He takes the preferences you would have in these conditions to be your moral preferences amongst the social situations.

If you are faced with the choice I have described, from your point of view it is a choice having uncertain results. The alternatives are gambles. When you compare the social situations A and B in Table 9, under the specified conditions of choice, the alternatives you face are really the ones shown in Table 10. Corresponding to each person in the social situation, there is, from your point of view, a state of nature. There must be some random device that will determine which position in the society you are going to

Table 10

States of nature					States of nature				
1	2	3	. . .	h	1	2	3	. . .	h
a_1	a_2	a_3	. . .	a_h	b_1	b_2	b_3	. . .	b_h

Gamble A　　　　　　　　　　　Gamble B

occupy, and a state of nature is a state of that device. You know, as one of the conditions of your choice, that each state has the same probability.

Amongst gambles like the ones in Table 10, you will form preferences. This is a matter of weighing or aggregating goods across the dimension of states of nature. Only your own goods are involved; the weighing is intrapersonal. But Harsanyi identifies your resulting preferences with your moral preferences amongst the given social situations. A social situation distributes goods to different people, across the dimension of people. Your moral preferences, then, involve weighing different people's goods against each other. A weighing of your own goods across the dimension of states of nature is being identified with a weighing of different people's goods across the dimension of people. That is the strategy of the argument.

Harsanyi next makes a particular assumption about the form of a rational person's preferences under uncertainty:

> *Bernoulli's hypothesis about rationality.* A rational and well-informed person prefers one alternative to another, or is indifferent between the two, if and only if the first gives her at least as great an expectation* of her good as the second.[19]

('Well-informed' means only that the person knows what her expectation of good is, from each of the alternatives.) Write the goodness for you of life a_1 as $g(a_1)$, of life a_2 as $g(a_2)$, and so on. Since all the states of nature have the same probability, the probability of each is $1/h$. So the expectation of your good from gamble A is

$$g(a_1)/h + g(a_2)/h + \ldots + g(a_h)/h.$$

From gamble B it is:

$$g(b_1)/h + g(b_2)/h + \ldots + g(b_h)/h.$$

---

* The expectation of any quantity is defined as follows. For each state of nature, take the value of the quantity in that state and multiply it by the probability of that state. Then add up the products, one for each state. The expectation is the total. So the expectation of a quantity z is
$$p_1 z_1 + p_2 z_2 + \ldots + p_s z_s,$$
where p_1, p_2 and so on are the probabilities of the states, and z_1, z_2 and so on are the values that z takes on in the states. The expectation is the weighted average of the values of z, weighted by the probabilities.

According to Bernoulli's hypothesis, if you are rational and well informed, you will prefer A to B, or be indifferent between the two, if and only if the expectation from A is at least as great as it is from B.

The goodness for you of a life is how good it would be for you to live this life. Living a life means taking over all the properties of the person who actually would live it in the social situation. It means losing all those properties of your own that could make the life better or worse for you than it would be for anyone else. How good it would be for you, therefore, must be the same as how good it would be for anyone else. It is simply how good the life would be. So $g(a_1)$ is the actual goodness of the life a_1, $g(a_2)$ the actual goodness of a_2, and so on. The expectation of good from gambles like A and B will consequently be the same for everyone, and every rational and well-informed person will have the same preferences amongst these gambles. These preferences Harsanyi identifies with her moral preferences amongst the corresponding social situations.[20]

Any rational and well-informed person, then, will morally prefer social situation A to social situation B, or be indifferent between them, if and only if gamble A gives at least as great an expectation of good as gamble B. In comparing expectations from these gambles, the factor $1/h$ will cancel out. (Harsanyi does not consider social situations with differing populations.) So gamble A will have at least as great an expectation of good as gamble B if and only if

$$g(a_1) + g(a_2) + \ldots + g(a_h)$$

is at least as great as

$$g(b_1) + g(b_2) + \ldots + g(b_h).$$

These sums are simply the totals of good in the corresponding social situations A and B. So we may conclude that

> Every rational and well-informed person will morally prefer one social situation to another, or be indifferent between them, if and only if the former has at least as great a total of good as the latter.

This is not the utilitarian principle of distribution, but it is as close as Harsanyi would aim to get. The utilitarian principle says that if, and only if, one social situation has at least as great a total of good as another, then it is actually at least as good. Harsanyi is confessedly a utilitarian.[21] But, with the modesty typical of economists in these matters, he shrinks from making assertions about the actual goodness of alternatives. This conclusion about moral preference is, for him, enough.

Harsanyi's argument, then, is effectively a defence of the utilitarian principle of distribution. What should we make of it?

Bernoulli's hypothesis is contentious. I shall be discussing a different form of it at length in Sections 6.5 and 10.3. It is doing especially contentious work here, when coupled with the succeeding step in the argument. The succeeding step claims that a particular life would be exactly as good for one person as it would be for anyone else. Consequently the expectation of good from gambles like A and B will be exactly the same for everyone. Given that, Bernoulli's hypothesis implies that every rational and well informed person must have the same preferences amongst such gambles. But it may seem that rationality cannot really impose such uniformity of preference. Different people, surely, might rationally have different attitudes to the same life. If a businessman and an academic have different preferences between the life of a businessman and the life of an academic, this surely need not result from ignorance or irrationality on the part of one of them. Bernoulli's hypothesis, then, may exaggerate the demands of rationality. In this application, it is covering up some profound difficulties.[22]

This is a weak link in the argument. But even if this link were to fail, the argument would still be important. It is an important step just to connect together the weighing of goods across the two dimensions of states of nature and people. In his 1953 article, that is all Harsanyi set out to do. And this step does not depend on Bernoulli's hypothesis.

There is, though, a more fundamental weakness in the argument. Harsanyi identifies a person's moral preferences about social situations with her preferences about the corresponding gambles. That is the very heart of his argument. And the grounds he offers for it are inadequate.

There is no point in arguing about the meaning of 'moral preference'. Harsanyi uses the term in his arguments, and he draws conclusions from his arguments, so the conclusions tell us implicitly what he must mean by it. Let us examine Harsanyi's conclusions, then. Look at the one I set out above. I am not now concerned with its utilitarian form. I am concerned with this: if every rational and well-informed person morally prefers one social situation to another, that is evidently supposed to tell us something significant. What?

The very least it can be supposed to tell us is that there is a reason for bringing about the social situation that everyone morally prefers, rather than the other, if ever there is a choice. It need not be an overriding reason; other considerations may defeat it. But there has to be *some* consideration in favour of the preferred situation. Harsanyi is engaged in an ethical argument, and ethics is concerned with how to act. He may be diffident about saying that one alternative is better than another. But however he chooses to express his conclusion, he must intend to record a reason for acting one way rather than another. There is no weaker ethical conclusion he could be drawing. If he does not intend this, we need not listen to him; his argument is not intended seriously.

Suppose every rational and well-informed person prefers gamble *A* to gamble *B* in Table 10. It follows, according to Harsanyi, that all these people morally prefer social situation *A* to social situation *B* in Table 9. And from that it must be supposed to follow that there is a reason for bringing about social situation *A* rather than *B* if ever there is a choice. But why should it follow? Why should people's preferences about the gambles give us any reason to favour one corresponding social situation over another?

Harsanyi's only answer is that the preferences between the gambles are impartial and impersonal. That was the point of setting up the gambles in the first place. It puts the people behind a 'veil of ignorance'.[23] A veil of ignorance certainly establishes impartiality and impersonality. But this is not enough to explain why the people's preferences about the gambles should give us any reason to favour one social situation rather than another. It is hard to see why these preferences about gambles should give a reason in favour of a social situation, even to the people whose preferences they are, let alone to anyone else. The preferences are about gambles, and it is hard to see what they have to do with social situations. As Brian Barry says:

> Suppose I am initially disinclined to believe that I must always be prepared to sacrifice my own interests whenever by doing so I can provide somebody else with a larger benefit . . . I do not see that I have been given any adequate cause for changing my mind if I am told that, as a utility-maximizer behind a thin veil of ignorance, that is what I would have endorsed as a principle. I may agree that I would indeed have done so but then ask: 'So what?'[24]

An argument certainly needs to be made here, and Harsanyi has not made one. 'No adequate reason', says Barry, 'has ever been given (by Harsanyi or anybody else) for identifying moral judgments with those made by someone trying to maximize his own prospects from behind a veil of ignorance.'[25] Until this difficulty is overcome, the significance of Harsanyi's argument is seriously in doubt.

The argument I have been describing was first presented by Harsanyi in 1953. My main reason for setting it out is to contrast it with Harsanyi's *other* argument, which first appeared in an article published in 1955.[26] The 1953 argument takes a view about aggregation in the dimension of states of nature – Bernoulli's hypothesis – and transfers it to the dimension of people. The transfer is justified by the veil-of-ignorance argument I have described. The 1955 argument, on the other hand, considers the aggregation of good in the two dimensions simultaneously. It is a formal proof that depends on separability in each dimension. Given separability, logic enforces a connection between aggregation in the two dimensions. It is exactly the sort of argument this book is about. Indeed, after some reinterpretation, it forms the main subject of a good part of the book. I have already mentioned it on page 28.

Not all authors have clearly distinguished Harsanyi's two arguments. One reason is that the arguments' conclusions are similar: both are aimed at the utilitarian principle of distribution. Also, Harsanyi often repeats them together; both are presented in Chapter 4 of *Rational Behavior and Bargaining Equilibrium*. Furthermore, in the 1955 article,[27] Harsanyi himself refers to his 1953 argument in a slightly misleading way. He seems to suggest that the 1955 argument requires the support of the 1953 one. But actually this is not so. The two arguments are entirely independent.

This means that the 1955 argument is not subject to the objection I have just made to the 1953 one. It makes no attempt to move from preferences formed behind a veil of ignorance to moral preference. No veil of ignorance plays any part in it. For this reason I much prefer the 1955 argument.

Harsanyi himself seems slightly to prefer the other. He says: 'This axiomatic approach [the 1955 argument] yields a lesser amount of philosophically interesting information about the nature of morality than the equiprobability model [the 1953 argument] does, but it has the advantage of being based on much weaker – almost trivial – philosophical assumptions.'[28] It is true that the 1955 argument works in slightly mysterious ways. A mathematical theorem does a lot of the work in it, and it is a little hard to figure out how. But it does require only weak assumptions, and that benefit is worth a little trouble in penetrating the mystery. I hope this book will help to clear it up. The 1953 argument does not really yield philosophically interesting information about the nature of morality. Instead, it makes a philosophically unsupported assumption about the nature of morality: that morality is to be found from people's preferences when they are placed behind a veil of ignorance.

Notes

1. For instance, Nozick, *Anarchy, State and Utopia*, p. 33.

2. *Reasons and Persons*, pp. 333–4.

3. Another example of a disuniting metaphysics, besides Parfit's, is in Lewis, 'Survival and identity'. An example of a uniting metaphysics is in Wiggins, *Sameness and Substance*. For a useful exposition, see Perry, 'Introduction', in his *Personal Identity*. A good critique of disuniting metaphysics is Haslanger, 'Persistence, change and explanation'. Another is Thomson, 'Parthood and identity across time'.

4. *A Theory of Justice*, pp. 26–7.

5. p. 27.

6. Parfit (p. 341) quotes J. Findlay, *Values and Intentions*, p. 294: 'the separateness of persons . . . is *the* basic fact for morals'.

7. Chapter 13.

8. pp. 307–8. See also pp. 342–3.

9. p. 343.

10. See, for instance, p. 333.

11. 'Comments', responding to criticisms made by Bart Schultz in 'Persons, selves and utilitarianism'.

12. pp. 341–5.

13. p. 341.

14. p. 341.

15. Nagel, 'Equality', note on pp. 124–5. Sen makes the same point in 'Utilitarianism and welfarism', p. 470.

16. p. 345. Parfit actually attributes the argument to Haksar, *Equality, Liberty and Perfectionism*, p. 111, but endorses it himself.

17. 'Cardinal utility in welfare economics and in the theory of risk-taking'. There is a similar argument in Vickrey, 'Risk, utility and social policy', which develops a remark in Vickrey's earlier paper 'Measuring marginal utility by reactions to risk', p. 329.

18. *Rational Behavior and Bargaining Equilibrium*, pp. 49–50.

19. Bernoulli's hypothesis is a version of expected utility theory, which is explained in Chapter 5 of this book. I attribute it to Bernoulli on the basis of his 'Exposition of a new theory on the measurement of risk'. Bernoulli, writing in Latin, uses the word '*emolumentum*' rather than 'good'. But I take it that, by the *emolumentum* of an outcome for a person, Bernoulli means how good that outcome is for the person.

I attribute Bernoulli's hypothesis to Harsanyi on the basis of Harsanyi's

Rational Behavior and Bargaining Equilibrium, Chapter 4. Harsanyi speaks of 'utility' rather than 'good', and unfortunately, his use of 'utility' is ambiguous. He sometimes uses the term as I shall use in this book, as a name for the value of a function that represents an ordering, specifically a preference ordering. 'Represents' here has a technical sense, which is defined by (4.2.1) on page 65 below. Utility in this sense is determined from previously given preferences. But take this sentence of Harsanyi's: 'If I want to compare the utility that I would derive from a new car with the utility that a friend would derive from a new sailboat, then I must ask myself what utility I would derive from a sailboat if I had taken up sailing for a regular hobby as my friend has done, . . .' (p. 59). Here, Harsanyi is discussing how I would form my preferences between different lives, such as mine with a new car and my friend's with a new sailboat. I am evidently supposed to do so by first assessing the utility of these lives. Utility, then, is evidently supposed to determine my preferences; it is not determined from previously given preferences. It is clear to me that in this sentence, and in many others, Harsanyi is using 'utility' to mean good. The ambiguity of 'utility' in economists' usage is described in my '"Utility"'.

20. This paragraph is a very liberal interpretation of Harsanyi's argument in *Rational Behavior and Bargaining Equilibrium*, pp. 57–60. I find the original argument hard to understand, because of the ambiguity of 'utility' mentioned in note 19.

21. pp. 62–4.

22. See Scanlon, 'The moral basis of interpersonal comparisons'; also Griffin, *Well-Being*, p. 113, and Skyrms, *The Dynamics of Rational Deliberation*, note 15 on p. 173.

23. This term was introduced, I think, by Rawls (*A Theory of Justice*, note on p. 137) in taking over the idea from Harsanyi.

24. *Theories of Justice*, pp. 334–5. T. M. Scanlon makes a similar point in 'Contractualism and utilitarianism', p. 123.

25. pp. 78–9.

26. 'Cardinal welfare, individualistic ethics, and interpersonal comparisons of utility'.

27. p. 14.

28. 'Morality and the theory of rational behavior', p. 48.

Chapter 4

The Separability Theorems

This chapter sets out the theorems that underlie the argument of this book. Section 4.1 presents two examples that show in a rough way how the theorems work. Section 4.2 defines separability precisely, and states the theorems. Section 4.3 starts the work of interpreting the theorems. It explains the significance of their conclusions from a formal, mathematical point of view. The rest of the book continues the work of interpretation, by giving content to the forms described in this chapter. Section 4.4 discusses a significant assumption that is used in the proofs of the theorems.

4.1 Two examples

Suppose that each week you earn £200. Each week your employer, in bringing round your pay packet, offers to toss with you for double or quits. Indeed, being a gambling sort, she offers you a premium of £20 to play. So if you win on the toss you get £420. If you lose you get £20. Your employer's coin is fair. But you dislike risk, and each month you decline the offer. You take home your pay of £200.

Let us look at your behaviour from the perspective of ten years taken together (call it five hundred weeks). By playing safe each week, over the five hundred weeks you get £100,000. What would have happened if, instead, you had regularly accepted the gamble? The risk to your total income over the whole period would have been very small. Wins in some weeks would have cancelled out losses in others. And each week there was the premium to be had. The chances that you would have done better than £100,000 by taking the gamble each week are about 98.75 percent. The chances that you would have done much worse are minute. So if you were concerned for your total income over the ten years, you should have taken the gamble each week. It would have been paranoid to play safe each week just to avoid such a tiny risk to your total income.

Does this mean that in refusing the gamble each week you are irrational? Not necessarily. Suppose your circumstances are these. For some reason you cannot carry money over from one week to the next. What you get each week is what you have to live off that week. So if you find yourself with only £20, that will have very serious consequences. You will be turned out of your house, and have to beg for food. If you were to gamble each week, you would, pretty certainly, do better in total. But your income over the ten years, though bigger in total, would be unevenly spread over the weeks. In some weeks you would be destitute. In others you would be supremely affluent, but those good weeks will not make up for the bad ones. That is a good reason for declining the gamble. You avoid risk each week, not in order to avoid risk to your total income, but in order to have your income evenly distributed across time. You are willing to sacrifice some part of total income for the sake of an even distribution. Your weekly risk aversion amounts to the same thing as a temporal unevenness aversion. If you had no reason to prefer an even distribution – if, say, you could keep income from one week to spend in another – then you would have no reason to avoid risk each week.

The next example tightens up the link between risk aversion and unevenness aversion.

Suppose your working life is shrunk to two weeks only. You still earn £200 each week. Again your employer offers double or quits, with a premium of £20 for playing. But she now also offers this guarantee: if (and only if) you lose in one week, you will win in the other. That is to say, she offers to toss once. If the coin falls heads, you get £20 in the first week and £420 in the second. If it falls tails, you get £420 the first week and £20 the next. But you can still take the safe option if you choose, and have £200 each week. In this example, the gamble poses no risk at all to your lifetime earnings. It only affects their distribution. The small risk to lifetime earnings was a complication in the previous example, and this example eliminates it.

Your alternatives are shown in Table 11 on the next page. (Suppose your employer tosses her coin even if you choose not to play, just to see what would have happened.) This is a two-

Table 11

		States of nature					States of nature	
		Heads	Tails				Heads	Tails
Weeks	1	£200	£200		Weeks	1	£20	£420
	2	£200	£200			2	£420	£20

Do not play   Play

dimensional problem of the sort I mentioned in Section 2.2. Goods distributed along the two dimensions of time and states of nature have to be weighed together simultaneously.

How are you to evaluate these alternatives? One way would be to look at them taking one state of nature at a time. Look, that is to say, at the results of the two alternatives in each state, and evaluate the alternatives on that basis. So take state heads first. In state heads, if you choose not to play, you get £200 each week. If you choose to play, you get £20 the first week and £420 the next. Which do you prefer? That depends on how much you care about having your income evenly distributed over time. If you care a lot, you will prefer the result of not playing. If you do not care so much, you will prefer the result of playing, because of the £40 premium.

Now take state tails. Again, if you choose not to play, you will get £200 each week. If you choose to play, you will get £420 in the first week and £20 the next. Which of these do you prefer? I am going to assume for simplicity that each week counts equally for you; you do not count future income for less than present income, or anything of that sort. Then this choice is effectively the same as the previous one. You will prefer the result of not playing if you care a lot about an even distribution of income over time. If you do not care much you will prefer the result of playing.

The example is conveniently symmetrical. You will prefer the result of playing in one state if and only if you prefer it in the other. This makes your choice between the alternatives of playing or not playing a fairly easy one. If you care a lot about an even distribution of income over time, you will prefer not to play, because you will prefer the result of not playing in both states. If you do not care much about evenness, you will prefer to play.

That is the conclusion we come to by looking at the problem one way: taking states of nature one at a time. An alternative way of looking at it is to take weeks one at a time. Look at the first week first. If you do not play, you will definitely have £200. If you play, you will have either £20 or £420. Which do you prefer? That is a matter of your attitude to risk. If you are strongly averse to risk, you will prefer the definite £200. If you are not, you will prefer the risky alternative.

Now look at the second week. The alternatives are effectively the same as in the first week, since the coin is fair. So your preferences will go the same way. The problem is symmetrical viewed this way too: you will prefer the result of playing in one week if and only if you prefer it in the other. Again the choice is a fairly easy one. You will prefer not to play if you are strongly averse to risk. You will prefer to play if you are not.

What I have done is to slice up the problem of Table 11 across the two different dimensions: state by state and week by week. Each led to a different conclusion. One: that you will prefer not to play if and only if you care a lot about evenness in the distribution of income across time. The other: that you will prefer not to play if and only if you care a lot about avoiding risk. Together, these conclusions tell us that risk aversion and unevenness aversion must be linked. They are really just two ways of describing the same pattern of preferences. But risk aversion is a feature of the way you aggregate goods across the dimension of states of nature, and unevenness aversion is a feature of the way you aggregate goods across the dimension of time. So our conclusion has connected up the aggregation of goods in the two dimensions.

I hope the example makes this seem unremarkable. It is an example of the working of the separability theorems. Of course, it is not meant to prove anything. It is only meant to suggest how the dimensions of aggregation come to be connected.

In the descriptions I gave of the two different slicings, I was implicitly assuming separability. Starting with one slicing, I considered your preferences about what happens in the two states of nature, taken separately. I assumed that your preferences about what happens in one state are not affected by what happens in the other. This is what it means to say that the states are separable. For states of nature, separability generally seems a plausible assumption; I shall be saying much more about it in Chapter 5. So I hope the argument in that case seemed straightforward.

Then I came to the other slicing, and considered your preferences about what happens in the two weeks, taken separately.
Here I assumed separability between weeks: your preferences
about what happens in one week are not affected by what happens
in the other. This seems a much less plausible assumption. It
seems very likely that what happens in one week will affect your
attitude to what happens in another. If we suppose, as I did for the
previous example, that money can be spent only in the week when
it is earned, separability may be a little more acceptable. But there
will still be all sorts of interconnections between the weeks. If, for
instance, you travel widely at one stage of your life, you might not
mind forgoing travel at another. So separability between weeks is
pretty implausible. And I think my argument, which assumed
separability, showed the strain when it came to slicing by weeks.
It is questionable that you could really settle your preferences
between playing and not playing by examining the results in each
week taken separately. Chapter 11 examines in more detail the
question of separability between times in a life.

Nevertheless, plausible or not, the argument above assumed
separability in both dimensions. The conclusion that risk aversion
and unevenness aversion are equivalent depended on it. First I
said you will prefer not to play if and only if you are averse to
unevenness, and that depended on assuming separability between
states of nature. Then I said you will prefer not to play if and only
if you are averse to risk, and that depended on assuming separability between weeks. From these two things the conclusion
followed. The conclusion is, in fact, the result of *crosscutting*
separability, which I shall define formally on page 69. I reached
this conclusion because I was able to cut the problem into separable slices across two dimensions, so that the slices cut across each
other. If separability fails in one or the other dimension, the
conclusion will fail too.

Table 12

		States of nature	
		Heads	Tails
Weeks	1	y_{1h}	y_{1t}
	2	y_{2h}	y_{2t}

Before going on to the general theory, I want to extend the example a little. I have been talking about only the two alternatives of playing and not playing. But we can imagine many other alternatives within the same framework of two weeks and two states of nature. A generic alternative is shown in Table 12. The ys stand for amounts of money. Let us suppose you have preferences, not just between playing and not playing, but amongst a range of alternatives like this. I shall be using this example later.

4.2 Definitions and theorems

Now I come to defining separability more precisely.[1]

Separability is a property of a relation. I shall only be concerned with relations that are transitive, reflexive and complete.* Let $\succeq$ be such a relation, and call it an *ordering*. Call the field of the ordering (the set of all things that are related to something by $\succeq$) the set of *alternatives*. Traditionally, in the discussion of separability, $\succeq$ has been taken to be a *preference* relation: '$A \succeq B$' has been taken to mean that A is preferred or indifferent to B. More often, I shall be taking $\succeq$ to be a *betterness* relation, so '$A \succeq B$' means that A is at least as good as B. But the interpretation of $\succeq$ does not matter for the definition of separability.

Granted some technical conditions that need not concern us, an ordering $\succeq$ can be *represented* by a function.[2] This means there is a function U that assigns a real number to each alternative in such a way that

(4.2.1) $\qquad U(A) \geq U(B)$ if and only if $A \succeq B$.

I call the function U a *utility function* and $U(A)$ the *utility* of A, for any alternative A.

This word 'utility' has been the source of great confusion amongst economists. Officially in economics, utility is defined as the value of a function that represents an ordering – specifically a preference ordering – in the way I have described. But unofficially economists also often use 'utility' to stand for a person's good. The ambiguity is very damaging.[3] I would not use this word if I could find a good alternative. But 'utility theory' and 'expected

---

* A relation $\succeq$ is transitive if and only if, for all A, B and C in its field, $A \succeq B$ and $B \succeq C$ imply $A \succeq C$. It is reflexive if and only if, for all A in its field, $A \succeq A$. It is complete if and only if, for all A and B in its field, either $A \succeq B$ or $B \succeq A$.

utility theory' are the thoroughly established names of theories that are central to this book – theories that deal with the structure of ordering relations between alternatives. It would be very odd to apply utility theory and expected utility theory without using the word 'utility'. I am therefore stuck with this word. But I must say with emphasis that the meaning I give it is entirely determined by the definition. By 'the utility of A', I mean the number assigned to A by a function that represents an ordering, and nothing else. If the ordering in question is a betterness ordering, then utility represents betterness: one alternative is at least as good as another if and only if it has at least as great a utility. It *may* also turn out that, by selecting a suitable utility function, utilities can be made to measure goodness more tightly than this. Levels of utility may give some indication of levels of goodness; I shall be saying much more about this later. But if so, that is something to be discovered; it is no part of the meaning of 'utility'.

We shall be dealing with alternatives that have some complexity. Each one I shall denote by a *vector*, say $(x_1, x_2, \ldots x_n)$. (A vector is simply a list.) Call each place in this vector a *location*, and the term occupying each place the *occurrence* at that location. So $(x_1, x_2, \ldots x_n)$ has n locations, at which the occurrences are x_1, x_2, x_3 and so on.

I shall assume that, in any particular problem we have to deal with, all the alternatives contain just the same locations. They differ only in the occurrences at those locations. All the alternatives, then, will be denoted by vectors of the same length.

For an example, look back to Table 2 on page 22. It shows two alternatives, A and B. Each has two locations, the states of nature good weather and bad weather. The alternatives are

$$A = \text{(enjoyable trip, enjoyable trip)}$$
and $$B = \text{(thrills and achievement, boredom)}.$$

The occurrences here are: enjoyable trip, thrills and achievement, and boredom. In Table 12 on page 64 the generic alternative is

$$(y_{1h}, y_{1t}, y_{2h}, y_{2t}).$$

I have simply written the rows in the table next to each other to form a vector. (Notice, then, that the vector of locations does not necessarily correspond to just one of my three 'dimensions'.) The alternatives in Table 11 on page 62 are

Do not play = (200, 200, 200, 200)

and Play = (20, 420, 420, 20).

Now, from all the locations, pick out any subset of them. (The subset may consist of one location only.) The occurrences at the locations in this subset can be collected together to form a subvector. For instance, from the n locations in $(x_1, x_2, \ldots x_n)$ let us pick out the subset consisting of the first and third. This gives us the subvector (x_1, x_3).

And now allow the occurrences at the selected locations to vary, but hold constant the occurrences at all the other locations. This means varying the subvector, keeping constant the other components of the original vector. It gives us a range of alternative subvectors. For instance, vary the values of x_1 and x_3, but give all the other components, x_2, x_4, x_5 and so on, constant values, say $\bar{x}_2$, $\bar{x}_4$, $\bar{x}_5$ and so on.

Given the occurrences that are held constant, the ordering of the alternatives determines, in an obvious way, an ordering of the subvectors. I shall call the latter a *conditional* ordering. To define it properly: one subvector ranks higher than another in the conditional ordering $\succeq'$ if and only if the alternative it is extracted from ranks higher than the alternative the other is extracted from in the original ordering $\succeq$. For instance, for any subvectors (x_1, x_3) and $(\hat{x}_1, \hat{x}_3)$:

$$(x_1, x_3) \succeq' (\hat{x}_1, \hat{x}_3) \text{ if and only if}$$
$$(x_1, \bar{x}_2, x_3, \bar{x}_4, \ldots \bar{x}_n) \succeq (\hat{x}_1, \bar{x}_2, \hat{x}_3, \bar{x}_4, \ldots \bar{x}_n).$$

The conditional ordering is an ordering of the subvectors conditional on the occurrences at the other locations. If the original ordering is someone's preference ordering, the conditional ordering tell us the person's preferences about the subvector, given what happens at the other locations. For example, take the four-component vectors $(y_{1h}, y_{1t}, y_{2h}, y_{2t})$ that come from Table 12. Pick out the first two locations – heads and tails in the first week – and keep the third and fourth components of the vector constant at, say, 200 each. You will have preference among vectors like (100, 400, 200, 200) and (150, 210, 200, 200), which have these constant values for the third and fourth components. In effect, these are your preferences amongst alternative gambles you might be offered in the first week, such as (100, 400) and (150, 210), given that you are going to get £200 for sure in the second week. They are your conditional preferences about gambles in the first week.

So far, we have picked out a subset of locations, and found the ordering of its subvectors conditional on some fixed occurrences at other locations. Next, keep the same subset, but pick new occurrences for the locations outside the subset. Then hold these new occurrences constant, and again vary the occurrences in the chosen subset. This will determine a new ordering of the subvectors, conditional on the new occurrences at other locations. Normally, this conditional ordering will be different from the previous one. But if it happens to be the same, and if, furthermore, it happens to be the same whatever the fixed occurrences at other locations, the subset is said to be separable.

That is: a subset of locations is defined to be *separable* under the ordering $\succeq$ if and only if the conditional ordering determined by $\succeq$ on the subvectors corresponding to this subset is the same whatever are the constant occurrences at the other locations.

Separability says that the ordering amongst the occurrences in the subvector is independent of what happens elsewhere. In the example of Table 12, the first week will be separable if your preferences about gambles in the first week are not affected by what is going to happen in the second.

There is a way of understanding separability in terms of a utility function representing the ordering. Since the alternatives are vectors $(x_1, x_2, \ldots x_n)$, a utility function will be a function of these vectors:

$$U(x_1, x_2, \ldots x_n).$$

Suppose the first and third locations form a separable subset. Then, and only then, the utility function will have the form

$$V(u(x_1, x_3), x_2, x_4, \ldots x_n),$$

where $u(x_1, x_3)$ is a real number. The function u is called a *subutility* function.

This formula means that a separable subvector, in this case (x_1, x_3), can be evaluated separately by a subutility function, independently of what happens at the other locations. The function assigns a subutility to the subvector. Then the subutility can be put together with the occurrences at the other locations to determine overall utility. I hope this conclusion will seem obvious from the definition of separability I have given.[4]

Many different subsets of locations may be separable. And the separable subsets may overlap and cut across each other. In Table 12, for instance, each week may be separable, and so may each state of nature. This means that a utility function

$$U(y_{1h}, y_{1t}, y_{2h}, y_{2t}),$$

representing the ordering, can be written in the form

$$W(w_1(y_{1h}, y_{1t}), w_2(y_{2h}, y_{2t})),$$

and also in the form

$$V(v_h(y_{1h}, y_{2h}), v_t(y_{1t}, y_{2t})).$$

I now have to define some more terms. First, an ordering is defined to be *weakly separable* if and only if every location is separable on its own. This means that what happens at one location can be evaluated according to a subutility function of its own, independently of what happens at the other locations. So if an ordering is weakly separable, a utility function that represents it will have the form

$$U(x_1, x_2, \ldots x_n) = V(u_1(x_1), u_2(x_2), \ldots u_n(x_n)).$$

(Notice that the occurrences x_1, x_2 and so on need not be real numbers, whereas the subutilities $u_1(x_1)$, $u_2(x_2)$ and so on must be.)

Next, an ordering is defined to be *strongly separable* if and only if every subset of locations is separable: every individual location is separable, every pair is separable, every triple, and so on.

An ordering is *additively separable* if and only if it can be represented by a sum of subutilities. That is to say: if and only if it can be represented by a function of the form

(4.2.2) $\quad U(x_1, x_2, \ldots x_n) = u_1(x_1) + u_2(x_2) + \ldots + u_n(x_n).$

(This is called an *additively separable function*.)

Finally, suppose the locations can be arranged on a rectangular grid with at least two rows and two columns:

$$
\begin{array}{cccc}
x_{11} & x_{12} & \cdots & x_{1J} \\
x_{21} & x_{22} & \cdots & x_{2J} \\
\cdot & \cdot & & \cdot \\
\cdot & \cdot & & \cdot \\
\cdot & \cdot & & \cdot \\
x_{I1} & x_{I2} & \cdots & x_{IJ}
\end{array}
$$

in such a way that each row and each column is separable in the ordering. If, and only if, this can be done, I shall say the ordering has *crosscutting separability*.

Now I can state the separability theorems.

First separability theorem. An ordering is strongly separable if and only if it is additively separable.

Second separability theorem. If an ordering has crosscutting separability, it is additively separable.

The first of these theorems was proved by Gérard Debreu,[5] the second by W. M. Gorman.[6] There are informal proofs in the appendix to this chapter.

For an example of the second separability theorem, take Table 12. If each week and each state of nature is separable, your preferences will have crosscutting separability. So you will have an additively separable utility function representing them:

$$(4.2.3) \quad U(y_{1h}, y_{1t}, y_{2h}, y_{2t}) = u_{1h}(y_{1h}) + u_{1t}(y_{1t}) + u_{2h}(y_{2h}) + u_{2t}(y_{2t}).$$

4.3 The significance of additive separability

What does additive separability of a utility function signify? This chapter is about form rather than content, and this section about significance will be formal too. The rest of the book discusses the concrete significance of additive separability in particular applications. But there are some important formal points to be made first.

If a utility function is additively separable, it has a property often known as *cardinality*. I shall explain what this means. Page 89 in the appendix mentions an alternative way of looking at it.

Increasing transformations and ordinal utility

As a preliminary, I need to explain the idea of *transforming* a utility function. A utility function U assigns a number $U(A)$ to each alternative A in the field of an ordering. A transformation of U assigns, to each value that U takes on, a different value V. It is a function from values of U to values of V. It can be shown in a graph such as Figure 3. For each alternative A we have a value of U, and now for each value of U we have a value of V. So we now have another function $V(A)$ defined on the field of alternatives A. V is called a *transform* of U.

Suppose the transformation is *increasing*. This means that whenever one value of U is higher than another, it is always assigned a higher value of V. The graph of an increasing transformation slopes upwards; Figure 3 shows an increasing transformation. Then, for any pair of alternatives A and B, it will be the case that

(4.3.1) $\qquad V(A) \geq V(B)$ if and only if $U(A) \geq U(B)$.

Consequently, if U is a utility function representing an ordering, V will also be a utility function representing the same ordering. This follows immediately from (4.3.1) and (4.2.1) on page 65. If a utility function represents an ordering, then, any increasing transform of it represents the same ordering.

So an ordering of alternatives will be represented, not just by one utility function, but by a whole family of utility functions. Each member of the family will be an increasing transform of every other member, and the family will include every increasing transform of each of its members. So the condition that a utility function represents a given ordering does not determine a single function; it determines a family like this. In the jargon, it determines a utility function *uniquely up to increasing transformations*.

Figure 3

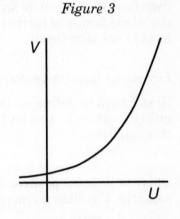

In practice, we often pick one function out of the family to work with. It stands in for the whole family. A utility function playing this role – standing in for a family whose members are all the increasing transforms of each other – is often called an *ordinal* utility function. The only *significant* properties of an ordinal function are those properties it shares with all the rest of the family. These properties are determined by the fact that the function represents the given ordering. Its other properties, peculiar to it, are the accidental result of our choice of this function, rather than some other, to stand in for the family.

Take the example of Table 12 again. Suppose it happens that your preferences can be represented by the following function, which is additively separable (it is a particular instance of (4.2.3) on page 70):

(4.3.2) $U(y_{1h}, y_{1t}, y_{2h}, y_{2t}) = \log(y_{1h}) + \log(y_{1t}) + \log(y_{2h}) + \log(y_{2t}).$

Let V be the antilog of U. Then

$$V(y_{1h}, y_{1t}, y_{2h}, y_{2t}) = \text{antilog}\{U(y_{1h}, y_{1t}, y_{2h}, y_{2t})\}$$
$$= \text{antilog}\{\log(y_{1h}) + \log(y_{1t}) + \log(y_{2h}) + \log(y_{2t})\}$$
$$= \text{antilog}\{\log(y_{1h}y_{1t}y_{2h}y_{2t})\}$$
$$= y_{1h}y_{1t}y_{2h}y_{2t}.$$

Taking the antilog of U is an increasing transformation. (Figure 3 happens to be its graph.) Therefore V represents your preferences as well as U. V is the product of the four components y_{1h}, y_{1t}, y_{2h} and y_{2t}. It is not additively separable. So the additively separable form of U is not shared by all its increasing transforms. If, therefore, U is taken as an ordinal utility function, standing in for the whole family of increasing transforms, its additively separable form is not significant.

Increasing linear transformations and cardinal utility

Next I need to define an increasing *linear* transformation. Take a utility function U, and let the values of V be determined from it by this equation:

$$V = aU + b$$

where a is some positive number and b any number, positive or negative. V is then an increasing linear transform of U. I shall call

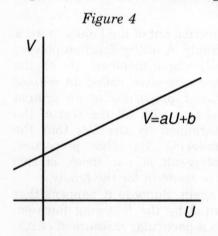

Figure 4

a the *scaling factor* of the transformation, for a reason that will appear on page 76. The fact that a is positive is what makes the transformation increasing. The graph of an increasing linear transformation is an upward-sloping straight line; Figure 4 shows one. Notice that if V is an increasing linear transform of U, U is an increasing linear transform of V.

Now suppose we are dealing with a strongly separable ordering. We know from the first separability theorem that it can be represented by an additively separable utility function – by a function having the form shown in (4.2.2), that is:

$$U(x_1, x_2, \ldots x_n) = u_1(x_1) + u_2(x_2) + \ldots + u_n(x_n).$$

Let V be an increasing linear transform of U: V is $(aU + b)$, where a is positive. Let $b_1, b_2, \ldots b_n$ be any collection of numbers that add up to b. And define functions $v_1, v_2, \ldots v_n$ by these equations:

(4.3.3)
$$v_1(x_1) = \{au_1(x_1) + b_1\},$$
$$v_2(x_2) = \{au_2(x_2) + b_2\},$$
$$\ldots$$
and
$$v_n(x_n) = \{au_n(x_n) + b_n\}.$$

Each v_r is $(au_r + b_r)$. And a is a positive number. So v_r is an increasing linear transform of u_r. Furthermore, notice, all the transformations share the same scaling factor a.

With these definitions in place, we can write V like this:

$$V = aU + b$$
$$= a\{u_1(x_1) + u_2(x_2) + \ldots + u_n(x_n)\} + \{b_1 + b_2 + \ldots + b_n\}$$
$$= \{au_1(x_1) + b_1\} + \{au_2(x_2) + b_2\} + \ldots + \{au_n(x_n) + b_n\}$$
$$= v_1(x_1) + v_2(x_2) + \ldots + v_n(x_n).$$

So V, an increasing linear transform of U, also turns out to be the sum of subutilities that are each increasing linear transforms of the subutilities of U. And all the transformations share the same scaling factor.

The converse is also true. Take the subutilities of U and put each through an increasing linear transformation, using the same scaling factor for each. That is to say, from u_1, u_2 and so on determine subutilities v_1, v_2 and so on that satisfy equations of the form (4.3.3). Then add up the resulting subutilities v_1, v_2 and so on. This is just working backwards through the above sequence of equations. So the result will be a new function V that is $(aU + b)$, an increasing linear transform of U.

In summary: V is an increasing linear transform of U if and only if V is the sum of subutilities that are increasing linear transforms of the subutilities of U, all having the same scaling factor.

Since V is the sum of subutilities v_1, v_2 and so on, it is additively separable. Since it is an increasing transform of U, it represents the same ordering as U. Starting from an additively separable function, then, an increasing linear transformation always produces another additively separable utility function that represents the same ordering.

Furthermore, *only* increasing linear transformations will work this trick. Any increasing transformation will produce another representation of the same ordering. But only a linear one will produce an additively separable function. The proof of this point is quite long, and I shall omit it.

Our conclusions about increasing linear transformations can be summarized like this:

> *Uniqueness theorem.* Let U be an additively separable utility function that represents an ordering. Then the following are all equivalent:
>
> V is an additively separable utility function representing the same ordering as U;
>
> V is an increasing linear transform of U;
>
> V is the sum of subutilities that are increasing linear transforms of the subutilities of U, all having the same scaling factor.

Why do I call this a uniqueness theorem? If an ordering can be represented by an additively separable utility function (as it can if it is strongly separable), the theorem shows it can be represented by a whole family of additively separable functions. Each member of the family is an increasing linear transform of the others, and the family includes every increasing linear transform of each of its members. The condition that a function represents the ordering, and the condition that it is additively separable, together determine such a family. That is to say, they determine a utility function *uniquely up to increasing linear transformations*. This is a tighter determination than is achieved by the simple condition that a function represents the ordering. That, I explained on page 71, determines utility uniquely only up to increasing transformations.

The tighter determination is only possible when the ordering is strongly separable, because only then can it be represented by an additively separable function. Furthermore, it is very important to understand that utility functions are determined this tightly *only* if we impose the condition of additive separability. The condition that the functions represent the ordering (even if it is a strongly separable ordering) is not enough. From an additively separable function, *any* increasing transformation will produce another function that represents the same ordering. But it will not be an additively separable function unless the transformation is linear.

Once again, in practice, we often pick one function out of the family to work with. A utility function playing this role – standing in for a family whose members are increasing linear transforms of each other – is often called a *cardinal* utility function. Requiring additive separability, then, (when it can be done) means that we have cardinal utility functions to work with. For a cardinal utility function, its significant properties are those it shares with all the rest of the family: with all increasing linear transforms of itself. If U in (4.3.2) were taken as a cardinal utility function, its additive separability would be a significant property, because all its increasing linear transforms are also additively separable.

The same two conditions – that the utility functions represent a given ordering and that they are additively separable – also determine subutilities uniquely up to increasing linear transformations. Each member of the family of utility functions will have subutilities that are increasing linear transforms of the subutilities of other members. Subutilities, then, are cardinal too. Furthermore, when the subutilities of one member are transformed into the subutilities of another, the scaling factor will be the same for each of them. Transformations of the subutilities have to keep in step with each other. Because of this, subutilities are said to be, not just cardinal, but *cocardinal*.

The shape of utility graphs

The important feature of cardinal utility and subutility functions is that, for them, *ratios of utility differences* are significant.

To see this, take two utility functions U and V that are increasing linear transforms of each other. Take any four alternatives A, B, C and D. It turns out that, because the transformation is increasing and linear, the ratio of the utility difference $\{U(A) - U(B)\}$ to $\{U(C) - U(D)\}$ is necessarily the same as the ratio of $\{V(A) - V(B)\}$ to $\{V(C) - V(D)\}$.* That is to say, the ratio of utility differences is preserved by an increasing linear transformation. If a utility function determines a particular ratio of utility differences for four alternatives, then all its increasing linear transforms will determine the same ratio. For a cardinal function, then, these ratios are significant.

The condition of additive separability makes subutility functions

---

* V is an increasing linear transform of U. So V is $(aU + b)$ for some a and b. Therefore

$$\frac{[V(A) - V(B)]}{[V(C) - V(D)]} = \frac{[(aU(A)+b) - (aU(B)+b)]}{[(aU(C)+b) - (aU(D)+b)]} = \frac{[aU(A) - aU(B)]}{[aU(C) - aU(D)]} = \frac{[U(A) - U(B)]}{[U(C) - U(D)]}.$$

not only cardinal but also cocardinal. This implies that the transformations preserve the ratio of utility differences, not only within a particular subutility function, but between different functions as well. For instance, let x_1 and $\hat{x}_1$ be two occurrences at the first location, and x_2 and $\hat{x}_2$ be two at the second. Suppose the subutilities u_1 and u_2 are transformed to v_1 and v_2. Then the ratio of $\{u_1(x_1) - u_1(\hat{x}_1)\}$ to $\{u_2(x_2) - u_2(\hat{x}_2)\}$ will be the same as the ratio of $\{v_1(x_1) - v_1(\hat{x}_1)\}$ to $\{v_2(x_2) - v_2(\hat{x}_2)\}$, provided the transformation is one that preserves additive separability.* (The *differences* must always be within one subutility function; it is the *ratios* of differences that are preserved between functions.) Ratios of utility differences, then, are significant even between different locations.

But why should we be interested in ratios of utility differences? To explain this I shall use once more the example of Table 12 on page 64. Let us assume that your preference ordering has crosscutting separability. So it has the additively separable representation shown in (4.2.3). The subutility functions, u_{1h} for instance, will be cardinal. Since u_{1h} is a function of amounts of money (the amount you get in the first week in state heads), I can conveniently draw a graph of it. It is shown in Figure 5. Let v_{1h} be some increasing linear transform of u_{1h}, so $v_{1h} = au_{1h} + b_{1h}$. This produces another function $v_{1h}(y_{1h})$ of y_{1h}. I have drawn that in Figure 5 too, and another transform $w_{1h} = a'u_{1h} + b'_{1h}$ with different coefficients. The coefficient a changes the scale of the graph on the vertical axis. That is why I called it 'the scaling factor'. A scaling factor greater than one stretches the scale; a factor smaller than one shrinks it. (Remember a has to be positive.) The coefficient b_{1h} moves the graph up and down; it shifts the origin. But neither coefficient alters the *shape* of the graph, or more exactly its pattern of curvature. If the graph curves downwards, for instance, an increasing linear transformation leaves it curving downwards.

Figure 5

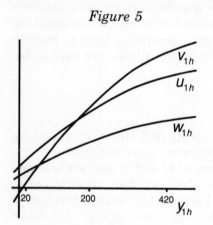

* The proof is the same as before.

The preservation of shape is the graphical manifestation of the preservation of the ratios of utility differences. According to all the functions u_{1h}, v_{1h} and w_{1h} in Figure 5, the difference in utility between £420 and £200 is less than the difference in utility between £200 and £20, and in the same proportion. (These are strictly subutilities rather than utilities. I shall often use 'utility' for either, and rely on the context to distinguish.) This is because the graphs all have the same strong downward curvature.

The shape and curvature of the graph of a subutility function is important. The curvature represents in graphical form the properties of preferences that I discussed at length in Section 4.1: attitudes to risk and attitudes to temporal unevenness. (It will also turn out to represent attitudes to inequality between people, but I shall leave this aside until Chapter 8.)

To explain why, I shall return once more to the problem shown in Table 11 on page 62: how to choose between the alternatives of playing and not playing? I am, in effect, going to repeat some of the steps I took in Section 4.1. But this time I am going to make the comparison in terms of utilities.

The utilities of the alternatives are

$$U(\text{Do not play}) = u_{1h}(200) + u_{1t}(200) + u_{2h}(200) + u_{2t}(200)$$

and $$U(\text{Play}) = u_{1h}(20) + u_{1t}(420) + u_{2h}(420) + u_{2t}(20).$$

When comparing the alternatives in Section 4.1, I first did it one state of nature at a time. These formulae for utility can be divided up one state at a time too:

$$U(\text{Do not play}) = \{u_{1h}(200) + u_{2h}(200)\} + \{u_{1t}(200) + u_{2t}(200)\}$$

and $$U(\text{Play}) = \{u_{1h}(20) + u_{2h}(420)\} + \{u_{1t}(420) + u_{2t}(20)\}.$$

Each curly bracket picks out a state. Take the state heads. The problem in this state is to compare together the first brackets in the two formulae: to compare

$$\{u_{1h}(200) + u_{2h}(200)\} \text{ with } \{u_{1h}(20) + u_{2h}(420)\}.$$

This amounts to comparing the utility difference

$$\{u_{1h}(200) - u_{1h}(20)\} \text{ with } \{u_{2h}(420) - u_{2h}(200)\}.$$

So we are comparing a utility difference at one location with a utility difference at another. (Since the utilities are cocardinal this is a significant comparison.) The comparison, in words, is this. Choosing not to play would give you £200 rather than £20 in the first week. That would be the benefit of this choice. Choosing to play would give you £420 rather than £200 in the second week. That would be the benefit of this choice. (We are only considering what would happen in the state heads, remember.) We have to compare these benefits. That is what this comparison of utility differences is doing.

Now assume for simplicity that the utility functions u_{1h} and u_{2h} are the same. (I assumed in my earlier discussion that you view the two weeks in the same way; that was effectively this assumption.) Then the graph of u_{1h} in Figure 5 will do for both. I chose to draw this graph curved downwards strongly enough to make $u_{1h}(200) - u_{1h}(20)$ greater than $u_{1h}(420) - u_{1h}(200)$ and therefore than $u_{2h}(420) - u_{2h}(200)$. The effect of this is that in the comparison we are making – the comparison between playing and not playing in state heads – not playing wins. This is the alternative that leads to an even distribution of income across time, but sacrifices the £40 premium. If the graph of utility had been less curved, playing would have won in the comparison. For the sake of the premium, you would have chosen the alternative that distributed income unevenly. The degree of curvature in the graph reflects the strength of your aversion to unevenness. A strongly curved graph reflects strong aversion. If the graph were a straight line, it would mean you had no aversion; you would pick the alternative that gave you the largest total income. You might conceivably have a graph that curved upwards. That would mean you liked unevenness, and were willing to sacrifice some income in total for the sake of having it unevenly distributed.

In Section 4.1, having compared the alternatives one state of nature at a time, I sliced the problem across the other dimension, and compared them one week at a time. The utilities of the alternatives, sliced this way, are:

$$U(\text{Do not play}) = \{u_{1h}(200) + u_{1t}(200)\} + \{u_{2h}(200) + u_{2t}(200)\}$$
and $$U(\text{Play}) = \{u_{1h}(20) + u_{1t}(420)\} + \{u_{2h}(420) + u_{2t}(20)\}.$$

Take the first week. The comparison here is between

$$\{u_{1h}(200) + u_{1t}(200)\} \quad \text{and} \quad \{u_{1h}(20) + u_{1t}(420)\},$$

which amounts to a comparison between

$$\{u_{1h}(200) - u_{1h}(20)\} \quad \text{and} \quad \{u_{1t}(420) - u_{1t}(20)\}.$$

Assume now that the functions u_{1h} and u_{1t} are the same, as the symmetry of the example makes almost inevitable. Then the graph of u_{1h} in Figure 5 will do for both. Once again the curvature of the graph as I have drawn it ensures that not playing wins. But whereas previously we were considering the results of the alternatives in the state of nature heads, we are now considering their results in the first week. In the previous paragraph, not playing was the alternative that represented evenness across time. Now it represents avoidance of risk. Not playing gives you £200 for sure in the first week, whereas playing gives you the gamble of either £20 or £420. In choosing not to play you are avoiding risk, and that is what the curvature of the graph of utility brings about. Looked at from this perspective, the curvature reflects your degree of risk aversion. If the graph were less curved you would prefer the risky alternative for the sake of the premium. A straight graph would reflect no risk aversion at all. An upward curving one would show a positive liking for risk.

Looked at one way, the curvature of the graph reflects unevenness aversion. Looked at another way, it reflects risk aversion. But it is the very same graph. So we have arrived at the conclusion that risk aversion and inequality aversion amount to the same thing. We reached the same conclusion in Section 4.1. But we now have the notions of risk aversion and unevenness aversion more precisely captured in the shape of the utility graph.

I must repeat that the whole of this argument rests on the assumption that preferences are separable in both crosscutting dimensions. Otherwise, we should not have additively separable utility functions, so we should not have cardinal subutilities.

Some definitions

This is the point to set down explicitly some definitions that we shall need.

An ordering (such as a preference ordering) is *risk neutral* about some quantity if and only if two gambles that have the same expectation of the quantity are always level in the ordering. An ordering is *risk averse* about the quantity if and only if, of two gambles with the same expectation of a quantity, the less risky one is always higher in the ordering. It is essential to understand that these notions are defined relative to the particular quantity in question. A person's preferences may be risk averse about money, for instance, and at the same time risk neutral about the person's wellbeing.

The technical term for a function with a downward-curving graph is *strictly concave*. A function with a straight graph is *linear*. A function with an upward-curving graph is *strictly convex*.

We have seen that a strictly concave subutility function of money implies risk aversion about money. It also implies unevenness aversion, and – we shall see in Chapter 9 – inequality aversion of a sort.

4.4 *The rectangular field assumption*

I have one final note to make. The published proofs of both the separability theorems (including the proofs in the appendix below) depend on an assumption that may be objectionable in some contexts. These theorems are about an ordering $\succeq$ defined on a field of alternatives. The alternatives are vectors $(x_1, x_2, \ldots x_n)$. Each component x_i of the vector, standing for an occurrence at the ith location, has a range of its own. Call it X_i. X_i is the set of all possible occurrences at the ith location. The assumption that may be objectionable is that the field of $\succeq$ is the whole of the 'product set' $X_1 \times X_2 \times \ldots \times X_n$. I shall call this the 'rectangular field assumption' (because a product set occupies a rectangle or a series of rectangles in vector space).

Here is what the rectangular field assumption means. Go through all the locations, and for each one, pick any one of the possible occurrences at that location. Then take the vector made up of all these occurrences, one for each location. The assumption is that this vector has a place in the ordering. So any occurrence at one location can be put together with any occurrences at other locations to make up a vector, and that vector will have a place in the ordering.

Whether or not this is an objectionable assumption will depend on the application. It will depend on what the locations are, what occurrences we are dealing with, and what the ordering represents. But there are certainly some contexts where one might doubt the assumption. Suppose, for example, that the locations are people, the occurrences for each person are what happens to her, and the ordering is a betterness relation. For each of a number of people, it is a possible occurrence that she is the first human being to stand on Mars. The assumption says that, in the ordering, there is one alternative in which each of those people is the first human being to stand on Mars. This alternative is impossible. That, by itself, may not necessarily prevent it from having a place in the betterness ordering; even some impossible alternatives might be better or worse than other alternatives. Nevertheless, it is at least grounds for worrying about the rectangular field assumption. Other examples are mentioned in Section 5.8.

So, in so far as the separability theorems depend on the rectangular field assumption, that diminishes their reliability. The published proofs of the theorems use this assumption. But it is by no means necessary for the theorems. Indeed, they may be proved on the basis of a much weaker assumption about the field of the ordering.[7] Nevertheless, possible doubts about the rectangular field assumption need to be borne in mind. Section 5.8 considers them further in the context of uncertainty.

Notes

1. My definition comes from Gorman, 'The structure of utility functions'.

2. A proof is in Debreu, 'Representation of a preference ordering by a numerical function'.

3. See my '"Utility"'.

4. There is a proof in Gorman, 'The structure of utility functions' pp. 387–8.

5. 'Topological methods in cardinal utility theory'. There is another proof in Kranz, Luce, Suppes and Tversky, *Foundations of Measurement: Volume 1*, pp. 309–10. In stating this theorem and the next, I am leaving out some technical conditions.

6. It is an extract from a more general theorem proved in 'The structure of utility functions'.

7. W. M. Gorman has an unpublished proof based on a weaker assumption, but I do not think one has been published.

Appendix to Chapter 4: Proofs

This appendix contains informal proofs of the first and second separability theorems. They use no mathematics beyond elementary algebra. The method is fundamentally that of Kranz, Luce, Suppes and Tversky in *Foundations of Measurement: Volume 1*, though these authors do not turn their method to proving the second separability theorem. I have ignored many complications, which they deal with rigorously.

Proof of the first separability theorem (strong separability is equivalent to additive separability)

It is obvious that additive separability implies strong separability. I need only prove that strong separability implies additive separability.

In the text of the chapter, I did not mention some minor conditions required for the truth of the first theorem. One is that there must be at least three locations. I shall prove the theorem on the assumption that there are exactly three. It is easy to see how the method can be extended to four or more locations.

So let there be three. Each alternative is a vector (x_1, x_2, x_3). The alternatives are ordered by a relation $\succeq$ that is strongly separable. I have to prove that the relation can be represented by an additively separable function

$$U(x_1, x_2, x_3) = u_1(x_1) + u_2(x_2) + u_3(x_3).$$

To put it another way: utilities (strictly subutilities) can be defined for each location in such a way that one alternative is at least as high in the ordering as another if and only if it has at least as big a total of utility. If utilities meet this condition I shall say they are *additive*.

I shall start by defining a scale of utility for each location: u_1, u_2, and u_3. Afterwards I shall show that the utilities I have defined are additive.

The first location is separable on its own. That means the outcomes x_1 have an order of their own that is independent of the outcomes in the other two locations. Imagine them arranged on a vertical line like the one in Figure 6. At each point on the line there may be several outcomes, all level in the ordering. For simplicity I shall speak as though there is only one, but if there are several, I mean to assign the same utility to each of them. Similarly we can arrange the outcomes in the second and third locations on vertical lines. These are shown in Figure 6 too.

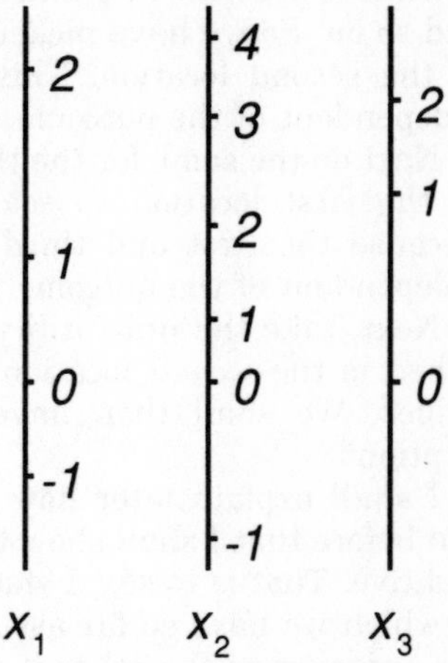

Arbitrarily pick an outcome from the first location, and define its utility to be nought. It is handy to call this outcome '*0*', so that $u_1(0) = 0$. Similarly pick an arbitrary outcome to have utility nought in each of the second and third locations. Call these '*0*' too, so that $u_2(0) = u_3(0) = 0$. In Figure 6, I have picked three *0*s level with each other.

Figure 6

Next, arbitrarily pick another outcome in the first location, above *0*, and define its utility to be one. Call this outcome '*1*', so that $u_1(1) = 1$.

The gap between *0* and *1* in the first location provides a unit for utility, which I shall now use to scale utility in the other two locations. Start with the second. In this second location, first of all find an outcome x with the property that $(0, x, 0)$ is level in the ordering with $(1, 0, 0)$. The way to do this is to try out various outcomes x up and down the line x_2 in Figure 6 until we find one that has this property. To make sure this can be done requires a particular assumption about the continuity of the ordering, but that is a technical matter I shall ignore. When we have an x that has this property, call it '*1*', and let its utility $u_2(1)$ be one.

The effect of all this is that $(0, 1, 0)$ is level with $(1, 0, 0)$ in the ordering. In these two vectors, the outcome in the third location is the same: *0*. So we are really comparing the subvectors $(0, 1)$ and $(1, 0)$ in the conditional ordering of the first two locations, conditional on *0* in the third location. We are effectively comparing the gaps between *0* and *1* in the two locations, and making them count the same in the ordering.

Since the ordering is strongly separable, the first two locations together are separable. Consequently, the ordering of subvectors in these locations is independent of the outcome in the third. I defined *1* in the second location keeping the outcome in the third location constant at *0*, but any constant outcome would have done equally well and led to the same result. In fact, now *1* is defined in the second location, we know that $(0, 1, x_3)$ will be level with $(1, 0, x_3)$ for any x_3.

Next define *2* in the second location by the property that *(0, 2, 0)* is level with *(1, 1, 0)*. Here we are comparing the subvectors *(0, 2)* with *(1, 1)*. In effect this is comparing the gap between *1* and *2* in the second location with the gap between *0* and *1* in the first, and making them count the same. Once more, I have used a constant outcome *0* in the third location, but any other outcome would have worked as well.

Similarly define *3*, *4* and so on in the second location, and also *–1*, *–2* and so on. So we have picked out all the outcomes with integral utilities in the second location. This integral scaling of the second location is independent of the outcome in the third.

Next do the same for the third location, again using the unit utility gap in the first location to scale the third for integral values of utility. Because the first and third locations are separable, this scale will be independent of the outcome in the second location.

Next, take the unit utility gap between *0* and *1* that has been established in the *second* location, and use that to scale the first for integral values. We shall then have a scale of integral utilities in all three locations.

I shall explain later how to assign nonintegral utilities to outcomes. But before that I shall show that the integral scales established so far are additive. That is to say, I shall show that if we take any two alternatives to which we have so far assigned utilities, one comes at least as high in the ordering as the other if and only if it has at least as great a total of utility.

This will require some elementary but slightly complicated manipulations. In what follows, the algebraic symbols '*a*', '*b*' and '*c*' all stand for integers.

First, I shall write down in symbols the properties of the scales of utilities by which I defined them. I defined the scale in the second location in terms of the unit in the first. The definition made sure that

$$(0, b+1, 0) \approx (1, b, 0) \quad \text{for all } b.$$

(The symbol '$\approx$' means level in the ordering.) Since the first two locations are separable, any outcome can be substituted for *0* in the third location. Therefore

(A.1) $(0, b+1, c) \approx (1, b, c)$ for all *b* and *c*.

Similarly the scaling of the third location ensured that

(A.2) $(0, b, c+1) \approx (1, b, c)$ for all *b* and *c*.

Finally, I scaled the first location by means of the unit in the second. This ensured that

(A.3) $(a+1, 0, c) \approx (a, 1, c)$ for all *a* and *c*.

We can generalize these formulae, using the facts of separability. First (A.1) and (A.2) imply

$$(0, b+1, c) \approx (0, b, c+1) \quad \text{for all } b \text{ and } c.$$

And because the second and third locations are separable, this equivalence will be preserved if any other outcome is substituted for 0 in the first location. That is to say:

(A.4) $\qquad\qquad (a, b+1, c) \approx (a, b, c+1) \quad \text{for all } a, b \text{ and } c.$

In particular, setting b to 0 in (A.4),

$$(a, 1, c) \approx (a, 0, c+1) \quad \text{for all } a \text{ and } c.$$

So, by (A.3),

$$(a+1, 0, c) \approx (a, 0, c+1) \quad \text{for all } a \text{ and } c.$$

Because the first and third locations are separable, it follows that

(A.5) $\qquad\qquad (a+1, b, c) \approx (a, b, c+1) \quad \text{for all } a, b \text{ and } c.$

The formulae (A.4) and (A.5) give us all we need. (A.4) shows that moving up one unit of utility in the second location (from (a, b, c) to $(a, b+1, c)$), is equivalent to moving up one unit in the third location (from (a, b, c) to $(a, b, c+1)$); it takes us the same distance up the ordering. So units in the second and third locations count the same. (A.5) says that units in the first and third locations count the same. Units of utility, then, count the same in all locations. This means they are additive. The manipulations below simply work out this point more formally.

Take any two alternatives (m_1, m_2, m_3) and (n_1, n_2, n_3) made up of integral outcomes. Suppose n_2 is more than m_2. (The argument is just as easy if it is not.) Apply (A.4) repeatedly:

$$\begin{aligned}
(m_1, m_2, m_3) &\approx (m_1, m_2+1, m_3-1) \\
&\approx (m_1, m_2+2, m_3-2) \\
&\quad \cdots \\
&\approx (m_1, n_2, m_3-(n_2-m_2)).
\end{aligned}$$

Suppose n_3 is more than $m_3-(n_2-m_2)$. (The argument is just as easy if it is not.) Apply (A.5) repeatedly:

$$\begin{aligned}
(m_1, m_2, m_3) &\approx (m_1, n_2, m_3-(n_2-m_2)) \\
&\approx (m_1-1, n_2, m_3-(n_2-m_2)+1) \\
&\approx (m_1-2, n_2, m_3-(n_2-m_2)+2) \\
&\quad \cdots \\
&\approx (m_1-(n_3-(m_3-(n_2-m_2))), n_2, n_3) \\
&\approx (n_1+(m_1+m_2+m_3)-(n_1+n_2+n_3), n_2, n_3).
\end{aligned}$$

Call this last vector N. We have found N to be level with (m_1, m_2, m_3) in the ordering. If $(m_1+m_2+m_3)$ is equal to $(n_1+n_2+n_3)$, N is just (n_1, n_2, n_3). If $(m_1+m_2+m_3)$ is greater than $(n_1+n_2+n_3)$, N is above (n_1, n_2, n_3) in the ordering, because its first component is greater and its other two are the same. Similarly, if $(m_1+m_2+m_3)$ is less than $(n_1+n_2+n_3)$, N is below (n_1, n_2, n_3) in the ordering. The outcomes, remember, were given names that coincide with their utilities. So the conclusion is that

$$(m_1, m_2, m_3) \succeq (n_1, n_2, n_3) \text{ if and only if}$$
$$u_1(m_1) + u_2(m_2) + u_3(m_3) \geq u_1(n_1) + u_2(n_2) + u_3(n_3).$$

This is what was required: utilities are additive.

The next step in the argument is to extend the utility scales to nonintegral values. The point here is that we can make the scale as fine as we like by making the arbitrary starting unit as fine as we like. Here is one way of proceeding.

Pick an outcome x somewhere between 0 and 1 in the first location. Use it to define an outcome x in the second location by the property that $(0, x, 0)$ is level with $(x, 0, 0)$. Then define $2x$ in the second location by the property that $(0, 2x, 0)$ is level with $(x, x, 0)$. Then define $3x$ in the second location, and so on, up to $10x$. Now compare $10x$ in the second location with 1 in that location. If $10x$ is above 1, choose a new lower outcome for x in the first location. If $10x$ is below 1, choose a new higher outcome for x in the first location. Then repeat the whole operation. Continue until we have an outcome x in the first location such that $10x$ in the second location is the same as 1. (The same continuity condition as I mentioned on page 83 ensures this can be done.) Call this x '0.1', and define its utility to be 0.1. We can now use the gap between 0 and 0.1 in the first location to scale all three locations in units of 0.1 of utility. The arguments I have gone through will show that these new finer scales are additive in the way that is required. And because we know that 1 in the second location is $10(0.1)$, the new scales will be consistent with the original integral scales.

Similarly we can establish scales in units of 0.01, of 0.001, and so on indefinitely. At every stage utilities will be additive. And, continued indefinitely, this process will determine a utility for every outcome. At each stage, the utility of any outcome is approximated by the point on the scale next below it. This approximation is a decimal number, which becomes longer at each stage. Successive approximations will converge on a value of utility for the outcome. Utilities will be additive throughout the process. So this completes the proof of the first separability theorem.

Proof of the second separability theorem (crosscutting separability implies additive separability)

I shall only deal with the case of alternatives that have just four locations: (x_1, x_2, x_3, x_4). It is not hard to extend the proof to bigger vectors. Suppose the ordering of these alternatives has crosscutting separability. Then the first and second locations together, the first and third, the second and fourth, and the third and fourth, are all separable. I need to prove the ordering is additively separable.

The first point is that it is weakly separable: each location is individually separable. Take the first location. Suppose, for some outcomes x_2, x_3, and x_4 in the other locations, that x_1 ranks at least as high as $\hat{x}_1$ in the conditional ordering. That is: $(x_1, x_2, x_3, x_4) \succeq (\hat{x}_1, x_2, x_3, x_4)$. Because the first and second locations are separable, $(x_1, x_2, \hat{x}_3, \hat{x}_4) \succeq (\hat{x}_1, x_2, \hat{x}_3, \hat{x}_4)$ for any $\hat{x}_3$ and $\hat{x}_4$. Therefore, because the first and third locations are separable, $(x_1, \hat{x}_2, \hat{x}_3, \hat{x}_4) \succeq (\hat{x}_1, \hat{x}_2, \hat{x}_3, \hat{x}_4)$ for any $\hat{x}_2$, $\hat{x}_3$ and $\hat{x}_4$. That is to say: x_1 ranks at least as high as $\hat{x}_1$ in the conditional ordering, whatever the outcomes in the other locations. So the first location is separable. Similarly, so are the others.

We can therefore arrange the outcomes at each location on a vertical line, as I did in Figure 6. For each of the four locations pick an outcome arbitrarily. Assign it utility nought, and call it '*0*'. In the first location, arbitrarily pick an outcome above *0*. Assign it utility one, and call it '*1*'. Use the gap between *0* and *1* in the first location to establish an integer scale of utilities in the second and third locations, in the way I described on pages 83–84. Use the gap now established between *0* and *1* in the second location to establish an integer scale in the fourth and first locations.

We now have integer scales of utility for all the locations. The scales can be refined in the way I described on page 86 to assign utilities to all outcomes. So all I need to do is show that the integer scales are additive. That will be enough to prove the theorem.

For this, I shall keep the outcome in the fourth location fixed at *0*. I shall show, given this, that the utilities in the first three locations are additive. When that is done, it will be obvious how to extend the argument to the fourth location too.

Since the outcome in the fourth location is always *0*, I need not trouble constantly to write it in the vectors. We can proceed as if we have vectors with three dimensions: (x_1, x_2, x_3). We have integer scales defined for the three locations. And we know that the first and second locations together are separable, and also the first and third. In proving the first separability theorem, we were given also that the second and third locations were separable, but that is not now given to us. Apart from that, we are now in exactly the position we were in on page 84 when proving the first theorem.

In our new problem, I defined the integer scales in exactly the way I did in the proof of the first theorem. That definition did not rely on the separability of the second and third locations. Therefore (A.1), (A.2) and (A.3) on page 84 are true in our new context. However, I did assume the separability of the second and third locations to prove (A.4), and I derived (A.5) from (A.4). These two equations remain true in our new context, but it will take a more complicated argument to prove them. I shall prove (A.5) first, and then derive (A.4). Equations (A.4) and (A.5) were enough to establish the additivity of utility, as the previous proof showed. So once I have proved them, my task will be done.

Equation (A.5), to repeat it, is this

$$(a+1, b, c) \approx (a, b, c+1) \quad \text{for all } a, b \text{ and } c.$$

(Remember that a, b, and c, are all integers.) We already know (A.5) is true when $a = 0$. That is,

$$(1, b, c) \approx (0, b, c+1) \quad \text{for all } b \text{ and } c,$$

because this is simply (A.2). I shall prove, step by step, that

(A.6) $(2, b, c) \approx (1, b, c+1)$ for all b and c,

which is (A.5) for $a = 1$, and that

(A.7) $(3, b, c) \approx (2, b, c+1)$ for all b and c,

which is (A.5) for $a = 2$, and so on. And I shall also prove that

(A.8) $(0, b, c) \approx (-1, b, c+1)$ for all b and c,

which is (A.5) for $a = -1$, and that

(A.9) $(-1, b, c) \approx (-2, b, c+1)$ for all b and c,

which is (A.5) for $a = -2$, and so on. This sequence of proofs will prove (A.5) for all integers.

In the steps that follow, the quantifiers 'for all a, b and c' are to be assumed. Here is the proof of (A.6).

From (A.3) with $a = 1$, $(2, 0, c) \approx (1, 1, c)$,
which, from (A.2) with $b = 1$, $\approx (0, 1, c+1)$,
which, from (A.3) with $a = 0$ and $c+1$ for c, $\approx (1, 0, c+1)$.
So $(2, 0, c) \approx (1, 0, c+1)$. Since the first and third locations are separable, it follows that $(2, b, c) \approx (1, b, c+1)$, which is (A.6).

Now, here is the proof of (A.7).

From (A.3) with $a = 2$, $(3, 0, c) \approx (2, 1, c)$,
which, from (A.6) with $b = 1$, $\approx (1, 1, c+1)$,
which, from (A.3) with $a = 1$ and $c+1$ for c, $\approx (2, 0, c+1)$.
So $(3, 0, c) \approx (2, 0, c+1)$. Since the first and third locations are separable, it follows that $(3, b, c) \approx (2, b, c+1)$, which is (A.7).

Similar proofs will establish (A.5) for all positive integral values of a. Each proof uses the conclusion of the previous proof. Now, here is the proof of (A.8).

From (A.3) with $a = -1$ and $c+1$ for c, $(-1, 1, c+1) \approx (0, 0, c+1)$,
which, from (A.2) with $b = 0$, $\approx (1, 0, c)$,
which, from (A.3) with $a = 0$, $\approx (0, 1, c)$.
So $(0, 1, c) \approx (-1, 1, c+1)$. Since the first and third locations are separable, it follows that $(0, b, c) \approx (-1, b, c+1)$, which is (A.8).

The proof of (A.9) is similar, using (A.8) instead of (A.2). And similar proofs will establish (A.5) for all negative integral values of a.

That concludes the proof of (A.5).

A similar proof will establish the symmetrical conclusion that

$$(a+1, b, c) \approx (a, b+1, c) \quad \text{for all } a, b \text{ and } c.$$

From this and (A.5), (A.4) immediately follows. And this, as I explained on page 87, is enough to prove the theorem.

Cardinality

A final note. Because these proofs have proceeded by constructing subutility functions, they display the functions' cardinality nicely. In constructing the scales, we chose arbitrarily the 0s in each location, and we chose arbitrarily the 1 in one location. We could have chosen any of these things differently. That means we could have chosen a different origin for any of the subutility functions, and we could have chosen a different unit. But the same unit, once chosen, applied to all the subutility functions. This is what it means for the functions to be cocardinal: the origins of each are arbitrary, and the unit is arbitrary but the same for all, and nothing else is arbitrary. Everything else is determined by the ordering that the utility is to represent.

Chapter 5

Expected Utility and Rationality

This chapter will be concerned with rational preferences in the face of uncertainty. Although the subject of this book is good rather than rationality, it will turn out in Chapter 6 that the goodness of uncertain prospects is best understood in terms of rational preferences. So this chapter does some necessary spadework.

Its particular purpose is to defend some parts of *expected utility theory* as an account of rational preferences. Section 5.1 explains the general idea of expected utility theory, and particularly how it is founded on axioms. The principal axiom is explained in Section 5.2. It is often called the 'sure-thing principle', and it amounts to an assumption of strong separability. Sections 5.3 to 5.7 defend this axiom. The argument turns on the individuation of occurrences; Section 5.3 explains why. Sections 5.4 and 5.5 develop an argument about individuation in the context of a simpler axiom, namely transitivity. Sections 5.6 and 5.7 extend the argument to the sure-thing principle. Section 5.8 discusses a threat to another of the axioms of expected utility theory, which is raised by my defence of the sure-thing principle.

5.1 Axiomatic expected utility theory

To model uncertainty, I shall work with a one-dimensional collection of locations. Each location is a state of nature. It is not known which state will come about; that is the uncertainty. Suppose there are s states. Each alternative is a vector $(x_1, x_2, \ldots x_s)$ of occurrences, one for each state. I shall often call alternatives like this *prospects*, and the occurrences *outcomes*. It is uncertain what the outcome of a prospect will be; a prospect is a vector of different possible outcomes. Examples of prospects are shown in Table 2 on page 22. A prospect can often be identified with an act, as the prospects in Table 2 can.

People often have preferences amongst uncertain prospects like this. For example, you might prefer visiting London in Table 2 to taking out your sailboard. So a person will often have a *preference relation*

$$\underline{\quad} \text{ is preferred or indifferent to } \underline{\quad}$$

defined on a field of prospects; the blanks in this formula are to be filled in with prospects. Expected utility theory is a theory about such preferences. It is sometimes taken as a theory about people's actual preferences, but in that role it performs rather badly.[1] Instead, I am going to take it as a theory about *rational* preferences. I shall take it that expected utility theory intends to describe the preferences a person would have if she were rational.

What expected utility theory says about rational preferences is no more nor less than this: that they can be represented by a utility function U having the form

$$(5.1.1) \qquad U(x_1, x_2, \ldots x_s) = p_1 u(x_1) + p_2 u(x_2) + \ldots + p_s u(x_s),$$

where p_1, p_2 and so on are nonnegative numbers that sum to one. What I mean by 'represented' is defined by (4.2.1) on page 65: U is such that one prospect is preferred or indifferent to another if and only if it has at least as great a value of U. Let us call the function u a 'subutility function', and its values 'subutilities' or, loosely, 'utilities'. Let us call the numbers p_1, p_2 and so on 'probabilities'. Then the right hand side of (5.1.1) is the expectation of utility, or expected utility. Equation (5.1.1) says, in brief, that one alternative is preferred or indifferent to another if and only if it has at least as great an expected utility. To put it another way, expected utility theory says that rational preferences maximize expected utility.

I shall call a utility function U that has the form of (5.1.1) *expectational*.

Expected utility theory claims only that rational preferences can be represented by an expectational utility function. It claims only that there *are* numbers p_1, p_2 and so on and a function u that allow the preferences to be represented in the manner of (5.1.1). It says nothing about what the numbers and the function signify.

At least, this is true of some versions of expected utility theory, but not all. I have already mentioned on page 53 Daniel Bernoulli's version: that a rational person maximizes the expectation of her good. Other authors have claimed that a rational person maximizes the expectation of some other specific thing, such as happiness or pleasure.[2] But in this chapter I am going to consider only the most stripped-down version of expected utility theory, which makes no such specific claims. For a reason that will appear in a moment, I shall call it the *axiomatic* version. Axiomatic expected utility theory asserts only that a rational person's preferences can be represented by an expectational utility function; nothing more.

This chapter tests out that claim.

How does the theory try to justify it? Its method is to specify some conditions for a preference relation that are sufficient to ensure it can be represented in the form of (5.1.1). The conditions are called 'axioms'. One part of the justification is to prove that (5.1.1) does indeed follow from the axioms. This part is not in doubt; the proof is sound. But it has also to be shown that rational preferences necessarily conform to the axioms. I shall describe the most important of the axioms, and consider whether rational preferences must really conform to them.

Various different sets of axioms have been proposed for the theory.[3] But they are similar enough to allow me to talk in a general way about the axiomatic structure.[4] We can quite easily identify in a general way some of the axioms that will be needed.

For one thing, there must be axioms to guarantee that the preferences can be represented by a utility function in the first place, whether or not the function is expectational. For this, I explained on page 65, the preference relation needs to be an ordering: it must be complete, transitive and reflexive. Is this acceptable? Reflexiveness is undeniable: each alternative must be preferred or indifferent to itself. Transitivity I shall be talking about in Sections 5.4 and 5.5. That leaves completeness.

Completeness is dubious. A person's preference relation is complete if and only if, of every pair of alternatives, either the person is indifferent between them, or she prefers one to the other. But it seems plausible that the reasons in favour of one alternative may sometimes be *incommensurable* with the reasons in favour of another. It may be that neither side dominates the other but they do not exactly balance either. In a choice between two careers, for instance, it seems plausible that the benefits of one – security and comfort, say – may be of such a different sort from the benefits of the other – excitement and the chance of a fortune – that they cannot be weighed against each other. And yet it is not a matter of indifference which one chooses. If this is so, it seems it would be rational to prefer neither of the alternatives to the other, and not to be indifferent either. So it seems that rational preferences need not be complete.[5]

This is a problem for expected utility theory, but I am sorry to say I am going to ignore it. Incommensurability will come up several times in this book, and on each occasion I shall note it as a difficulty and set it aside. Incommensurability is a well-recognized problem, and this book is about other problems. Simply for the sake of moving on, I shall assume that rational preferences are indeed complete.

Given that, rational preferences will be representable by a utility function $U(x_1, x_2, \ldots x_s)$ defined on the field of alternative prospects. The next question is whether the function will have the expectational form (5.1.1). Suppose the preferences happen to be *strongly separable*. Then the first separability theorem on page 70 says they can be represented by a utility function that is additively separable:

$$(5.1.2) \qquad U(x_1, x_2, \ldots x_s) = u_1(x_1) + u_2(x_2) + \ldots + u_s(x_s).$$

This is already a long way towards (5.1.1). All that is required to move from (5.1.2) to (5.1.1) is to show somehow that the subutility functions u_r are proportional to each other.

One way of making this move is to assume some symmetry between states of nature. The idea, roughly, is to assume that any outcome can occur in any state, and that the preferences are indifferent to which state it occurs in. Then the outcomes x_1, x_2 and so on in (5.1.2) may be permuted amongst the states without affecting the overall utility U. Therefore the subutility functions u_r must be the same in every state. But this is only a rough idea, because it actually *does* matter which state an outcome occurs in. The states may have differing probabilities, and it is preferable for a good outcome to occur in a likely state than in an unlikely state. The subutility functions u_r should actually *not* all come out the same. They should come out proportional, with the constant of proportionality capturing the state's probability. So the argument needs to be more elaborate than the rough one I sketched.

But I am not going to concern myself with this argument. I shall take the move from (5.1.2) to (5.1.1) for granted. To achieve the additively separable form (5.1.2) is really the essence of expected utility theory. And this form is achieved by assuming the preferences are strongly separable. Expected utility theory is, in a way, simply an application of the first separability theorem. Strong separability is the principal axiom of the theory. It is also the most controversial and the one this chapter is chiefly concerned with.

Expected utility theory requires a few other axioms besides the ones I have mentioned. One is dealt with in Section 5.8. Others are technical axioms such as continuity. Still others may be called axioms of 'consistency'. Transitivity is an axiom of consistency, and we shall see that strong separability comes in that class too. There are also some other consistency axioms besides those; I shall mention one on page 153. But I have never seen any of these other consistency axioms questioned. I am simply going to take them and the technical axioms for granted.

5.2 The sure-thing principle

In expected utility theory, strong separability goes by other names. It is sometimes called 'strong independence'.[6] Leonard Savage calls it 'the sure-thing principle',[7] and I am going to adopt that name. But it is nothing other than strong separability, set in the context of states of nature.

It will be helpful if I set up a table to show what the sure-thing

Table 13

States of nature							States of nature					
1	...		r	$r+1$	...	s	1	...		r	$r+1$	...	s
w_1	...		w_r	y_{r+1}	...	y_s	w_1	...		w_r	z_{r+1}	...	z_s

Prospect A Prospect C

States of nature							States of nature					
1	...		r	$r+1$	...	s	1	...		r	$r+1$	...	s
x_1	...		x_r	y_{r+1}	...	y_s	x_1	...		x_r	z_{r+1}	...	z_s

Prospect B Prospect D

principle requires. Pick a group consisting of the first r states of nature, and compare the four alternatives in Table 13. Compare the prospects A and B first. These prospects have the same outcomes y_{r+1}, y_{r+2} and so on, in states $r+1$ to s. So A is preferred or indifferent to B if and only if the subvector $(w_1, w_2, \ldots w_r)$ is conditionally preferred or indifferent to $(x_1, x_2, \ldots x_r)$, conditional on these outcomes y_{r+1}, y_{r+2} and so on. Similarly C is preferred to D if and only if the subvector $(w_1, w_2, \ldots w_r)$ is conditionally preferred or indifferent to $(x_1, x_2, \ldots x_r)$, conditional on the outcomes z_{r+1}, z_{r+2} and so on, in the states $r+1$ to s. But if the first r states are separable, the conditional preferences will be independent of outcomes in the other states. So A will be preferred or indifferent to B if and only if C is preferred or indifferent to D. The first r states are separable if and only if this is true for *any* four prospects having the configuration shown in Table 13.

The preferences are *strongly* separable – they satisfy the sure-thing principle – if and only if the same thing is true for any group of states, not just the first r.

Is this a requirement of rationality?[8]

5.3 *Individuation of outcomes*

Here is one way of arguing that it is. We have already assumed away incommensurability of reasons. Given that, it must be a principle of rationality that you should prefer one alternative to another, or be indifferent between them, if and only if the reasons for preferring the one are, on balance, at least as strong as the reasons for preferring the other. What reasons are there for preferring A to B in Table 13, or alternatively for preferring B to A? These reasons can only derive from what happens in one or other of the states of nature. And no reasons for either preference can derive from what happens in any of states $r+1$ to n, because what happens in these states is the same in A as in B. So the reasons can only derive from what happens in states 1 to r. Similarly whatever reasons there are for preferring C to D or D to C can only derive from what happens in states 1 to r. But in states 1 to r, what happens in A is the same as what happens in C, and what happens in B is the same as what happens in D. Therefore, any reason for preferring A to B will also be a reason for preferring C to D. And any reason for preferring B to A will also be a reason for preferring D to C. So the reasons for preferring A to B will, on balance, be at least as strong as the reasons for preferring

B to *A* if and only if the reasons for preferring *C* to *D* are, on balance, at least as strong as the reasons for preferring *D* to *C*. Consequently, rationality requires you to prefer *A* to *B*, or be indifferent between them, if and only if you prefer *C* to *D*, or are indifferent between them. That is the sure-thing principle.

This argument, however, starts by begging the question. It assumes that every reason there is for preferring one alternative to another must derive from what happens in some state of nature, taken by itself. And this is the essence of the sure-thing principle: what happens in one state can be evaluated separately from what happens in the others. Granted this assumption, the argument simply recites the obvious. So it does not give the sure-thing principle much support.

The crucial question is whether outcomes in different states can be evaluated independently. Many authors, most notably Maurice Allais,[9] have denied that they can. They have insisted that there may be interactions between the states: 'complementarities', they are often called.[10] A quick answer to them is Paul Samuelson's: 'Either heads *or* tails must come up: if one comes up the other cannot.'[11] Samuelson's point is this. The value you assign to what happens in one state of nature should depend on what it will be like if that state occurs. But if that state occurs, no other does. So what would have happened in other states should make no difference to the value. For a rational person there should be no complementarity. There may be complementarity in other dimensions. I suggested on page 25, for instance, that there may be complementarity between people. If inequality is a bad thing, that means the value of one person's income may well depend on other people's income. But that is because these people live in the same world. In this respect, the dimension of states of nature is not analogous at all, because two states never exist together.

Samuelson's remark is by no means a conclusive argument. But I do think it is enough to establish a prima facie presumption in favour of the sure-thing principle. The burden of proof is on its opponents. Complementarity between different states of nature is, prima facie, puzzling; if there is complementarity, it needs to be explained how.[12] How can something that never happens possibly affect the value of something that does happen? A modal realist such as David Lewis believes that everything that might happen does happen: it happens in some possible world that is as real as the actual world.[13] So a modal realist may be less impressed than the rest of us by Samuelson's remark. But even a modal realist, I think, should recognize that it calls for explanation how events in one world can affect the value of events in another. In response to this puzzle, Allais and others have exhibited examples where what would have happened in one state does seem to make a decided difference to the value of what happens in another. I shall examine some of these examples to see exactly what they prove.

I shall start with Allais's own example.[14] A number of alternative lotteries are available, and you have to decide your preferences between them. For each, the procedure will be the same: you are to draw a ticket out of a hat containing a hundred tickets, numbered from one to a hundred, and you will receive a prize determined by the number on the ticket. Each lottery offers you a different range of prizes. The alternatives are shown in Table 14 ('m' stands for 'million'). It turns out that Allais prefers A to B and also D to C, and so do many other people. Allais insists these preferences are rational. If they are, then that conflicts with the sure-thing principle, because Table 14 is an instance of Table 13 (with $r = 11$ and $s = 100$). So Allais believes this example shows that rational preferences need not conform to the sure-thing principle.

Table 14

States of nature (ticket numbers)			States of nature (ticked numbers)		
1	2–11	12–100	1	2–11	12–100
£1m	£1m	£1m	£1m	£1m	0

Lottery A Lottery C

States of nature (ticket numbers)			States of nature (ticket numbers)		
1	2–11	12–100	1	2–11	12–100
0	£5m	£1m	0	£5m	0

Lottery B Lottery D

According to Allais, this is a case where there is complementarity between different states of nature. There is a reason for preferring *A* to *B* that does not derive from what happens in any individual state. It derives from what happens in all the states taken together. Taking them together, it emerges that *A* gives a certainty of winning £1 million. Certainty does not show up in any of the states separately. And certainty, Allais believes, has a special value. This value provides a reason for preferring *A* to *B* that is not also a reason for preferring *C* to *D*.

Before this argument can completely rationalize Allais's preferences, we need to be told what the special value of certainty is. Why does the certainty of *A* constitute a reason for preferring *A* to *B*? The literature contains several more detailed rationalizations that answer this question,[15] and anyone who feels the appeal of Allais's preferences can easily supply one for herself. For instance, because the result of *A* is certain, choosing *A* may be a way to avoid anxiety. Alternatively, it may be a way to avoid the chance of suffering bitter disappointment: if you picked *B* instead of *A* and happened to end up with nothing, perhaps your extreme bad luck – missing a 99 percent chance of becoming rich – would distress you. On the other hand, if you have a choice between *C* and *D*, you are unlikely to win whichever you pick. So you will not be particularly upset if you happen to lose.

All the rationalizations of Allais's preferences point out a good or bad feeling you may experience. This feeling, they claim, can rationally be taken into account, as well as the money prizes, in determining your preferences. Let us write the feeling into our table of lotteries. If we pick disappointment as an example (any other would do for the argument), Table 15 shows the result. It describes the alternatives available more fully than does Table 14. But Table 15, unlike Table 14, is not an instance of Table 13. So preferring *A* to *B* and *D* to *C* does not conflict with the sure-thing principle. The threat to the principle has been removed. So here is a defence of the sure-thing principle against Allais's example.

Rewriting the table like this is a matter of refining the individuation of the outcomes. In Table 14, outcomes are individuated by money prizes only. Any outcome in which you receive no money is identified with any other. But Table 15 individuates more finely. It treats getting nothing as a different outcome from getting nothing and also feeling disappointment.

That, then, is a response to Allais's example. Decision theorists, however, have generally been suspicious of refining the individua-

Table 15

States of nature (ticket numbers)			States of nature (ticket numbers)		
1	2–11	12–100	1	2–11	12–100
£1m	£1m	£1m	£1m	£1m	0

    Lottery *A*   Lottery *C*

States of nature (ticket numbers)			States of nature (ticket numbers)		
1	2–11	12–100	1	2–11	12–100
0 and disapp-ointment	£5m	£1m	0	£5m	0

    Lottery *B*   Lottery *D*

tion of outcomes as a method of defending the sure-thing principle. 'Where will it end?', they ask. Whenever you meet anybody whose preferences conflict with the sure-thing principle, you could always refine away the conflict by this device. There will always be *some* difference between the results of different choices, which could be used to distinguish them as different outcomes. So, the worry is, the sure-thing principle will turn out to be consistent with any preferences at all. The principle can only be rescued by this device at the cost of draining it of content.[16]

One might ask what there is to be afraid of? The role of the sure-thing principle is to stand as one of the axioms from which expected utility theory can be derived. And what could be better than an axiom that is empty in the sense that it cannot be false? But actually there are genuine grounds for worry. Too much weakening of the sure-thing principle would really put expected utility theory at risk. Section 5.8 explains why. And in any case, the sure-thing principle is intended to be a constraint that rationality imposes on preferences. It would be an unwelcome conclusion if it turned out not to constrain preferences at all. I shall say more about that in Section 5.5.

So the worry is reasonable. But it is not enough simply to point out the danger of individuating too finely. We have to know what principle of individuation *should* be applied. We must have *some* principle for deciding when to take outcomes as different, and when the same. Critics of the sure-thing principle have always implicitly adopted some coarse scheme of individuation. Allais individuated outcomes on the basis of money prizes only. Mark Machina at one time individuated by 'physically observable aspects',[17] Amartya Sen by 'everything in the real world (except in [the] mind)'.[18] But none of these schemes has been defended by argument. And in principle the need for a finer individuation has always been recognized.[19] What is needed is not some arbitrary scheme but one that is properly set up to support an account of rational preferences.

Sections 5.4 to 5.7 describe and defend such a scheme. Sections 5.4 and 5.5 do so in the context of transitivity, a simpler condition of rationality than the sure-thing principle. Sections 5.6 and 5.7 extend the same scheme to the sure-thing principle.

5.4 Transitivity of preferences

I shall begin, then, by looking at a parallel argument about a simpler axiom of expected utility theory: the axiom that rational preferences are necessarily transitive. To keep things as simple as possible, let us abstract from uncertainty. Let us consider only alternatives that each lead to a particular outcome whatever the state of nature. Then we can think of the alternatives as simply the outcomes themselves.

I shall not argue positively for the transitivity axiom; instead I shall concentrate on apparent counterexamples.[20] All that matters for the general argument of this book is that *betterness* relations are transitive, and my case for that claim does not depend on the transitivity of rational preferences. So I have no need to prove that rational preferences are transitive. I am turning to transitivity in this section only because it provides a simple context for discussing the individuation of outcomes.

Here is a counterexample to transitivity.[21] Maurice prefers visiting Rome to mountaineering in the Alps, and he prefers staying at home to visiting Rome. However, he does not prefer staying at home to mountaineering; if he had a choice between

those two alternatives, he would take the mountaineering trip. So
Maurice's preferences are intransitive. Write 'M' for mountaineering, 'R' for visiting Rome and 'H' for staying at home. Since
Maurice prefers R to M and H to R, transitivity requires him to
prefer H to M. And he does not. Yet Maurice claims his preferences are rational. If he is right, then transitivity is not a requirement of rationality. Or so it seems.

Maurice's claim to rationality is this. Mountaineering frightens
him, so he prefers visiting Rome. Sightseeing bores him, so he
prefers staying at home. But to stay at home when he could have
gone mountaineering would, he believes, be cowardly. That is why,
if he had the choice between staying at home and going mountaineering, he would choose to go mountaineering. (To visit Rome when
he could have gone mountaineering seems to him cultured rather
than cowardly.)

Let us distinguish four alternatives where previously I distinguished only three: M, mountaineering; R, visiting Rome; H_1,
staying at home without having turned down a mountaineering
trip; and H_2, staying at home having turned down a mountaineering trip. H_2, Maurice believes, would be cowardly, and H_1 would
not. He prefers R to M and H_1 to R. Transitivity therefore requires
him to prefer H_1 to M. But if he had a choice between staying at
home and mountaineering, that would be a choice between H_2 and
M. And transitivity does not require him to prefer H_2 to M.

If, therefore, Maurice is right to claim his preferences are
rational, then they are not intransitive, despite appearances. So
this example poses no threat to the transitivity axiom, after all.

Here, then, is a defence of transitivity against the Maurice
example, parallel to my defence of the sure-thing principle against
the Allais example. It also works by refining the individuation of
outcomes. And it is subject to the same worry: where will it all
end? Whenever you meet anyone who has intransitive preferences,
it will always be possible to individuate outcomes more finely and
thereby restore transitivity. Indeed, we could have made the
distinction between the two outcomes H_1 and H_2 even without
hearing Maurice's rationalization of his preferences. His views
about cowardice played no essential part in restoring his preferences to transitivity. If this sort of fine individuation is always
allowed, transitivity will truly be an empty condition.

It is not exactly that transitivity will impose no requirements on
preferences. Since Maurice prefers M to R and R to H_1, transitivity
will require him to prefer H_1 to M. But this is a preference of a
sort I call *nonpractical*. I call a person's preference between two

alternatives *practical* if and only if the alternatives are ones the person might possibly have a choice between. Maurice could not possibly have a choice between H_1, staying at home without having turned down a mountaineering trip, and M, a mountaineering trip. So his preference between these alternatives is nonpractical. Only practical preferences can have practical effects; only they can determine choices. If outcomes are individuated this finely, then, transitivity does not constrain preferences in a practically significant way. This is the sense in which allowing too fine an individuation makes transitivity empty.

We need a principle for individuating outcomes that wards off this danger.

Look again at Maurice's claim to rationality. It is that H_1 and H_2 are different outcomes, and it is rational for him to have a preference between them. They differ, not just in that one involves rejecting a mountaineering trip and the other not, but in that one involves cowardice and the other not. And this, he claims, is enough to make it rational for them to occupy different places in his preferences.

Either we accept this claim to rationality, or we do not. If we do, then we must accept that H_1 and H_2 are indeed different outcomes. Maurice has justified himself in distinguishing them and having a preference between them. We cannot accept that Maurice's preference between H_1 and H_2 is rational, and at the same time deny that H_1 and H_2 are different outcomes. The example really raises no possibility of rational intransitivity. The grounds that make the preferences rational, if they succeed, make them transitive. The Maurice example cannot possibly damage the transitivity axiom.

Suppose, on the other hand, we reject Maurice's claim to rationality. (Suppose, for instance, we think he is mistaken about cowardice: staying at home is just good sense if you are frightened of mountaineering.) So we believe his preferences are irrational. What is irrational about them? Presumably what we first thought of: they are intransitive. But they cannot be condemned for intransitivity if we accept that H_1 and H_2 are different outcomes. The only way to bring home the charge of intransitivity is to reject that claim. We shall have to deny Maurice the right to distinguish H_1 and H_2 as different outcomes. We shall have to set this limit to the individuation of outcomes.

It is now clear what, in general, the limit has to be. Sometimes two putative outcomes differ in a way that makes it rational to have a preference between them, and sometimes they do not. Only if they do should they be counted as different outcomes. This is the only way of making sure the transitivity axiom rules out as intransitive just those preferences it should rule out. So this is the principle I offer for individuating outcomes:

> *Principle of individuation by justifiers.* Outcomes should be distinguished as different if and only if they differ in a way that makes it rational to have a preference between them.

By a *justifier*, I mean a difference between two putative outcomes that makes it rational to have a preference between them.

Now, actually, what I have just been saying is inaccurate. Maurice's claim to rationality is a conjunction. He claims, first, that H_1 and H_2 are different outcomes and, second, that it is rational for him to have a preference between them. If we think his preferences are irrational, we do not have to deny that H_1 from H_2 are different outcomes. We could simply deny that it is rational for Maurice to have a preference between them. We could say that rationality requires him to be indifferent. That would be enough to convict him. If rationality requires him to be indifferent between H_1 and H_2, it requires him to prefer H_2 to M, because (by transitivity) it requires him to prefer H_1 to M. Since he does not prefer H_2 to M, he is irrational. Instead of setting a limit to individuation, this second way of convicting Maurice imposes a *rational requirement of indifference*.

So there are two ways of dealing with the problem of emptiness. One is to limit individuation to justifiers; the other is to recognize rational requirements of indifference. Either will ensure that the transitivity axiom has the effect it should have.

I prefer the second way. It is awkward to deny that H_1 and H_2 are different outcomes. There *is* a difference between staying at home having rejected a mountaineering trip and staying at home without having rejected one. Furthermore, Maurice does actually have a preference between them. Even if this preference is irrational, he has it. To deny that H_1 and H_2 are different outcomes, then, makes it impossible to give an accurate description of the preferences that he actually has. Nevertheless, despite the awkwardness, previous arguments about the sure-thing principle have generally been conducted in terms of individuation.[22] For the sake of continuity with them, I shall continue to speak in those terms too.

In any case, either way of proceeding relies on the existence of rational requirements of indifference. If Maurice's preferences are irrational, what makes them so is that it is irrational for him to have a preference between staying at home having rejected a mountaineering trip and staying at home without have rejected one. This is a rational requirement of indifference, even if it is expressed as a principle of individuation. I offered a principle of individuation based on justifiers. And a justifier is simply the opposite of a rational requirement of indifference. If rationality requires one to be indifferent between two alternatives, then the alternatives do not differ in a justifier: they do not differ in any way that justifies a preference between them. If, conversely, there were no rational requirements of indifference, then *any* difference between putative outcomes would be a justifier. So the principle of individuation by justifiers would not limit individuation at all. And, we have seen, that would mean the axiom of transitivity imposes no restrictions on practical preferences.

5.5 *Rational requirements of indifference*

Fine individuation saves transitivity. But the worry was: where will it all end? Now we have an answer: it will end at rational requirements of indifference, which limit the fineness of the individuation that is allowed.

However, it is a common opinion that rationality allows you to prefer anything to anything else. For instance, it is not contrary to reason to prefer the destruction of the whole world to the scratching of your finger, or your own acknowledged lesser good to your greater. So there can be no such things as rational requirements of indifference. This is part of the Humean tradition. It implies that any difference between outcomes would be enough to justify a preference between them; any difference is a justifier. I cannot respond properly to this Humean opinion here. I have made a fuller response elsewhere,[23] and here I shall only sketch the beginning of it.

Most Humeans moderate their opinion a little. They believe rationality does impose some conditions on preferences. It imposes conditions of consistency, but nothing more. Rationality, these moderate Humeans say, allows you to have any preferences, provided only that they are consistent with one another. In particular, there are no rational requirements of indifference. Allais is a moderate Humean. He says: 'It cannot be too strongly emphasized *that there are no criteria for the rationality of ends as such other than the condition of consistency.* Ends are completely arbitrary.'[24]

But if there are no rational requirements of indifference, then any difference is a justifier, and nothing could ever stop somebody like Maurice from escaping the requirement of transitivity. Without requirements of indifference, transitivity would not constrain practical preferences in any way. Only these requirements give transitivity its bite. Yet transitivity is the central condition of consistency; without it, consistency is nothing. If rationality really requires only consistency, then, it requires nothing at all of practical preferences. So the moderate Humean view is untenable. There are two alternatives: either the extreme Humean view that rationality imposes no constraints at all on practical preferences, not even constraints of consistency, or else the non-Humean view that rationality imposes some requirements of indifference. I assume that few people will be attracted to the extreme Humean view. Leaving it aside brings us to the conclusion that there must be rational requirements of indifference.[25]

There *must* be such things, if rationality is to constrain practical preferences in any way. That is my argument for the existence of rational requirements of indifference. It turns around the 'Where will it end?' worry. The strategy of fine individuation *must* be brought to an end somewhere, and rational requirements of indifference determine where. It is no part of my argument to exhibit examples of rational requirements of indifference. Nor would I expect examples to contribute much to the argument, because they are likely to be controversial. I would not expect everyone to agree readily about what particular requirements of indifference rationality imposes. That is likely to be discovered only by debate. But still, it may be useful to have an example of a rational requirement at work.

On page 15, I described the case of a couple wondering whether to have a second child. Because of the considerations I described there, the couple may find themselves preferring alternative A in Table 1 to B, B to C and C to A. So their preferences seem intransitive. Can they restore them to transitivity by finer individuation? Can they say, for instance, that B having rejected A occupies a different place in their preferences from B not having rejected A? This may actually be true. As I described the couple's reasoning, by which they arrived at their preferences, comparing B with C brought into play a consideration that was not present in comparing B with A: the good of the second child. This may have led the couple to put B in two different places in their preferences, according to what it was being compared with. But is it *rational* for them to make this distinction? Not as far as I can see. If outcome *B* comes about, I cannot see that it makes any difference to its value whether it comes about as a result of rejecting *A* or not. What matters about *B* is that there are two children living equally good lives. I cannot see that it matters what choices their parents are faced with in bringing about this result. Comparing *B* with different alternatives may *bring to mind* different considerations, but it does not alter *B*'s *actual* goodness. In this case, the difference in the rejected alternatives is not a justifier. Therefore, the couple ought not to split the outcome *B* and put it in two different places in their preference ordering. According to the principle of individuation by justifiers, their preferences are truly intransitive.

The couple's position is not like Maurice's. If Maurice is correct in his opinion about cowardice, it really does make a difference to the value of staying at home whether or not he has rejected a mountaineering trip. If he has, this is a cowardly thing to do, but not otherwise.

In criticizing the couple's preferences, I took it for granted that it is rational to have a preference between two alternatives only if they differ in some good or bad respect: only good or bad features can be justifiers. Although concrete examples of rational requirements of indifference are likely to be controversial, this minimal connection between preference and good is surely innocuous. Even a Humean could accept it, though in a backhanded way. A Humean believes that goodness is in some way determined by people's preferences. If a person prefers *A* to *B*, then that by itself is a good feature of *A* that *B* does not possess. So, if a person has a preference (whether rational or not) between two alternatives, those alternatives do indeed differ in a good or bad respect. This, of course, makes the preference rational; any preference is self-justifying in Humean thinking.

This connection between rational preference and good explains why I said on page 19 that internal conditions of consistency require external criteria of goodness to give them meaning. Justifiers give meaning to consistency conditions; they determine exactly what the consistency conditions amount to. And justifiers are good or bad features of the alternatives.

It follows from the same connection that any theory about what good consists in implies a view about justifiers. Some utilitarians, for instance, believe that the only intrinsically good or bad things in the world are feelings. So it is rational to have a preference between two alternatives only if they differ in some good or bad feeling. On page 112 there is an example of this view in operation.

5.6 *Individuation and the sure-thing principle*

Now let us return to the sure-thing principle, and start by reviewing the case against it. The burden of proof, as I said, is on the principle's opponents. Their case, using the example of Table 14 on page 97, is that Allais's preferences are rational on the one hand, and inconsistent with the sure-thing principle on the other. Both halves of this conjunction need to be proved.

What is the argument that Allais's preferences are rational? I described one way of rationalizing these preferences. It pointed out that, in Table 14, the outcome alternative *B* leads to in state 1 is different from the outcome *D* leads to. Both outcomes are labelled '0' in the table, but one involves disappointment and the other does not. Furthermore, it is rational to prefer one of these outcomes to the other. Therefore it is rational to have Allais's preferences about the lotteries. This is only one amongst many possible rationalizations, but all the others work in the same way. They make a distinction between outcomes that are given the same label in Table 14, and treat them as different outcomes that it is rational to have a preference between.

And what is the argument that Allais's preferences are inconsistent with the sure-thing principle? It is that all the outcomes given the same label in Table 14 are in fact the same outcome. If they are not, Table 14 will not be an instance of Table 13, and will have nothing to do with the sure-thing principle.

Plainly, therefore, the case against the sure-thing principle is absurd. It depends on making a distinction on the one hand and denying it on the other. I said on page 102 that the Maurice example, despite appearances, really raises no possibility of rational intransitivity. Similarly, Allais's example raises no possibility that rational preferences may fail to satisfy the sure-thing principle. If we make the distinction, Allais's preferences do not conflict with the sure-thing principle. If we do not make it, they are irrational.

But there is still the worry about allowing too fine an individuation of outcomes, and so leaving the sure-thing principle empty. The question is: should we make the distinction or not? Should we treat getting nothing and feeling disappointed as a different outcome from getting nothing without disappointment? The answer depends on whether or not Allais's preferences are rational. If they are, we certainly have to make the distinction. Unless these are distinguished as different outcomes, it is not possible, rationally, to prefer one to the other, and the fact that one is rationally preferred is what makes Allais's preferences rational.

But suppose alternatively that Allais's preferences are irrational. This is Leonard Savage's view.[26] What is irrational about them? Well, they are inconsistent with the sure-thing principle; there can hardly be any objection to them apart from that. But these preferences are only inconsistent with the sure-thing principle if those outcomes given the same label in Table 14 are in fact the same. The preferences will only be irrational, then, if we decline to distinguish getting nothing and feeling disappointed as a different outcome from getting nothing without disappointment.

It may seem implausible that Allais's preferences might be irrational. Surely a person could rationally prefer an outcome without disappointment to an outcome with disappointment. Savage's view, presumably, was that a rational person should not have this feeling of disappointment in the first place. It does not matter for my argument. My only point is that Allais's preferences are irrational if and only if we decline to distinguish outcomes that are given the same label in Table 14.

So this is where we have got to. The attempt at rationalizing Allais's preferences distinguishes outcomes, and claims it is rational to have a preference between them. If this attempt succeeds, and Allais's preferences are indeed rational, then the distinction must be allowed. If the attempt fails, it must not. Our principle for individuating outcomes has to be this: take one outcome as different from another if and only if it is rational to have a preference between them. This is exactly the conclusion I reached for transitivity. It is the principle of individuation by justifiers. The very same scheme of individuation is exactly appropriate for both the sure-thing principle and transitivity. It does not leave the sure-thing principle empty. It gives the principle exactly the content it ought to have, and it ensures that a rational person will conform to the principle.

In 'Expected utility and risk', Paul Weirich recommends individuating outcomes by the riskiness of the prospect that led to them, quite independently of any feelings that the riskiness gives rise to. In Table 14, for instance, he would treat the £1,000,000 that lottery *A* leads to as different from the £1,000,000 that lottery *C* leads to, just because *C* is more risky than *A*. But I doubt that a mere difference in riskiness is a justifier by itself. To defend

Allais's preferences as rational, it does not seem enough merely to point out that *A* and *C* differ in their riskiness. It also needs to be explained *why* this difference should justify a difference in preference. Allais's defenders normally do this by pointing to a feeling such as disappointment (though I do not mean to suggest that only feelings are justifiers). So I think Weirich's scheme of individuation is too fine: it will count as conforming to the sure-thing principle preferences that ought not to be counted. It is wide open to the accusation of leaving the principle empty. Weirich himself escapes this accusation to some extent by adopting specific formulae for defining the riskiness of a prospect. But this procedure is arbitrary unless it is properly aimed at making a distinction when and only when a distinction is justified. Otherwise, it will not give the sure-thing principle exactly the force it ought to have.

We should individuate by justifiers, then. I do not want to be misunderstood. I would not deny anyone the right, in developing a theory of rational preferences, to individuate outcomes in any way that suits her. Suppose, for instance, that a person has preferences amongst a range of money gambles. Each gamble is a vector of amounts of money $(y_1, y_2, \ldots y_s)$; y_2, for instance, is the amount the person will receive in state 2. It may be that the person has a rational preference ordering amongst these gambles that can be represented by a utility function $U(y_1, y_2, \ldots y_s)$. If the preferences are like Allais's, the function will not have the expectational form

$$U(y_1, y_2, \ldots y_s) = p_1 u_1(y_1) + p_2 u_2(y_2) + \ldots + p_s u_s(y_s).$$

But Mark Machina has shown that a different function of the vector may represent the preferences perfectly well.[27] This function will then provide a useful theory of rational preferences. It would be silly to object to it. And in a sense it individuates outcomes by money prizes only.

I would only object if the theory was held to refute expected utility theory and the sure-thing principle.[28] Individuating by money prizes, one may not be able to come up with a utility function that has the expectational form. But that does not mean expected utility theory is wrong. Utility can only be expected to have the expectational form when outcomes are individuated by justifiers. For many purposes, this may not be the most convenient way of individuating. But it is the best way for the theoretical purpose of understanding rationality. Furthermore, because it preserves separability between states of nature, I hope to show in this book that it gives access to important discoveries about the structure of good.

5.7 *The dispersion of value amongst states of nature*

Let us step back a bit. Allais's fundamental objection to the sure-thing principle is that there may be interactions or complement-arities between states of nature. The sure-thing principle requires outcomes to be assessed individually, one state at a time. But if there are interactions between states, they will not show up in such a state-by-state assessment. How did my argument overcome this objection?

The answer is that I presumed the effects of the interaction – or at least those effects that influence rational preferences – would show up as properties of the outcomes in the individual states of nature. I presumed, specifically, that they would show up as feelings that would occur in one or more of the states. The value that Allais associates with interactions between states, is really *dispersed* amongst the states themselves. In this, I was faithfully following all the available rationalizations of Allais's preferences; they all depend on feelings of some sort. Consequently, when the outcomes were properly individuated to take account of the feelings, the threat to the sure-thing principle disappeared.

Indeed, Allais's example scarcely exhibits any genuine interact-ion between states. The full story is this. In a particular state, if it occurs, events in that state (the numbering of the tickets, the solemn shaking of the hat, the presence of witnesses, and so on) will cause you, the subject, to have particular beliefs about what would have happened in other states. These beliefs will in turn cause you to have particular feelings such as disappointment. All of this will occur within the causal nexus of the single state. There is not really any interaction between states at all. There are simply causal processes within states that involve beliefs about other states. And the effects of these processes, which influence the preferences, are feelings that lie within a state.

Nearly all the published counterexamples to the sure-thing principle are like this. They depend on feelings that occur in one or more of the states.[29] They therefore pose little threat to the sure-thing principle; the principle is protected from them by the dispersion of value amongst the states. But it is easy to suspect there is something fishy about the dispersion of value.[30] The worry is most clearly brought out in a different example, which does not depend on feelings: Peter Diamond's.[31] Diamond's example is more effective than the others, because it exploits a more substantial interaction between states.

I mentioned Diamond's example in Chapter 2, but I shall repeat it here. There is a kidney available for transplant, and two people who need it to survive. The choice facing a hospital administrator is between tossing a coin to decide who is to get the kidney and giving it directly to Q. The alternatives are A and B in Table 16. (I have also included C and D, for a reason that will appear.) In certain circumstances Diamond prefers A to B and D to C, and he believes this would be rational. His reason is that in A and D the selection of who is to get the kidney is random, and he believes that in certain circumstances it is best to choose randomly, because it gives each person 'a fair shake'. If he is right, this seems to be a counterexample to the sure-thing principle. Table 16 is an instance of Table 13 on page 94, which defines the principle.

Diamond's stylized example represents a widespread practical

Table 16

		States					States	
		Heads	Tails				Heads	Tails
People	P	Lives	Dies		People	P	Lives	Lives
	Q	Dies	Lives			Q	Dies	Dies

Alternative A — Alternative C

		States					States	
		Heads	Tails				Heads	Tails
People	P	Dies	Dies		People	P	Dies	Lives
	Q	Lives	Lives			Q	Lives	Dies

Alternative B — Alternative D

problem. For a given quantity of risk, is it better to have it more rather than less equally distributed? Radiation leaking from nuclear power stations will kill a number of people. Should nuclear policy be designed so that the risk of death is evenly distributed across the population, rather than concentrated on a smaller group of people? Suppose one hundred people will die; is it better to have ten million people exposed to a .00001 chance of dying, than ten thousand exposed to a .01 chance? It is commonly believed that it is,[32] and this view is embedded in the practice of the British National Radiological Protection Board and other government organizations.[33] But if this is so, it raises the same difficulty for the sure-thing principle as Diamond's example. The example is the very same problem restricted to two people. Alternative A distributes the risk of death equally between the people, and B concentrates it on one. Diamond prefers the equal distribution of risk.

The example does not depend on feelings. I assume that the fairness of A and D (if Diamond is right that they are fair) consists in the fact that these alternatives give each person an equal chance of survival. And this, I assume, is Diamond's reason for preferring them to B and D. His reason is not that in A and D one or the other person may feel better (perhaps because she believes she is being fairly treated). To purify the example, it is best to exclude differences of feelings. Imagine that neither person will know anything about how the decision is made; each person will either receive a kidney or not, without explanation. The process of choice, then, cannot affect their feelings.

Some authors, discussing Diamond's example, have argued that in this purified case (and provided also that there is no risk of prejudice or corruption on the part of the administrator), there are no good grounds for Diamond's preferences.[34] This would follow from the view – common amongst utilitarians – that good and bad feelings are the only justifiers. If these authors are right, then the purified example fails immediately as an objection to the sure-thing principle.

We do not need to settle here whether they are right or not.[35] I think at least that Diamond's case is strong enough to be worth pursuing. So let us suppose that, indeed, Diamond's preferences are rational. The example still does not damage the sure-thing principle. It can be given the treatment I gave Allais's example. The unfairness of B and C can be written into the table in some way, as it is in Table 17. The difference between a person's dying without being treated unfairly and her dying having been treated unfairly is a justifier: it makes it rational to have a preference

Table 17

People		States Heads	States Tails		People		States Heads	States Tails
	P	Lives	Dies			P	Lives	Lives
	Q	Dies	Lives			Q	Dies and treated unfairly	Dies and treated unfairly

Alternative A   Alternative C

People		States Heads	States Tails		People		States Heads	States Tails
	P	Dies and treated unfairly	Dies and treated unfairly			P	Dies	Lives
	Q	Lives	Lives			Q	Lives	Dies

Alternative B   Alternative D

between these outcomes. That is why, we are supposing, Diamond's preferences are rational. So the individuation of outcomes shown in Table 17 is required by my principle of individuation by justifiers. And it means that Diamond's preferences do not really conflict with the sure-thing principle.

However a serious objection may be raised when this method of argument is applied to Diamond's example. Sure enough, the principle of individuation by justifiers requires outcomes to be distinguished if they differ in a justifier. And fairness is certainly a justifier. But, the objection is, the fairness and unfairness in Diamond's example are not really properties of the outcomes at all. So the principle of individuation by justifiers does not apply.

The objection is not, or not simply, that the fairness is a

property of the process of choice rather than a property of the results of the process. It is true that what makes A fairer than B is that the process of choice in A is random. Nevertheless, this by itself does not prevent us from treating the fairness as a property of the outcome. My term 'outcome' may be a little misleading. It does not refer particularly to the results of an act rather than the act itself. The outcome in a state of nature includes everything that happens in that state, both before the state is revealed and after. It includes history. If alternative A is chosen rather than B, and state heads comes up, then the outcome includes the fact that A is chosen. If A is fair, its fairness will be a part of the value of the outcome. I said on pages 3–4 that there is little to be gained by trying to separate an act from its consequences. Any value an action or process possesses can perfectly well be counted into the value of its outcome. So that is not the real objection.

The real objection is this. In Diamond's example, states of nature interact more significantly than they do in Allais's. Under B, P is treated unfairly in state heads (in which she dies). What makes this so is what happens in state tails: in state tails she also dies. This makes it the case that she has no chance of surviving, and that is what is unfair. So the fact that P is treated unfairly in one state is made true by what happens in the other state. This suggests that the unfairness may not be genuinely a property of the outcome in a particular state. Perhaps the interaction between states has to be understood as Allais would have us understand it: it supplies a reason for choosing between alternatives that is not contained within any state on its own, but only appears when the states are taken together.

My answer to the objection is that unfairness is genuinely a property of an outcome, despite the interaction between states. It is a property with modal elements. What makes it the case that an outcome possesses the property of unfairness is a counterfactual conditional: that if the coin had fallen differently, the result would have been the same. Many properties are like this. Many dispositions are, for instance. A wooden ship is inflammable, even if it never burns but instead decays at the bottom of the sea. What makes it inflammable is that if it had been exposed to fire it would have burnt. Still, inflammability is a genuine property of the ship.

Furthermore, the property of inflammability supervenes on the nonmodal properties of the ship. The ship could only have failed to have this property if it had been different in some structural or chemical way from how it actually is. Likewise the unfairness of an outcome supervenes on its nonmodal properties. The choice was unfair, and it could not have been fair unless the process of choice had been different in some nonmodal way. Normally it would not have been fair unless the hospital administrator's intentions had been different: unless her intention had been to make the allocation of the kidney depend on the fall of the coin. As it happens, the intentions of the administrator do not completely determine whether the choice is fair or unfair. It might be, for instance, that the administrator has a sort of dyslexia that would have made her believe the coin had fallen tails, whichever way up it actually fell. That would make the choice unfair, whatever her intentions. Nevertheless, in one way or another, the nonmodal properties of the outcome will determine whether the choice is fair or unfair.

So there are really no good grounds for denying that fairness or unfairness is a property of the outcome. I therefore think that my argument in defence of the sure-thing principle is sound for Diamond's example as well as for Allais's.

5.8 The rectangular field assumption

That concludes my defence of the sure-thing principle. The role of the principle in expected utility theory is to stand as one of the axioms from which the expected utility formula (5.1.1) can be derived. So it would be a hollow victory if the sure-thing principle was rescued from attack in a way that puts one of the other axioms at risk. That would leave expected utility theory without the foundation that the sure-thing principle and the other axioms were intended to supply. And there is serious danger of that. One of the other axioms becomes progressively more doubtful the finer is the individuation of outcomes.

The axiom at risk is a version of the rectangular field assumption I mentioned in Section 4.4. The existing proofs of the first separability theorem depend on this assumption, and the first separability theorem is the basis of expected utility theory. In Leonard Savage's theory, this assumption is implicit in his first postulate.[36] Here is what it says. Take the set of all outcomes: the set of all the possible outcomes that any prospect may lead to. Now let us go through the states of nature one by one, and to each assign, quite arbitrarily, some outcome from this set. This operation will define an arbitrary prospect: the prospect that delivers, in each state, the outcome we have assigned to that state. The assumption says that *any* arbitrary prospect constructed this way has a place in the preference ordering. This is the rectangular field assumption as I described it in Section 4.4, with the added assumption that any outcome can appear in any state of nature. I shall continue to call it the 'rectangular field assumption'.

Refining the individuation of outcomes makes this axiom less plausible. Take, for instance, the outcome shown in Table 15 on page 99 as '0 and disappointment'. The rectangular field assumption says your preference ordering includes all arbitrary prospects. Amongst them is the prospect that leads to this particular outcome for sure. This prospect determines, whatever lottery ticket you draw, that you get no money and also feel disappointment. But this feeling of disappointment is supposed to be one you get as a result of bad luck in the draw. It is hard to see how you could feel it if every ticket in the lottery would lead to the same boring result. So this prospect seems causally impossible, and that may make it doubtful that it will have a place in your preferences.

Or take Diamond's example. Table 17 on page 113 includes an outcome where P lives and Q dies and is treated unfairly. It also includes an outcome where Q lives and P dies and is treated unfairly. The rectangular field assumption requires there should be a prospect, with a place in the preference ordering, that leads to the first of these outcomes in state heads and the second in state tails. This prospect is shown in Table 18. Yet what makes it true in one of these outcomes that the person who dies is treated unfairly is that in the other state of nature she also dies. So the prospect in Table 18 is impossible. The rectangular field assumption requires this impossible prospect to have a place in the preference ordering. And this time the impossibility is more than causal. It casts, perhaps, more serious doubt on the rectangular field assumption.

So the refinements I introduced into the individuation of

Table 18

		States	
		Heads	Tails
People	P	Lives	Dies and treated unfairly
	Q	Dies and treated unfairly	Lives

outcomes, in order to preserve the sure-thing principle, make the rectangular field assumption dubious. This is no accident. I introduced the refinements in order to absorb into individual outcomes the interactions that occur between outcomes in different states of nature. To individuate finely, I therefore used properties that the outcomes possess only because of particular sorts of interaction. These properties will exist only when there are particular configurations of outcomes across the states of nature. They cannot exist with just any configuration, as the rectangular field assumption requires them to. There is therefore a direct tension between the sure-thing principle and the rectangular field assumption.

This is a problem. It is the real problem that is raised by the objections to the sure-thing principle. However, it is not such a serious problem for expected utility theory as an genuine difficulty with the sure-thing principle itself would be. The sure-thing principle can be derived from the expected utility formula (5.1.1). Therefore, if the sure-thing principle is false, so is expected utility theory.[37] But if the rectangular field assumption is false, expected utility theory may be true nonetheless.

And there is a good chance, I think, of proving the expected utility formula on the basis of a less dubious assumption about the field. I mentioned on page 81 that the separability theorems can be proved on the basis of a weaker assumption. And there are several proofs of the expected utility formula, specifically, that use alternative axioms. The rectangular field assumption has never seemed very plausible, for reasons that are unconnected with the problem I have raised.[38] This has motivated the search for an alternative. I do not think any of the existing proofs quite solves the problem I have described, but they give good reason to think it is soluble.[39] I shall not pursue the problem any further here.

Notes

1. See, for instance, Kahneman and Tversky, 'Prospect theory' or 'Rational choice and the framing of decisions'.

2. Jevons, *The Theory of Political Economy*, p. 99. Marshall, *Principles of Economics*, p. 843.

3. A useful survey is Fishburn, 'Subjective expected utility theory'. Fishburn does not cover theories that assume objective probabilities, such as Neumann and Morgenstern, *Theory of Games*, Section 3.

4. An exception is the axiomatization provided for Richard Jeffrey's version of expected utility theory (*The Logic of Decision*) by Ethan Bolker in 'Functions

resembling quotients of measures' and 'A simultaneous axiomatization of utility and subjective probability'. In particular, the Bolker-Jeffrey theory does not assume the sure-thing principle. In this chapter, which concentrates on the sure-thing principle, I shall set the Bolker-Jeffrey theory aside.

5. Incomplete rational preferences are discussed more thoroughly in my 'Choice and value in economics', and much more thoroughly in Morton, *Disasters and Dilemmas*.

6. Samuelson, 'Probability, utility and the independence axiom'.

7. *The Foundations of Statistics*, pp. 21–4. To understand the name 'sure-thing principle' look back to Diamond's example described on pages 26–27 above. For Diamond, the results of B are preferred or indifferent to the results of A in both states of nature. It is a sure thing, that is to say, that the results of B are preferred or indifferent to the results of A. So, according to the sure-thing principle, B itself should be preferred or indifferent to A. But Diamond, disagreeing with the principle, thinks it rational to prefer A to B.

8. Some parts of the argument that follows are developed more fully in my 'Rationality and the sure-thing principle'. There is a similar argument in Jeffrey, 'Risk and human rationality'.

9. 'Foundations of a positive theory of choice'.

10. Other authors, besides Allais, who have spoken particularly of complementarities include: Loomes and Sugden in 'The importance of what might have been', Manne in 'The strong independence assumption', and Sen in 'Rationality and uncertainty'. The term 'complementarity' comes from economics. One commodity is complementary to another if, the more you have of one, the more you value the other. Horses and wellies are complementary commodities.

11. 'Probability, utility and the independence axiom'. Neumann and Morgenstern make the same point in *The Theory of Games and Economic Behavior*, p. 18.

12. The sure-thing principle is the claim that what happens in one state can be evaluated independently of other states. If there are no complementarities between states, the sure-thing principle follows. This is not, as Edward McClennen says in 'Sure-thing doubts', a non sequitur.

13. See Lewis, *On The Plurality of Worlds*.

14. 'Foundations of a positive theory of choice', p. 89. I shall be using Savage's formulation of the example, from *The Foundations of Statistics*, p. 103.

15. For instance: Bell, 'Regret in decision making under uncertainty', p. 962; Eells, *Rational Decision and Causality*, pp. 39–40; Loomes and Sugden, 'Disappointment and dynamic consistency in rational choice under uncertainty', pp. 273–5.

16. This worry is mentioned by: Macrimmon and Larsson in 'Utility theory: axioms versus "paradoxes"', p. 398; Machina in 'Dynamic consistency and non-expected utility models' and in '"Rational" decision making versus "rational" decision modelling', p. 173; Samuelson in 'Utility, preference and probability', p. 136; and Tversky in 'A critique of expected utility theory', p. 171.

17. '"Rational" decision making versus "rational" decision modelling', p. 173.

18. 'Rationality and uncertainty', p. 121.

19. See Samuelson, 'Probability, utility and the independence axiom', and Drèze, 'Axiomatic theories of choice, cardinal utility and subjective probability', p. 8. In *Essays in the Theory of Risk-Bearing*, p. 45, Kenneth Arrow says: 'In the description of a consequence [i.e. an outcome] is included all that the agent values.'

20. In *Rationality and Dynamic Choice*, p. 66, Edward McClennen correctly points out that, in a previous discussion of mine in 'Rationality and the sure-thing principle', I offered no positive argument for transitivity. I shall not attempt one here either. If I was to attempt one, it would make no use of Dutch books or money pumps; I think McClennen successfully shows the inadequacy of these devices. Roughly, I think that a rational person has transitive preferences because she prefers what is better, and betterness is transitive. But this is not quite right, because (I think) it is rational to be neither perfectly altruistic nor perfectly egoistic. So a rational person need not always prefer what is generally better, and nor need she prefer what is better for herself only.

21. Other interesting examples appear in Pettit, 'Decision theory and folk psychology', in Schumm, 'Transitivity, preference and indifference', and in Sugden 'Why be consistent?'.

22. For instance: Drèze, 'Axiomatic theories of choice, cardinal utility and subjective probability', p. 15; Eells, *Rational Decision and Causality*, pp. 39–40; Machina, '"Rational" decision making versus "rational" decision modelling', p. 173; Macrimmon and Larsson, 'Utility theory: axioms versus "paradoxes"', pp. 397–8; Samuelson, 'Utility, preference and probability', p. 136; Tversky, 'Additivity, utility and subjective probability', p. 198, and 'A critique of expected utility theory', pp. 170–3. (Few of these authors use the word 'individuation'.)

23. 'Can a Humean be moderate?'

24. 'The foundations of a positive theory of choice', p. 70.

25. Amos Tversky, in 'A critique of expected utility theory', presents an argument that is, if I understand it, similar to this one. He reaches much the same conclusion: 'I believe that an adequate analysis of rational choice cannot accept the evaluation of consequences as given, and examine only the consistency of preferences.' (p. 172.) See also the arguments in Susan Hurley's *Natural Reasons*, especially Chapter 5. Hurley's arguments are close to mine, but she is particularly concerned with the question of 'radical interpretation'. This question (which has been examined by, amongst others, Davidson in *Truth and Interpretation* and Lewis in 'Radical interpretation') is about how a person's preferences can come to be understood by an observer. It is related to the question of this chapter: what does rationality require of a person's preferences. But a note in my 'Can a Humean be moderate?' explains that there are also important differences.

26. *The Foundations of Statistics*, p. 103.

27. Such a function appears in Machina, '"Expected utility" analysis without the independence axiom', and Machina, 'Dynamic consistency and non-expected utility models', contains a list of others.

28. At the end of 'Dynamic consistency and non-expected utility models', Machina explicitly declines to make this claim. He takes the same peaceable attitude towards expected utility theory as I am taking towards his theory.

29. For instance, Drèze, 'Axiomatic theories of choice, cardinal utility and subjective probability', p. 15, and two of the examples in Sen, 'Rationality and uncertainty'. Ellsberg's examples in 'Risk, ambiguity, and the Savage axioms' have been given a treatment in terms of feelings by Bell in 'Disappointment in decision making under uncertainty' and Eells in *Rational Decision and Causality*, p. 39. But I have to say I find this treatment less convincing for these examples.

30. This suspicion is expressed in MacLean, 'Rationality and equivalent redescriptions'.

31. 'Cardinal welfare, individualistic ethics and interpersonal comparisons of utility'.

32. See Maclean, 'Social values and the distribution of risk'.

33. Clark, Fleishman and Webb, 'Optimisation of the radiological protection of the public'.

34. Deschamps and Gevers, 'Separability, risk-bearing and social welfare judgements'; Harsanyi 'Nonlinear social welfare functions', pp. 68–71; Mirrlees, 'The economic uses of utilitarianism', p. 82.

35. This is the subject of my two papers 'Fairness' and 'Selecting people randomly'. I think a good case can be made out in Diamond's favour.

36. *The Foundations of Statistics*, p. 18.

37. Apart from Bolker–Jeffrey theory, which does not rely on this axiom. See note 4.

38. See: Eells, *Rational Decision and Causality*, pp. 83–4; Fishburn, 'Subjective expected utility theory', pp. 162–3; Jeffrey, *The Logic of Decision*, pp. 156–62.

39. There is, for instance, Fishburn's theory, where preferences are derived from act-event pairs (*The Foundations of Expected Utility*, Chapter 12). This theory fails to solve the problem completely because Fishburn assumes the existence of 'mixed acts'. If B is the act of giving the kidney to the first person, and C the act of giving it to the second person, there is the mixed act that is 'implemented by flipping a fair coin and using [B] if "heads" and [C] if "tails"'. (Fishburn, 'On the foundations of decision making under uncertainty', p. 33.) This mixed act is assumed to lie in the preference ordering between B and C. But we have learned from Diamond's example that it may not.

The main problem is to make sure that the given preferences are rich enough to determine probabilities and utilities. One approach to this problem is to build more structure into the theory, so that it needs fewer data to work on. This approach is exemplified by the work of Loomes and Sugden ('Disappointment and dynamic consistency in choice under uncertainty', 'Regret theory'). These authors make specific assumptions about what determines people's feelings of regret and disappointment. Where it is feelings that are causing the problem, as it is in Allais's example, this it enough to allow utilities and probabilities to be determined. ('Regret theory', appendix.) Another example is in Weirich's 'Expected utility and risk', pp. 438–41. But this approach is obviously not general enough to be a complete solution.

Hammond's new proof of expected utility theory ('Consequentialist foundations for expected utility') is based on very weak assumptions. The sure-thing principle is, indeed, proved by Hammond rather than assumed. He individuates outcomes finely enough to allow this. His approach, however, does not solve our problem either. He makes an assumption of unrestricted domain, which has much the same effect as the rectangular field assumption. With fine individuation it is equally unacceptable.

Jeffrey's radically different version of expected utility theory contained in *The Logic of Decision* offers an alternative way of coming at the problem. It is discussed more fully at the end of my 'Rationality and the sure-thing principle'.

Chapter 6

The Coherence of Good

Having disposed of preliminaries, I now come my main subject: the structure of good.

More exactly, as I explained in Chapter 1, my subject is the structure of the betterness relation:

__ is at least as good as __.

To avoid ambiguity, I shall sometimes call this the *general* betterness relation. A substructure within it is formed by each *individual* betterness relation, the betterness relation of a person:

__ is at least as good for the person as __.

Chapters 8 and 9 examine the connection between the general relation and the individual relations. The present chapter aims to establish one point about all of these relations: they all conform to the axioms of expected utility theory. I shall call a relation that conforms to these axioms *coherent*. I aim to show that the betterness relations are coherent or, as I shall sometimes put it, that good is coherent.

Expected utility theory was originally intended as a theory of preferences. But it is only a collection of axioms and a proof. It can be applied to any relation that satisfies the axioms. I aim to apply it to betterness relations. The theory proves that, if a relation satisfies the axioms, it can be represented by an expectational utility function – that is, a function having the form of (5.1.1) on page 91. I aim to show that betterness relations can be represented in this way. The details of the representation and its significance are spelt out in Sections 6.4 and 6.5.

The argument for coherence is in Section 6.3. The difficult

121

axiom, once more, is the sure-thing principle. Chapter 5 defended this principle for rational preferences, and Section 6.3 extends the defence to betterness relations. The most straightforward way of showing the coherence of betterness would be to show first the coherence of rational preference relations, and then identify each betterness relation with some rational preference relation. Section 6.2 explores that route, and explains that it cannot be completely successful. So the argument in Section 6.3 has to be slightly more circuitous.

Before I can come to the question of coherence, however, one problem needs to be ironed out first. Expected utility theory is concerned with uncertainty. If betterness relations are to conform to the theory, they must be defined over a field of uncertain prospects. I am therefore taking betterness to be a relation that holds between prospects when the state of nature is unknown. And there are reasons for thinking this may be illegitimate. Section 6.1 reviews these reasons, and argues, oppositely, that there are good reasons to adopt my practice.

6.1 The goodness of uncertain prospects

Table 2 on page 22 shows two prospects you can choose between. You can choose to go to London or to go sailing. After consulting the sky and the weather forecast, suppose you conclude that the weather will probably be good. So you decide that sailing is the better option, and you head for the coast. But you find fog and a dead calm.

In this example, the only good in question is your own. Your conclusion, after consulting the sky and the forecast, is that sailing is better *for you*. Discussions of good and right, like the one that occupies this section, are traditionally set in a moral context. But there is nothing essentially moral about them, and that is why I have chosen this example. Everything I shall say about good in this section applies equally to the good of individuals and to general good.

Reflecting philosophically upon your mishap, you may well come to the view that it would have been better to go to London. Previously you judged it was better to go sailing. Now you judge it was not. So you may well feel you have to conclude that your previous judgement was false. That judgement was based on probabilities, and it was the very best judgement that could have been made on the basis of probabilities. Yet, you now think, it was false. So you may well conclude that probabilities are not an adequate basis for judgements of goodness. The goodness of a prospect such as going sailing is determined, not by probabilities, but by what would actually happen if it was chosen. It depends on what state of nature actually emerges, not on the probabilities of states of nature. Until you know the state of nature, you are not in a position to make judgements of goodness. You should have judged only that going sailing was *probably* the best option, not that it was actually the best.

The conclusion of your line of thought, then, is that the notion of goodness cannot be applied on the basis of probabilities. Goodness must be determined by what would actually happen. Whether or not one prospect is better than another cannot be determined when the state of nature is uncertain.

This is a common opinion. It does, however, create a difficulty for teleological ethics. In Chapter 1 (setting satisficing aside), I identified teleology as the view that the right act is the best. Now in practice, at a time when you have to make a decision between alternative acts, it is never certain what the results of any of them would actually be. If the goodness of an act is determined by what would actually happen, you will therefore never know which act is the best. Yet teleology says the best act is the right one – the one you ought to do. So you will never know what you ought to do. This threatens to make teleological ethics unworkable.

Should right be separated from good?

The common response of teleologists has been to drop the claim that the right act is the best. The notion of goodness is not applied to acts. Goodness is taken to be a property only of final outcomes, which contain no uncertainty. The rightness of acts with uncertain results is determined from the goodness of their possible results, taking probabilities into account. So, when it confronts uncertainty, teleology is conceived as a two-stage theory. In making a choice, you are supposed to proceed in two steps. First, work out the goodness of each act's possible consequences. Then apply a formula that takes account of probabilities, to find out which act you ought to do. The formula generally offered is a variant of Bernoulli's hypothesis mentioned on page 53: you ought to do the act that leads to the greatest *expectation* of good. You ought to maximize expected good. Derek Parfit says: 'What we ought . . . to do is the act whose outcome has the greatest *expected* goodness.'[1]

I see two things wrong with this response. The first is that the formula of maximizing expected goodness is, on the face of it at least, very implausible. The second is that it does not solve the problem anyway.

First the implausibility. The formula is open to two objections. One is that it presumes too much arithmetical precision in the notion of good. To form an expectation, good must be an arithmetic quantity. (To be more precise, if the formula of maximizing expected good is to determine properly what you should do, the scale of goodness must be defined uniquely up to an increasing linear transformation.) We know, certainly, that the betterness relation must be an ordering. But to operate on good arithmetically requires it to have much more structure than simply being an ordering. One might reasonably doubt it has as much. But suppose for a moment that good *is* an arithmetic quantity. Then comes the other objection. Consider an example. Suppose you have to choose between two acts. One will lead for sure to a hundred units of good; the other will lead, with equal probability, to either no units or two hundred and one units. The latter has the greater expectation of good. But you might reasonably doubt it is the right one to choose. It is a risky choice, and playing safe might well be better. Maximizing expected good implies *risk neutrality* about good: that only the expectation of good matters, and the degree of riskiness makes no difference. (See the definition on page 79.) But it seems implausible that teleological ethics should insist on risk neutrality. It seems perfectly reasonable for it to give value to safety.

The formula of maximizing expected good, then, seems wrong. But what can be put in its place? What *should* we say teleology requires in the face of uncertainty? Within the two-stage scheme, it is hard to find the right alternative formula.

My second complaint is that separating right from good does not solve the original problem. Let us return to your reflections on the foggy beach. Originally, after consulting the sky and the forecast, you thought it was right to go sailing. Now you may well conclude it was wrong; you ought to have gone to London. You may conclude that your original judgement was false: it was not right to go sailing, after all. You should not have tried to base a judgement of rightness on probabilities. The judgement you should have made was only that it was *probably* right to go sailing, not that it was actually right. All this is perfectly parallel to your thoughts about goodness that I mentioned previously. If goodness can only be determined by what would actually happen, and not by probabilities, why should rightness be any different?

Some authors at this point appeal to two senses of 'right'. They say that in one sense it was indeed wrong to go sailing, but in another sense it was right. The senses are often called 'objective' and 'subjective'.[2] From the objective standpoint of what would actually happen, it was wrong. From your subjective standpoint when you had to make the decision, knowing only probabilities, it was right. If, though, there can be objective and subjective senses of 'right', there can be objective and subjective senses of 'good' too. From the objective standpoint, going sailing was not the best thing to do. From the subjective standpoint, it was. I see no reason to treat rightness and goodness differently in this respect.

I think it is unnecessary and unwise for teleology to separate right from good in the way I have described. Uncertainty need make no difference to the formula that defines teleology: teleology is the view that the right act is the best. The major advantage of sticking to this formula is that it permits a simple and unified account of teleology. A two-stage theory is an unnecessary complication. As I see it, the question of how to act in the face of uncertainty is not a matter of deriving right from good, but a matter of the internal structure of good: how does the goodness of an act depend on the goodness of its possible results? This makes the question parallel to other questions about the structure of good, in other dimensions: how does general good depend on the good of individuals? and how does overall good depend on good at times? Treating all these questions within a unified structure is the way to get clear about the connections between the three dimensions. That is how I explained the connections in Chapter 2.

A second, and immediate, advantage of sticking to my formula is that it easily frees teleology from a commitment to risk neutrality about good. The right act, I say, is the best. But the best act is not necessarily the one with the greatest *expectation* of good. The goodness of an act need not be the expected goodness of its consequences. It may depend on the act's riskiness as well. A safe act with a smaller expectation of good may be better than a risky act with a greater expectation.

We can alternatively assign goodness to uncertain *prospects*, and say that the right act is the one that leads to the best prospect.[3] This has just the same benefits. Once again, the problem of how to act in the face of uncertainty is not a matter of deriving right from good. That is immediate: the right act is the one that leads to the best prospect. The problem is internal to good: how does the goodness of a prospect depend on the goodness of the final consequences that may result? The goodness of a prospect is not necessarily the expected goodness of the consequences.

I shall use this terminology. But I am also taking the step of identifying the goodness of an act with the goodness of the prospect it leads to. (Both will include any intrinsic value the act may have.) This follows the practice I adopted on page 4 of assigning goodness to acts, and identifying the goodness of an act with the goodness of the consequences it leads to. Now, in the context of uncertainty, I am retreating from final consequences to prospects. To identify the goodness of act with the goodness of the prospect it leads to is a convenient and harmless simplification of terminology. Leonard Savage, indeed, identified an act itself with the prospect it leads to,[4] and that too seems harmless in the context.

My formula, of course, leaves open the substantive question of how, exactly, the goodness of an act *does* depend on the goodness of its possible consequences. I shall pursue this question later in the book, starting in Section 6.5. On investigation, the goodness of an act might yet turn out to be just the expected goodness of its consequences. Risk neutrality might turn out to be correct. But we are not committed to it just by our definition of teleology.

Probability-relative right

Still, the original problem remains. If teleology is ever to tell you what to do, it must assign rightness to an act at a time when it is uncertain what the results of the act will be. Yet I suggested that you, on the beach, might well come to the conclusion that this cannot properly be done. Goodness and rightness must depend on what would actually happen. G. E. Moore took this view. He concluded that you can never know what is the right thing to do.[5] Judith Thomson agrees. 'Surely', she says, 'what a person ought or ought not to do, what it is permissible or impermissible for him to do, does not turn on what he thinks is or will be the case, or even on what he with the best will in the world thinks is or will be the case, but instead on what *is* the case.'[6]

In deciding whether or not to go sailing, you did the very best you could, taking account of all the information available. But unluckily things turned out badly. Your act turned out to have bad results. According to Moore, you acted wrongly. Moore recognizes that there is something paradoxical about this claim. You do not deserve blame; you may even deserve praise for your careful deliberation. And yet, Moore says, you ought not to have done what you did.[7]

I have already mentioned one route out of the paradox: to say
that your act was subjectively right but objectively wrong.
Thomson, however, denies the existence of subjective rightness.
She says:

> But I greatly doubt that there is such a subjective sense of 'ought'.
> On those rare occasions on which someone conceives the idea of
> asking for my advice on a moral matter, I do not take my fieldwork
> to be limited to a study of what he believes is the case; I take it to
> be incumbent on me to find out what *is* the case. And if both of us
> have the facts wrong, and I therefore advise him to do what turns
> out a disaster, I do not insist that in one sense my moral advice was
> all the same true, though in another sense it was false.[8]

Suppose someone was to conceive the idea of asking for Thomson's
advice on a matter of investment. Suppose she asked whether
International Glutamates was likely to do well. Thomson would
similarly extend her fieldwork beyond a study of what her friend
believes to be the case; she would feel it incumbent on her to find
out what *is* the case. *Is* it likely to do well or not? And if neither
she nor her friend realized that IG was on the verge of bankruptcy,
and Thomson's advice was that it was likely to do well, she would
not later insist that in one sense this advice was true, though in
another false. Yet, according to subjectivism about probability,
likelihood is nothing other than a degree of belief. So external
fieldwork should be unnecessary. If Thomson's argument is
effective, then, it will be effective against subjective probability as
well as subjective rightness.

I expect it would take more of an argument than this to disturb
a subjectivist about probability. Perhaps Thomson has raised a
genuine problem for subjective probability, and perhaps she has
not. But she has certainly not raised a *separate* problem for
subjective rightness. In so far as we are entitled to subjective
probability, we are entitled to subjective rightness. At least,
Thomson's argument does not show we are not.

I do not wish to take sides about the existence of subjective
probability or subjective rightness. I do wish, though, to claim a
right to a *probability-relative* notion of rightness. Whenever there
are probabilities, whatever sort they are, there is an associated
rightness. The rightness will inherit the status of the probabilities.
If, indeed, International Glutamates is likely to do well, then,
indeed, Thomson's friend ought to buy its shares. If the likelihood
is subjective, then so is the rightness. If, on the other hand, the
likelihood is in some way objective, then the rightness is too.

For every set of probabilities, I suggest, there is an associated rightness. It is not really that 'right' has many senses. It has one sense, which is relative to particular probabilities. 'It was right to go sailing' and 'It was not right to go sailing' do not contradict each other, unless they are meant to be understood relative to the same probabilities. Let us write 'right relative to probabilities p' as 'right$_p$'. Originally you concluded it was right$_p$ to go sailing, where p is the set of your original probabilities. On the beach you conclude it was not right$_q$ to go sailing, where q is the set of probabilities you have then (which assign probability one to bad sailing weather). Obviously, you are not forced to conclude that your original opinion was false. Normally we do not need to bother with the subscripts, because the context sets the probabilities for us.

The rightness that Moore speaks of, which is determined by what would actually happen, may be thought of as the limit of probability-relative rightness. It is rightness relative to the set of probabilities that gives probability one to what would actually happen and nought to everything else. It gives probability one, that is, to the actual state of nature.

We cannot do without probability-relative rightness. Moore denied its existence, but there is a worse problem for his position than the paradox I mentioned above. The conclusion of practical reasoning is a judgement of what ought to be done. And, also, it has to be a judgement one can act on. But the only judgement one can act on is relative to the probabilities available. Suppose, when wondering whether to go sailing, having consulted the sky and the weather forecast, you now consult Moore. You ask him what you should do. He replies that you cannot possibly know what you should do, but that probably you should go sailing. You, though, need to know what to do. Impatient with Moore's shilly-shallying, you ask him 'So what do you suggest I do, then?' Pressed like this, Moore will certainly tell you to go sailing. This is not simply an ungrounded whim on his part. He believes that practical reason, given the probabilities, requires you to go sailing; it would be irrational on your part not to. Another way of expressing this belief of Moore's is that you ought to go sailing. If it is irrational for you not to go sailing, then you ought to go sailing. Moore is debarred by his official doctrine from expressing it this way, but nevertheless this is what he believes. Indeed, he himself is sometimes careless enough to express his real opinion. He says at one point (speaking of a moral rule): 'Though we may be sure there are cases where the rule should be broken, we can never know which those cases are, and ought, therefore, never to break it.'[9] This looks like a contradiction: there are cases where we ought to break the rule, and there are no cases where we ought to break the rule. But actually it is not a contradiction, because the second 'ought' is meant to be understood relative to our probabilities, and the first is not. In this sentence, then, Moore himself uses a probability-relative 'ought'.

Not all probabilities have equal status. According to subjectivism, probabilities derived from more information have a higher status than those derived from less. Objective probabilities, if there are such things, have a higher status than subjective ones. At the extreme, what would actually happen has the highest status of all. It is a matter for probability theory to give an account of the status of probabilities, and of the logical relations between probabilities of different status. Higher-status probabilities do not necessarily contradict lower-status one. But in some way or other they certainly *supersede* them. This at least is true: you ought not to found your judgements on lower-status probabilities when higher-status probabilities are available.

The status of probabilities is inherited by their associated rightnesses. For instance, claims of rightness associated with false probabilities will be false claims. The rightness associated with what would actually happen, which is not really probability relative at all, has the highest status. Higher-status rightness supersedes lower-status rightness. The conclusion you reach on the beach supersedes your earlier judgement. If you had originally possessed your present knowledge of high-status probabilities, you would not have been right to go sailing. Rightness relative to what would actually happen supersedes all lower-status rightness. Moore thought it contradicted all lower-status rightness. But that is only so if what would actually happen contradicts all other probabilities. So long as it is true that good weather was probable (even though, actually, the weather was going to be bad), it is true, relative to that probability, that you ought to have gone to the beach.

Even if there is no contradiction between different rightnesses, the fact that they supersede each other means we cannot be neutral amongst them all. On the one hand, there is the superiority of higher status. On the other, our state of knowledge limits our access to high-status probabilities, and our knowledge changes with time. The resulting dialectic is documented by Frank Jackson in 'Decision theoretic consequentialism'. Jackson calls the different probability-relative rightnesses an 'annoying profusion', and plumps for a particular one as the 'most immediately relevant to action'. But for my purposes, I do not have to be partisan.

Probability-relative good

I said that teleology should not separate rightness from goodness. It should therefore take good as probability relative, like right. And everything I have been saying about rightness will apply to goodness too.

We very commonly use a probability-relative notion of good. For instance, if International Glutamates is likely to do well, then we say it is a good investment. Indeed, nearly all our judgements of good are probability relative, because the consequences of virtually everything are uncertain. If we were denied a probability-relative sense of betterness, we should never be able to say that one act was better than another, even long after the event; although we may come to find out reasonably well what actually did happen, we shall generally never know what would have happened if the other act had been done. Without a probability-relative notion of good, the only judgements of good we should be entitled to make in practice would be judgements of *intrinsic* goodness, because these are independent of causal consequences. But most of our judgements are not like that.

In any case, I do not need to insist that the notion of probability-relative goodness is in common use. It is certainly useful; I have already explained on page 125 its value in unifying the account of teleology.

Nevertheless, it does need to be treated with care. It is essential to keep in mind that not all probabilities have equal status. Good relative to what would actually happen has the highest status. Indeed, its status is unique because it is what ultimately matters. When the account is finally made up of how well the world went, it will be an account of the good that actually happens. Lower-status goodness is a sort of interim goodness, which has to be revised in the final account.

This means it is a mistake to assume that our intuitions about goodness may be extended without question to probability-relative goodness. Suppose, for instance, you think it a bad thing if some people lead much better lives than others. So you value equality in the distribution of good relative to what actually happens. There is no reason why this intuition should lead you to favour equality in probability-relative good. Even if people have equally good prospects relative to some probabilities, some people may nevertheless turn out to enjoy much better lives than others. And you may see no value in probability-relative equality that does not lead to actual equality. Even if you do value probability-relative equality, it is likely to be for different reasons from the ones that lead you to value actual equality.[10] I need to draw attention to the need for care here, because many economists are inclined to treat probability-relative equality, or 'ex-ante equality' as they call it, as a surrogate for actual, or 'ex-post', equality, as though the value achieved by the latter may be just as well achieved by the former.[11]

Here is another example of the need for care. I shall later be defending something I call 'the principle of personal good', which says, roughly, that one alternative cannot be better than another unless it is better for someone. Intuitively, this principle seems very plausible. However, Sections 8.2 and 9.3 show that it encounters serious difficulties when applied to probability-relative good. I shall provide arguments that, I hope, overcome the difficulties. But arguments are certainly required, and a direct appeal to intuition is not enough.

I need to make one other point about probability-relative good, because it will become important later. Good, both individual and general, may be assessed relative to different probabilities. Consequently, talk about good is ambiguous until a context has been set by fixing on some particular probabilities. Normally in a statement or argument, the probabilities will remain constant throughout, unless a switch of context is made explicit. Normally, the probabilities implied will be the speaker's own. The statement 'A is better than B for P, but worse for Q' normally means that A is better for P and worse for Q relative to the speaker's probabilities. Certainly it means that A is better for P and worse for Q relative to the same probabilities. In ordinary circumstances, it never means that A is better for P relative to P's probabilities and worse for Q relative to Q's probabilities. At any rate, this is true of my usage in this book. Statements and arguments about good are to be understood relative to probabilities that are held constant throughout.

6.2 Betterness and rational preferences

The aim of this chapter is to show that individual and general betterness relations satisfy the axioms of expected utility theory: they are coherent. Chapter 5 argued that rational preference relations satisfy the sure-thing principle, and it also gave some qualified support to the other axioms of expected utility theory, when applied to rational preference relations. It would be nice,

therefore, if each betterness relation happened to coincide with a
rational preference relation of some sort. Then, supposing the
arguments of Chapter 5 could be boosted to show the full coherence
of rational preferences, the coherence of betterness would follow.
With that idea in mind, in this section I shall take an individual's
betterness relation, and ask whether a rational preference relation
can be found that coincides with it. I shall not be concerned with
the general betterness relation in this section; I shall come back to
that at the end of Section 6.3. Also, for the sake of discussion in
this section, I shall take for granted what I have not fully demon-
strated: that rational preferences are coherent.

The links between preferences and betterness are intimate and
much debated. I shall need to survey some theories about them.

One theory takes a person's betterness relation to coincide with
her actual preference relation:

> *The actual-preference-satisfaction theory of good.* Of two
> alternatives A and B, A is at least as good for a person as B
> if and only if the person prefers A to B or is indifferent
> between them.

This theory might be defended in either of two very different ways.
The first is to say that a person's good actually *consists in* the
satisfaction of her preferences, and nothing else: getting what you
prefer is in itself good for you, and this, for you, is the only sort of
good. The second defence is to concede that some sorts of good, at
least, can be identified independently of preferences. But it says
that, as it happens, people always prefer what is better for them.

The actual-preference-satisfaction theory is false. It can be
refuted by pointing out the undeniable fact that people sometimes
prefer, of two alternatives, the one that is worse for them, because
they are misinformed about the merits of the alternatives. This
answers the second defence by showing it makes a false empirical
claim. It answers the first defence by showing, since this is indeed
an undeniable fact, that there *must* be a sort of good other than the
satisfaction of preferences. Otherwise it could not be a fact at all.

It is fortunate for me that this theory is false. The evidence from
psychologists is that people's actual preferences are often not
coherent.[12] If they coincided with betterness, then, betterness
would not be coherent either. But I want to show it is.

A second theory takes a person's betterness relation to coincide
with what her preference relation would be if she were rational
and well informed:

The rational-preference-satisfaction theory of good. Of two alternatives *A* and *B*, *A* is at least as good for a person as *B* if and only if the person would prefer *A* to *B* if she were rational and well informed.

This, too, might be defended in two very different ways. The first is to say that a person's good actually *consists in* the satisfaction of what her preferences would be if she were rational and well informed: getting what you would prefer if you were rational and well informed is in itself good for you, and this, for you, is the only sort of good.[13] The second defence concedes that some sorts of good, at least, can be identified independently of rational and well-informed preferences. But it says that, nevertheless, a rational and well-informed person will always prefer what is better for her. The second defence divides at this point on the question of whether this is a necessary or a contingent truth. One division says it is necessary, because rationality requires a person to prefer what is better for her. The other division says it is just a contingent fact that rational and well-informed people always prefer what is better for them.

One might try to refute the rational-preference-satisfaction theory of good in the same way as I refuted the actual-preference-satisfaction theory: by pointing out an undeniable fact. The fact I have in mind is that rational and well-informed people sometimes prefer, of two alternatives, the one that is worse for them, because it is better for someone else and they want to promote that person's good. This fact, however, is evidently not undeniable, since it is often denied. So the refutation will fail.

For the moment, though, I have no need to reject the rational-preference-satisfaction theory. In the spirit of neutrality I adopted in Section 2.4, I shall leave it alone. However, I shall not accept it either. Although the fact I mentioned is not undeniable, it is at least plausible. Therefore the rational-preference-satisfaction theory of good is insecure. It would be possible to make it the foundation of an argument for the coherence of good, but I shall not do so.

A third theory:

The self-interested-preference-satisfaction theory of good. Of two alternatives *A* and *B*, *A* is at least as good for a person as *B* if and only if the person would prefer *A* to *B* or be indifferent between them if she were rational, well informed and self-interested.

This theory is not very far from the truth. As it stands, though, it is open to the following objection. Self-interested people, like other people, sometimes discount their own future good in forming their preferences. Suppose that alternative A offers a person plenty of fun in the near future, but not so much when she becomes old. Suppose B on the other hand, requires some sacrifices in the near future but will produce excellent benefits in old age. Then it might well be that B is better for the person overall, but that she would prefer A, even if she were self-interested. One might try to counter this objection by arguing that discounting is irrational, so it would not be rational for the person to prefer A to B. But that could be a hard argument to make. Derek Parfit, for one, has presented strong arguments on the other side.[14]

The objection plays on some ambiguity in the notion of self-interest. We generally call people self-interested if they ignore the interests of others. People who are self-interested in this sense may not pursue exactly their own interest, because they may discount their future good.[15] So let us narrow down the notion, and refuse to call a person self-interested if she discounts. Let us adopt this definition:

> A self-interested person is someone who, if she were also rational and well informed, would, of two alternatives A and B, prefer A to B or be indifferent between them if and only if A was better for her than B.

This definition seems, at first sight, to give us the self-interested-preference-satisfaction theory of good on a plate. So it seems to give us an argument for the coherence of a person's betterness relation. This relation, it seems, coincides with what the person's preference relation would be if she were rational, well informed and self-interested. Since we are supposing the latter relation is coherent, the argument goes, so is the former.

Unfortunately, though, this argument fails. Two obstructions stand in its way.

The first is that my definition of 'self-interested' implicitly assumes it is possible for a person to be both rational and self-interested. (Otherwise no one could ever fit the definition.) And this is something we cannot rely on in arguing for the coherence of good.[16] What grounds could we have for supposing a person can be both rational and self-interested? They would have to be grounds of intuition and experience: we see around us people who appear fairly rational and fairly self-interested, and we imagine it would be possible to purify the type. Now, these grounds have to be adequate to support the conclusion that the person's good is coherent. How could they, though? Suppose people's good was actually not always coherent. Suppose, say, that people's betterness relations did not always conform to the sure-thing principle. Would that fact have impinged on our intuition and experience, so as to make us doubt that a person could be both rational and self-interested? Conceivably it might have if we were using 'self-interested' in its common or garden sense, because we have experience of people who are self-interested in that sense. But we are now taking 'self-interested' to be defined simply by the coincidence between the person's betterness relation and what her preference relation would be if she were rational and well informed. I do not believe that our intuition and experience are adequate grounds to establish that self-interest in this sense is consistent with rationality. If a person's betterness relation happened not to be coherent, then if she were rational her preference relation could not coincide with her betterness relation. To be sure it can coincide, we should have to know in advance that the betterness relation was coherent. But that is what we are trying to prove.

The second obstruction is that the definition of 'self-interested' does not actually imply the self-interested-preference-satisfaction theory of good. It implies this instead:

> If a person were rational, well informed and self-interested, she would, of two alternatives A and B, prefer A to B or be indifferent between them if and only if A was better for her than B.

A person's preference relation, if she were rational, well informed and self-interested, would coincide with what her betterness relation would be if she were rational, well informed and self-interested. But it is unlikely to coincide with her actual betterness relation. And that is what the self-interested-preference-satisfaction theory requires. If I were rational, well informed and self-interested, a quite different range of things would be good for me than are actually good for me as I am.[17]

These two obstructions prevent the self-interested-preference-satisfaction theory from supplying a defence of my claim that a person's good is coherent.

The second is a problem with the form of the counterfactual condition. It is possible to fix up a condition that overcomes it. Here is one way. Presumably, it would be possible for a person to have a private angel who wants this person's good and nothing else. The angel's preference relation would coincide with the person's betterness relation as it actually is. Then, if the angel were rational, she would have coherent preferences, and it would follow that the person's betterness relation is coherent. But would the angel be rational? The first obstruction is still standing in the way, or one like it. The angel has been identified simply by the coincidence between her preferences and the person's betterness. To have good grounds for thinking she would be rational, and have coherent preferences, we should need to know in advance whether the person's betterness relation is coherent. And that is what has to be proved.

Nevertheless, we are now very close to a successful argument. All we need do is enquire a little more deeply into the structure of the angel's preferences, to check they are really coherent. In effect, that is what Section 6.3 does.

6.3 The argument for coherence

I have been trying to find an easy way of defending the claim that a person's good is coherent. I was looking for a rational preference relation that coincides with the person's betterness relation. If that could be found, it would allow us to apply the conclusion of Chapter 5 wholesale. But I think that by now we should recognize that this line of argument is unlikely to succeed. What we shall have to do instead is step back from the conclusion of Chapter 5 into its actual arguments, and rework them for our new purposes.

For the moment I shall continue to deal with an individual's good only, not general good. I need to show it satisfies the axioms of expected utility theory. I shall consider only the more important and controversial axioms, which are described in Sections 5.1 and 5.2. They are transitivity, completeness and the sure-thing principle. Does an individual's betterness relation conform to these axioms?

It is certainly transitive. Here we are on even firmer ground than we were in Chapter 5. Logic requires betterness to be transitive, as I explained on page 11.

On the other hand, one might well doubt that the relation is complete. It is natural to think there may be incommensurable goods. Suppose one alternative (one possible career, say) will bring a person the goods of security and comfort, and another the goods of excitement and perhaps a fortune. It may not be possible to weigh these goods against each other. Then neither alternative will be better for the person than the other, and they will not be equally good for her either. In this book, I regret to say, I have to leave the problem of incommensurability aside.* I mention it here, and pass on. I shall simply assume that a person's betterness relation is complete.

What about the sure-thing principle? Table 13 on page 94 shows what the sure-thing principle requires. Applied to a person's betterness relation, it requires, for any four prospects with the configuration shown in Table 13, that *A* is at least as good as *B* if and only if *C* is at least as good as *D*.

On pages 95–96 I presented an argument for the sure-thing principle when it is applied to rational preferences. The argument compared the reasons a person has for preferring *A* to *B* or *B* to *A* with those she has for preferring *C* to *D* or *D* to *C*; I do not have to go into the details. I now want to use the same argument again, but confine it to one class of reasons only: those that are directed at the person's own good. A person may have reasons of many different sorts for preferring one alternative to another. Some will be directed at her own good; some may be directed at the good of other people; if teleology is false, some may not be directed at good at all. But now I want to concentrate only on reasons of the first sort. These are the reasons that would motivate the person's private angel, if there were such a thing, in forming *her* preferences.

I am going to assume that

A prospect *A* is at least as good for a person as another *B* if and only if the reasons directed towards the person's good for preferring *A* to *B* are at least as strong as the reasons directed towards her good for preferring *B* to *A*.

This may seem obvious, but it is a significant move all the same. *A* and *B* are uncertain prospects. As Section 6.1 explained, betterness between prospects is a notion that cannot be taken for

---

* Before it can be dealt with properly, mathematical work will be required to reconstruct as much as possible of expected utility theory on the basis of an ordering relation that allows for incommensurability. This will be very difficult. We have scarcely even the beginning: a suitable mathematical model of a relation with incommensurability. The closest model is a 'partial ordering', which is a transitive and reflexive relation that is incomplete. Being incomplete means that for some *A*s and *B*s it is false that $A \succeq B$ and also false that $B \succeq A$. But betterness is what may be called a 'vague relation'. For some *A*s and *B*s, it is sometimes neither definitely true nor definitely false that $A \succeq B$.

granted. The statement above fixes its meaning in terms of good-directed reasons. The reasons come first, and betterness follows. Each reason emanates from the goodness of what would happen in a particular state of nature, once the uncertainty has been resolved. Together the reasons determine goodness for uncertain prospects. So goodness for prospects is determined from the direction of rationality. What is better for the person is determined by what it would be rational to prefer, taking account only of reasons directed at the person's own good. To put it another way, A is at least as good for the person as B if and only if the person's private angel would prefer A to B or be indifferent between them.

Given this determination of goodness, the argument on pages 95–96 quickly shows that A is at least as good for the person as B if and only if C is at least as good for her at D. All that is needed is to take that argument and confine it to reasons directed towards the person's good. I shall not repeat the steps here. The conclusion is what we want: the sure-thing principle applied to the person's betterness relation.

It is true, as I said on page 96, that this argument begs the crucial question about the sure-thing principle: can there be interaction or complementarity between states of nature? But that question was thoroughly dealt with in Chapter 5, in the context of rationality. Now we have betterness for prospects determined by rationality, the whole argument of that chapter is available for betterness too. The whole argument supports the sure-thing principle applied to a person's betterness relation.

Furthermore, it is now easy to extend the argument to general betterness too. I have to show that the general betterness relation conforms to the axioms of expected utility theory. Once again, I shall concern myself only with the three contentious axioms: transitivity, completeness and the sure-thing principle.

Transitivity, once more, comes directly from logic. Completeness, once more, is dubious. Indeed, there may be more reason to doubt it for the general betterness relation than for the individual relations. It is a popular opinion in some circles that one person's good cannot be compared with another's.[18] Take two prospects and suppose one is better for one person and the other for someone else. If the good of these two people cannot be compared, then the goodness of the prospects cannot be compared either. The betterness relation will be incomplete. As I did before, I shall simply note this difficulty and pass on.

Does the betterness relation conform to the sure-thing principle? Once again I can use the argument on pages 95–96 to show it does. Consider the reasons there are for preferring one prospect to another, but consider only the *teleological* reasons. These are the reasons aimed at good (and not, now, just the good of one person). If there are genuinely nonteleological reasons, exclude them. Now,

A prospect *A* is at least as good as another *B* if and only if the teleological reasons for preferring *A* to *B* are at least as strong as the teleological reasons for preferring *B* to *A*.

This statement actually *determines* a notion of good for prospects. As for individual good, so for general good: good for prospects is determined from reasons – from the direction of rationality. A better prospect is one that it would be rational to prefer, taking account of teleological reasons only. It is one that would be preferred by a *public* angel, motivated only by teleological reasons.

The argument on pages 95–96 can now be run, restricted to teleological reasons only. It will show that the general betterness relation conforms to the sure-thing principle. And all the other arguments in Chapter 5 will be available to support this conclusion.

6.4 *Representing betterness by utility*

I conclude, then, that the individual and general betterness relations are coherent. That is to say, they conform to the axioms of expected utility theory. Now, expected utility theory says that any relation that conforms to its axioms can be represented by an expectational utility function. The theory is normally applied to preference relations, but it will work equally well for betterness relations. So we may conclude that each of the individual and general betterness relations can be represented by an expectational utility function. This section says more about what that means.

Take any one of the betterness relations, individual or general. (If it is an individual's relation, 'good' in the rest of this section refers to this individual's good.) This betterness relation is a relation amongst prospects such as $(x_1, x_2, \ldots x_s)$, where x_1, x_2 and so on are the outcomes in the different states of nature. Expected utility theory tells us that this relation can be represented by a utility function U that has the special form

(6.4.1)　　$U(x_1, x_2, \ldots x_s) = p_1 u(x_1) + p_2 u(x_2) + \ldots + p_s u(x_s)$.

where u is a subutility function, and p_1, p_2 and so on are probabilities. This equation is (5.1.1) from page 91. It defines a utility function U, and a subutility function u.

We need not fuss about distinguishing utilities from subutilities, for the following reason. For any outcome x, there is a corresponding 'certain prospect' $(x, x, \ldots x)$, which leads to the outcome x in every state of nature. Equation (6.4.1) tells us that the utility of the certain prospect is

$$U(x, x, \ldots x) = p_1 u(x) + p_2 u(x) + \ldots + p_s u(x)$$
$$= (p_1 + p_2 + \ldots + p_s)u(x)$$
$$= u(x),$$

because the probabilities add up to one. So the value assigned to an outcome by the subutility function u is just the value assigned to the corresponding certain prospect by the utility function U. We can treat this value as the utility of the outcome. The subutility function u is in effect an extract out of the full utility function U. U assigns a utility to every prospect, and u picks out the values assigned to just the certain prospects.

Now, the utility function *represents* the betterness relation. That means that one prospect is at least as good as another if and only if it has at least as great a utility. The same goes for outcomes: one outcome is at least as good as another if and only if it has at least as great a utility (or subutility). This follows from the obvious fact that one outcome is at least as good as another if and only if the certain prospect corresponding to the one is at least as good as the certain prospect corresponding to the other. For the sake of what comes in Section 6.5, it is worth attaching the term *ordinal* to this type of representation. The utility function represents the betterness relation *ordinally*. It represents good ordinally, as I shall sometimes put it. This means simply that the order of utilities is the same as the order of goodness: better prospects have higher utilities.

Next, the utility function is *expectational*. This means that the utility of a prospect is the expectation of the utilities of its possible outcomes. This is what (6.4.1) says. Of two prospects, then, the better one is the one with the greater expected utility. Consequently, we can express our conclusion in a convenient formula: *it is best to maximise expected utility*. This is so only because utility is defined precisely to make it so. It is defined, in effect, as that which it is best to maximize the expectation of. For an individual, her utility is defined as that which is best for her to maximize the expectation of. Expected utility theory tells us it is possible to define a utility function that has this property, provided the person's betterness relation is coherent.

One other property of the utility function is important. The function is *cardinal*. What this means is defined on page 75: it means that the function is standing in for a whole family of functions that are increasing linear transforms of each other. This needs some more explanation in our present context.

Because it is expectational, the function U is additively separable; see (5.1.2) on page 93 if this is not obvious. The uniqueness theorem on page 74 tell us, therefore, that any increasing linear transform of U is another additively separable function that represents the same betterness relation. And actually, rather more than this is true. It is also true that any increasing linear transform of U is another *expectational* utility function that represents the same betterness relation. To see this, let V be an increasing linear transform of U. Then V is $aU + b$ for some number b and positive number a. So

$$V = aU + b$$
$$= a\{p_1 u(x_1) + p_2 u(x_2) + \ldots + p_s u(x_s)\} + \{p_1 + p_2 + \ldots + p_s\}b$$
$$= p_1\{au(x_1) + b\} + p_2\{au(x_2) + b\} + \ldots + p_s\{au(x_s) + b\}$$
$$= p_1 v(x_1) + p_2 v(x_2) + \ldots + p_s v(x_s),$$

where v is an increasing transform of u, specifically $au + b$. This shows that V is expectational: like U it has the expected utility form shown in (6.4.1). And it represents the same relation as U, simply because it is an increasing transform of U.

The converse is true too. Any expectational utility function that represents the same betterness relation as U is an increasing linear transform of U. This follows directly from the uniqueness theorem. Any expectational utility function V is additively separable. Therefore the theorem tells us V is an increasing linear transform of U, if it represents the same betterness relation as U.

There are, then, many expectational utility functions that represent the betterness relation. Each is an increasing linear transform of the others. The function U is standing in for this whole family of functions; we say it is unique up to increasing linear transformations. So it is a cardinal utility function. Exactly the same is true of the subutility u. Section 4.3 explains what the cardinality of utility signifies in general. Section 6.5 considers what it particularly signifies when utility represents betterness.

6.5 Bernoulli's hypothesis

In this section I shall leave the general betterness relation aside, and concentrate on an individual's betterness relation. I shall ask whether we have any reason to believe:

> *Bernoulli's hypothesis about good.* One alternative is at least as good for a person as another if and only if it gives the person at least as great an expectation of her good.

Bernoulli's hypothesis has been taken for granted by many decision theorists.[19] I first mentioned a version of it – concerned with rationality rather than good – on page 53. I briefly criticized another version on page 124. This section begins a more thorough examination of Bernoulli's hypothesis, an examination that is continued in Chapters 10 and 11. I shall show in those chapters that the hypothesis has a much wider importance than appears at first sight. It explicitly makes a claim about the aggregation of good across the dimension of states of nature. But I shall show it has implications for aggregation across people and times as well.

Bernoulli's hypothesis says, put briefly, that it is best for a person to maximize the expectation of her good. And, as I said on page 141, a person's utility is in effect defined as that which it is best for the person to maximize the expectation of. Consequently, if Bernoulli's hypothesis is true, that seems to imply a person's utility will coincide with her good. And this is almost correct. It is not exactly correct, however, because a person's utility is not defined strictly uniquely, but only up to increasing linear transformations. The most we can derive from Bernoulli's hypothesis is therefore that utility is an increasing linear transform of good. The next paragraph spells this out more fully.

Suppose Bernoulli's hypothesis is true. This means that for any outcome x there is some quantity $g(x)$ that is the goodness of x for the person, and that, if we write the expected goodness of a prospect $(x_1, x_2, \ldots x_s)$ as

$$(6.5.1) \quad G(x_1, x_2, \ldots x_s) = p_1 g(x_1) + p_2 g(x_2) + \ldots + p_s g(x_s),$$

then one prospect is better than another if and only if it has a higher value of G. The function G, that is to say, represents the person's betterness relation ordinally.* So G is a *utility* function representing the betterness relation. Furthermore this equation shows it is an *expectational* utility function; it has the expected utility form, with g its corresponding subutility. Therefore, the uniqueness theorem tells us that G is an increasing linear transform of any expectational utility function that represents the same betterness relation. So, for any expectational utility function that represents the person's betterness relation, the goodness $g(x)$ of an outcome is an increasing linear transform of its utility $u(x)$.

If a utility function is such that the goodness of outcomes is an increasing linear transform of the outcomes' utility, I shall say the function *represents good cardinally*. We are, all the time, dealing with utility functions that represent good *ordinally*. As I explained on page 140, this means simply that one prospect or outcome is better than another if and only if it has at least as great a utility. We have just found that, if Bernoulli's hypothesis is true, then any expectational utility function that represents good ordinally also represents it cardinally.

The converse is also true. Suppose we have an expectational utility function that represents good cardinally. Then $g(x)$ is an increasing linear transform of $u(x)$. Therefore the function G defined by (6.5.1) is an increasing linear transform of U. So G is itself a utility function that represents the betterness relation: one prospect is at least as good as another if and only if it has a greater value of G. But G is simply the expected goodness of a prospect. So one prospect is at least as good as another if and only if it has a greater expected goodness. And this is Bernoulli's hypothesis.

In summary: Bernoulli's hypothesis is equivalent to the hypothesis that, if an expectational utility function represents good ordinally, it also represents it cardinally.

Should we believe Bernoulli's hypothesis? Should we believe that utility represents good cardinally? Figure 7 shows utility graphed

---

* For any prospect A, $G(A)$ is its expected goodness. Strictly, Bernoulli's hypothesis does not imply that $G(A)$ is also the goodness of A. But let us make the assumption (which I think is obviously correct) that the goodness of a certain prospect $(x, x, \ldots x)$ is just the goodness $g(x)$ of the outcome x. We know $g(x)$ is equal to $G(x, x, \ldots x)$ (because probabilities add up to one). So the expected goodness $G(A)$ of any *certain* prospect A is indeed the goodness of A. This, together with Bernoulli's hypothesis, is enough to ensure that the expected goodness $G(A)$ of *any* prospect A is also its actual goodness.

Figure 7

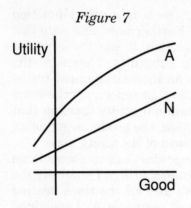

against goodness. According to Bernoulli's hypothesis, this graph is a straight line, like the one labelled 'N' in the diagram. Have we any reason to think this is necessarily the right form?

One mistake needs to be avoided at the start. As I said on page 141, an expectational utility function is itself cardinal. And our utility function is defined to represent good. It may therefore be tempting to think it must represent good cardinally. But this is a mistake. Our utility function is defined to represent good *ordinally*. That is to say, one prospect or outcome has more utility than another if and only if it is better. Increasing goodness implies increasing utility. Suppose goodness is an arithmetical quantity (a contentious assumption I shall soon be discussing). Then utility is an *increasing* transform of *goodness*. Our utility function is also cardinal, and that means it is a *linear* transform of any other expectational *utility* function. But nothing says utility is a *linear* transform of *goodness*.

And the prima-facie evidence is against Bernoulli's hypothesis. I have mentioned this evidence already on page 124, in discussing a different version of the hypothesis. First of all, the hypothesis implies that a person's good is an arithmetical quantity; otherwise the notion of expected goodness would not make sense. And on the face of it this is implausible. Second, even if the person's good *is* an arithmetic quantity, on the face of it it does not seem it must necessarily be best for the person to maximize the expectation of her good. Maximizing the expectation of good implies risk neutrality about good. But it might be better for the person, say, to avoid risk.[20] Suppose she has a choice between, on the one hand, one hundred units of good for sure and, on the other hand, a gamble at equal odds of either no units or two hundred and one units. It might well be better for the person to have the hundred units for sure, even though the risky alternative has a greater expectation of good.

I explained in Section 4.3 how the shape of a utility graph reflects an attitude to risk. (In that section, I dealt with risk to money rather than risk to good, but the point is the same.) A straight line graph, like the one labelled 'N' in Figure 7, implies risk neutrality. This is a consequence of Bernoulli's hypothesis. But a downward-curving graph, like the one labelled 'A', seems just as plausible. According to graph A, it is good for the person to avoid risk to good.

That is the prima-facie evidence against Bernoulli's hypothesis. There is, however, a response.

The response starts by pointing out that the way I presented the hypothesis may be misleading. I said the hypothesis implies that, for any outcome x, there is a quantity $g(x)$ that is the goodness of x, and that utility $u(x)$ is an increasing linear transform of $g(x)$. That is how utility represents good cardinally. This way of putting it may suggest that we must have in advance a quantitative notion of good, and that utility, representing the betterness relation, must then turn out to be an increasing linear transform of good. This would mean that, having found the family of utility functions that represent good cardinally, it would then make sense to ask which of the family is actually the goodness function itself. It is, indeed, implausible that we have such a definite quantitative notion of good. So if Bernoulli's hypothesis really implied as much, it would be objectionable. But actually it does not imply as much. Utility may represent good cardinally in a different way.

The measurement of hotness by temperature supplies an analogy. (Not a perfect one because there is an absolute zero of temperature, but I shall ignore that.) We have a primitive notion of hotness, and we can identify some things as hotter than others. The notion is not a precise quantitative one, though, until it comes to be measured by temperature. Scales of temperature can be based on the thermal expansion of metals. Many different scales are possible, distinguished by different calibrations; the Celsius and Fahrenheit scales are amongst them. Each of the scales is an increasing linear transform of the others. We take temperature to represent hotness cardinally. But this does not mean that one of the family of temperature scales coincides with a pre-existing quantitative scale of hotness. Instead, we think our quantitative notion of hotness is determined in the course of setting up the temperature scales based on the expansion of metals. Temperature is all there is to quantitative hotness. Having found the family of scales, it therefore makes no sense to ask which one of the family is really hotness itself. Quantitative hotness is not a particular scale, but is best understood as the entire family together. Nevertheless, in practice we shall have to pick a single scale to work with. Our choice will be arbitrary, but whichever we choose it will, genuinely, measure hotness. If we pick Celsius, the Celsius scale will measure hotness, and all the other scales will be increasing linear transforms of hotness.

Perhaps utility represents good cardinally in just this way. If so, then it will be true that one of the person's utility functions measures good, and the others are increasing linear transforms of good. But it will be arbitrary which one measures good, and the entire family of utility functions is really the best depiction of quantitative goodness. We need not have a quantitative notion of good in advance of its measurement by utility; the utility scales themselves will determine our quantitative notion. This makes it much less implausible than it seemed at first that utility represents good cardinally.

And a good case can be made out in detail for thinking that utility represents good cardinally in this way. Utility embodies the results of weighing good across states of nature, and this weighing may well be what determines our quantitative notion of good.

Take the example set out in Table 19. The amounts of money in the table are, let us say, your income for a week. Assume the

Table 19

States of nature		States of nature	
H	T	H	T
£100	£200	£20	£320

Prospect *A*	Prospect *B*

states are equally likely. Which prospect is better for you? This is a matter of weighing against each other differences in good located in different states of nature. The consideration in favour of prospect *A* is that if state *H* occurs, it gives you the good of £100 rather than the good of £20. The consideration in favour of *B* is that if state *T* occurs, it gives you the good of £320 rather than the good of £200. These two considerations – each a difference in good – have to be weighed against each other.

Your utility is defined to express the result of this weighing. Suppose, for instance, that the result is an exact balance, so that the two prospects are equally good for you. Then utility is defined in such a way that the expected utility of A is the same as the expected utility of B:

$$\tfrac{1}{2}\{u(100) + u(200)\} = \tfrac{1}{2}\{u(20) + u(320)\}.$$

Therefore $\quad\quad u(100) - u(20) = u(320) - u(200);$

the utility difference between £100 and £20 is the same as the utility difference between £320 and £200. The fact that the two utility differences are the same tells us, from the definition of utility, that the consideration in favour of A exactly balances the consideration in favour of B. Utility, that is to say, tells us how much the differences in good *count* in determining the overall goodness for you of the alternative prospects.

Since the two differences in good are exactly balanced in determining the overall goodness of the prospects, it would be very natural to express this fact by saying that the differences are actually the same. That is:

$$g(100) - g(20) = g(320) - g(200).$$

These differences count the same in determining overall goodness. So to deny they are actually the same would be to insist on a distinction between amounts of good and how much those amounts count in determining overall goodness. And it is natural to think this an empty distinction. To say that two differences in good are the same may mean nothing more than that they count the same when weighed against each other; they are evenly balanced in determining overall good. This would mean that two differences in good are the same whenever the corresponding differences in utility are the same. And that would be enough to ensure that utility is an increasing linear transform of good.* Utility, then, would measure good cardinally. Bernoulli's hypothesis would be true.

In brief, the suggestion is that our metric of good may be determined by weighing across states of nature.

If this suggestion is right, it overcomes both the prima-facie objections I raised against Bernoulli's hypothesis. In response to the first objection, it shows how good can be an arithmetic quantity, despite first appearances: quantities of good acquire their

---

* Strictly, this is not quite so. To ensure that utility is an increasing transform of good, we actually require slightly more: the ratio of two differences in good is always the same as the ratio of the corresponding differences in utility. The same argument could achieve this conclusion too, simply by considering gambles with unequal probabilities.

meaning in the course of weighing differences of good against each other. In response to the second, it shows that the way quantities of good acquire their meaning implies Bernoulli's hypothesis, and therefore makes sure of risk neutrality about good. The second objection implicitly assumed a metric of good that is independent of weighing across states of nature. But if the metric is determined by the weighing, risk neutrality about good is automatic.

The suggestion that the quantitative notion of good is determined in the course of weighing goods might be mistaken for operationalism.[21] But it is not that. According to an operationalist, a quantitative notion of good must be determined by the operations that are used to measure it empirically. But the weighing of good that I am speaking of is not empirical. The test of whether one difference in good outweighs another is whether one prospect is better for a person than another, and this is not an empirical matter. I am assuming a much less restrictive and controversial principle: simply that the meaning of our quantitative notion of good must be determined by the use we have for it.

So there is a defence of Bernoulli's hypothesis. It is by no means conclusive. It depends on the claim that our quantitative metric of goodness is determined by weighing across states of nature. It may be answered by showing that actually we find this metric elsewhere. It certainly seems plausible that weighing up of some sort is the source of our metric of goodness.[22] But it need not necessarily be weighing up across the dimension of states of nature; perhaps it might be across a different dimension. In Chapters 10 and 11, I shall come to the question of weighing across the dimensions of time and people. In those chapters I shall return to Bernoulli's hypothesis once again. For the moment I shall leave it suspended: the hypothesis is defensible, but the defence is inconclusive.

Notes

1. *Reasons and Persons*, p. 25. Frank Jackson takes a similar view in 'A probabilistic approach to moral responsibility'.

2. For instance, Jackson, 'A probabilistic approach to moral responsibility', and Parfit, *Reasons and Persons*, p. 25.

3. This is the terminology used by Peter Vallentyne in 'Utilitarianism and the outcomes of actions', except that what I call a 'prospect' Vallentyne calls an 'outcome'. (What I call the 'outcome' of an act, he calls 'what happens'.)

4. *Foundations of Statistics*, p. 14.

5. *Principia Ethica*, p. 149.

6. 'Imposing risks', p. 129. But Thomson takes a less strong line than Moore.

7. *Ethics*, pp. 99–101.

8. 'Imposing risks', p. 129.

9. *Principia Ethica*, pp. 162–3.

10. See my 'Uncertainty and fairness'.

11. Milton Friedman in *Capitalism and Freedom*, pp. 162–3, is the most explicit. There are many commentaries on these issues. Three examples are: Hammond, 'Utilitarianism, uncertainty and information'; Kanbur, 'The standard of living'; and Myerson, 'Utilitarianism, egalitarianism, and the timing effect in social choice problems'.

12. See, for instance, Kahneman and Tversky, 'Prospect theory', or 'Rational choice and the framing of decisions'.

13. This is close to Richard Brandt's view, expressed in *A Theory of the Good and the Right*. I am not sure, however, whether Brandt is really talking of rational preferences or of "rational" preferences, where ' "rational" ' is a term of art with a specially defined meaning. On p. 113, Brandt appears to be defining a term of art ' "rational" '. But elsewhere he drops the quotes and speaks as though he meant to offer an analysis of the actual meaning of 'rational'.

14. *Reasons and Persons*, Part II. One attempt to argue that discounting is irrational is Harrison, 'Discounting the future'.

15. As Derek Parfit reminded me.

16. Thomas Nagel argues in *The Possibility of Altruism* that rationality rules out self-interest. 'There are rational requirements on action,' he says on p. 3, 'and altruism is one of them.' But my point is different from Nagel's.

17. Nicholas Denyer made this point to me. It is made by James Griffin in *Well-Being*, p. 11.

18. See, for instance, Jevons, *The Theory of Political Economy*, p. 85. See also the discussion on pp. 219–220 below.

19. Few authors distinguish Bernoulli's hypothesis about good from his hypothesis about rationality stated on page 53, so this remark refers to the two together. I have given my grounds in note 19 on page 58 for attributing the hypothesis to Daniel Bernoulli and John Harsanyi. W. S. Jevons (*Theory of Political Economy*, p. 99) and Alfred Marshall (*Principles of Economics*, p. 843) both seem to have accepted it. It is implicit in John von Neumann and Oskar Morgenstern's *Theory of Games* (see the discussion in Ellsberg, 'Classic and current notions of "measurable utility"'). Richard Jeffrey, in *The Logic of Decision* claims that the desirability of a prospect is the expected desirability of its outcomes; this is Bernoulli's hypothesis if 'desirability' means good. Economists are often confused by their ambiguous use of the word 'utility'. They use the word both as it is defined in this book (on page 65), and also to mean good. They are consequently unable to distinguish between expected utility theory in general, which says that the utility of a prospect is the expected utility of its outcomes, and Bernoulli's much stronger hypothesis that the goodness of a prospect is the expected goodness of its outcomes. So they often assume incorrectly that expected utility theory implies Bernoulli's hypothesis. This confusion is documented in Ellsberg's 'Classic and current notions', in Ellingsen's 'Cardinal utility' and in my ' "Utility" '.

20. This view is implicit in Arrow, *Social Choice and Individual Values*, p. 10.

21. In economics, there has been an extensive discussion of the quantitative notion of good. But it has been dominated by operationalism and the search for empirical measurement. Ellingsen's 'Cardinal utility' is an excellent guide.

22. In 'Cardinal utility', Tore Ellingsen considers some alternative sources, but they are unconvincing.

Chapter 7

Coherence Against
the Pareto Principle

I said in Chapter 2 that the interesting discoveries are to be made
by taking two dimensions of locations together. This chapter and
the next three are all concerned with the dimensions of people and
states of nature taken together. Chapter 11 brings in the dimension of time too.

The first discovery to be made, however, is a problem. In
Chapter 6, I argued that general good is coherent. But taking
together the dimensions of people and states of nature seems to
reveal a reason for doubting that conclusion. The coherence of
general good turns out to conflict with the widely accepted Pareto
principle. Section 7.1 explains the conflict. Section 7.2 resolves it
in favour of coherence.

We have, in fact, already encountered one argument that
suggests general good is not coherent. It, too, results from taking
together the two dimensions of people and states of nature. It is
Peter Diamond's argument, which I examined in Section 5.7.
Diamond thinks that alternative A in Table 16 on page 111 is
better than B and also that D is better than C. This seems to deny
the sure-thing principle for general good. But I hope I dealt
adequately with Diamond's argument in Section 5.7, and I shall
say no more about it here. This chapter is about a quite different
problem.

Section 7.3 connects the argument of this chapter with traditional thinking in welfare economics. It also explains why I have
organized this book around good rather than preferences, the
staple of welfare economists.

151

7.1 The conflict

The Pareto principle. (a) Two alternatives are equally good if everyone is indifferent between them, and (b) if everyone either prefers the first of two alternatives to the second or is indifferent between the two, and someone definitely prefers the first, then the first is better than the second.

Call a betterness relation *Paretian* if it conforms to the Pareto principle. Then this is a true theorem:

The probability agreement theorem. Suppose that each person has coherent preferences. Then the general betterness relation cannot be both coherent and Paretian, unless everyone agrees about the probability of every state of nature.

Here is a proof.[1] Suppose there are only two people, P and Q. (It is easy to extend the proof to many people.) Suppose the general betterness relation is both coherent and Paretian. And suppose P and Q disagree about the probability of some state of nature. Divide the states of nature into two events (a set of states of nature is called an *event*) in such a way that P thinks the first event more likely than the second, and Q thinks the second more likely than the first. This can certainly be done whenever P and Q disagree about the probability of some state of nature, but proving this point is difficult, and requires a lot of the technical apparatus of expected utility theory.[2] So I shall simply take it for granted. I shall use the notation (x, y) to stand for a prospect that leads to the outcome x in all the states of nature included in the first of these events, and to the outcome y in all the states included in the second.

I shall assume there is some pair of outcomes, x_P and y_P, such that P prefers x_P to y_P but Q is indifferent between them.* Similarly, I shall assume there is some pair of outcomes, x_Q and y_Q, such that Q prefers x_Q to y_Q but P is indifferent between them. These are very mild assumptions. They say that neither person is indifferent between all the outcomes, and that the two people do

---

* So far, I have defined preference relations only between *prospects*. When I say one *outcome* is preferred or indifferent to another I mean that the certain prospect of the one (see page 140) is preferred or indifferent to the certain prospect of the other. Here, then, I am assuming P prefers the certain prospect (x_P, x_P) to the certain prospect (y_P, y_P) and Q is indifferent between these two certain prospects.

not have exactly the same preferences (or exactly opposite preferences) amongst the outcomes. These assumptions are necessary for the probability agreement theorem; without them the theorem would be false.

Since P prefers x_P to y_P and Q is indifferent between the two, the Pareto principle implies that x_P is better than y_P. Now compare the prospects (x_P, y_P) and (y_P, x_P). Because P thinks the first event is more likely than the second, she will think (x_P, y_P) gives her a greater chance of her preferred outcome x_P than does (y_P, x_P). She will therefore prefer (x_P, y_P) to (y_P, x_P). Q will be indifferent between the two. So the Pareto principle implies that (x_P, y_P) is better than (y_P, x_P). Since x_P is better than y_P, it follows that the general betterness relation must assign a higher probability to the first event than to the second. (By this I mean that, in the expected utility representation of the betterness relation, the first event is assigned a higher probability.)

Next compare (x_Q, y_Q) and (y_Q, x_Q). Symmetrical reasoning applied to these prospects shows that the betterness relation must assign a higher probability to the second event than to the first. So we have found a contradiction. Because the people disagree about probabilities, the Pareto principle has forced the general betterness relation to be incoherent. In Savage's theory, it has violated Postulate 4.[3] That concludes the proof.

I hope this proof will make the probability agreement theorem seem obvious. If the betterness relation is to be coherent, it must be possible to attribute probabilities to it. But the Paretian condition forces the betterness relation to follow individual preferences to some extent. So if individual preferences reflect differing probabilities, it is not going to be possible for the betterness relation to reflect consistent probabilities of its own.

The proof shows something else too. The theorem requires as a premise that everyone's preferences should be coherent. But actually the proof relies very little on the coherence of individual preferences. All it requires is that the people have some preferences that show up their disagreement about probabilities. P's preference for (x_P, y_P) over (y_P, x_P) and Q's for (y_Q, x_Q) over (x_Q, y_Q) were enough to do that. The rest of their preferences need not be coherent at all. So we cannot hope to escape the theorem's implications by dropping the assumption that individual preferences are coherent.

And the theorem's implications are serious. People do not agree about the probability of every state of nature. So the probability agreement theorem implies that coherence of general good is

incompatible with the Pareto principle. Since the Pareto principle
is widely accepted, this presents a serious challenge to coherence.
Either the Pareto principle or coherence will have to go. Which
should it be?

7.2 Two better principles

I shall centre the discussion around an example of a head-on
collision between coherence and the Pareto principle. The example
relies on an auxiliary assumption, but one that is very plausible.
Consider the prospects shown in Table 20. The numbers in the

Table 20

		States					States	
		M	*N*				*M*	*N*
People	*P*	2	2		People	*P*	3	0
	Q	2	2			*Q*	0	3

Prospect *I*   Prospect *J*

table stand for the people's wealth. Both people are interested only
in their own wealth, and both prefer more to less. Furthermore,
they are both risk neutral about their wealth: of two alternative
prospects, they always prefer the one with the greater expectation
of wealth. *P* attaches probability 0.7 to state *M* and 0.3 to *N*. *Q*
attaches probability 0.3 to *M* and 0.7 to *N*. Consequently each
person finds that prospect *J* gives her a greater expectation of
wealth than *I*, calculated according to her own probabilities. So
both people prefer *J* to *I*.

The Pareto principle therefore says *J* is better than *I*. But
suppose we assume – this is the auxiliary assumption – that the
distribution (2, 2) is better than both (3, 0) and (0, 3). This is very
plausible because (2, 2) has a greater total of wealth, and has it
equally distributed. Now, prospect *I* yields (2, 2) as a sure thing,
whereas *J* is a prospect of either (3, 0) or (0, 3). So the sure-thing
principle, applied to the betterness relation, that *I* is better than *J*.
Yet the Pareto principle says the opposite. So there is the collision

between the Pareto principle and the coherence of general good.

I think the attraction of coherence in the example is very strong. Since (2, 2) is better than both (3, 0) and (0, 3), it is hard to doubt that (2, 2) for sure is better than a gamble on (3, 0) and (0, 3). Furthermore, we have the argument of Chapters 5 and 6 supporting the coherence of general good.

What, then, is the appeal of the Pareto principle on the other side? I think it results from a muddle. The Pareto principle is a muddled conflation of two other principles that are each genuinely appealing. Its appeal is a confused reflection of theirs. The genuinely appealing principles are:

The principle of personal good. (a) Two alternatives are equally good if they are equally good for each person. And (b) if one alternative is at least as good as another for everyone and definitely better for someone, then it is better.

The democratic principle. If everyone either prefers the first of two alternatives to the second or is indifferent between them, and someone definitely prefers the first, then the first should come about.

I shall be defending the principle of personal good (with some qualifications) in Chapters 8 and 9. And the democratic principle is a plausible minimal condition of democracy. Neither of these principles conflicts with coherence of general good. But each may seem to, because from each a line of thought sets out that seems to show J is better than I in the example. So each may seem to give support to the Pareto principle. Both lines of thought, however, are confused.

The principle of personal good

The line of thought that sets out from the principle of personal good is this. Since both people prefer J to I, J is better than I for both. So it follows from the principle of personal good that J is better than I.

This line of thought contains a non sequitur. Both people prefer J to I, but it does not follow that J is better than I for both. And actually J cannot be better than I for both people. It is only better for P if state M is a lot more probable than N, and in that case it is not better for Q.

I am, of course, using the probability-relative notion of good that I defended in Section 6.1. And, as I said on page 131, this implies a context of fixed probabilities. The individual and general betterness relations mentioned within the principle must be understood relative to the same probabilities. In the example, relative to P's probabilities, prospect J is better than I for P, but worse for Q. Relative to Q's probabilities, the opposite is true. There are no probabilities that would make J better than I for both people. So the principle of personal good does not imply, relative to any probabilities at all, that J is better than I.

The principle of personal good is immune to the difficulty raised by the probability agreement theorem. The theorem shows the Pareto principle to be inconsistent with the coherence of general good, because the Pareto principle collates the preferences of different people, and these preferences may reflect differing probabilities. But the principle of personal good is about good rather than preferences, and the notion of good implies a context of fixed probabilities. Differing probabilities are ruled out. So the principle of personal good does not conflict with coherence.

The example reveals another reason to be cautious with the preference-satisfaction theory of good (the theory, roughly, that one alternative is better for a person than another if and only if the person prefers it to the other). I mentioned objections to various versions of this theory in Section 6.2. But some versions are undeniable. For instance, if 'self-interested' is given the definition on page 134, at least this fragment of the preference-satisfaction theory follows: if a rational, well-informed and self-interested person prefers J to I, then J is better for her than I. In this statement, however, 'better for' must be understood relative to the person's own probabilities. And that will have to be true in any version of the theory; it is obvious that good must be understood this way in the preference-satisfaction theory, because a person's own probabilities are the ones that determine her preferences. Therefore, if different people have different probabilities, then the 'better for's that emerge from the preference-satisfaction theory will be relative to different probabilities. Consequently, they must not be put together in an unqualified statement about betterness, because such a statement implies a context of fixed probabilities.

That is why it is a non sequitur to deduce, from the fact that both people in the example prefer J to I, that J is better than I for both. It is implicit in the conclusion 'J is better than I for both people' that J is better for both relative to the same probabilities. But even if both people are rational, well informed and self-interested, and both prefer J to I, it will only follow that J is better than I for each person relative to her own probabilities. (The fact that the people differ over probabilities does not necessarily rule out their both being well informed. In Bayesian probability theory, people may have different probabilities even if they have the same information, because they started with different priors.) The preference-satisfaction theory of good can never be detached from a person's own probabilities and used in a broader statement about good.

The democratic principle

The line of thought that sets out from the democratic principle is this. Since both people prefer alternative J to I, the democratic principle requires that J should come about rather than I. Therefore J is better than I.

This line of thought also contains a non sequitur. Suppose it is true that J should come about rather than I. (I mean: if I and J were the only two possibilities, J should come about.) It does not follow that J is better than I. We have to separate what is better from what should come about. The probability agreement theorem, I think, forces this conclusion on us. I shall explain it by outlining the thinking that underlies the democratic principle.

A democrat values a particular sort of social system. She sees the social system as a mechanism that coordinates and mediates people's preferences. It is not a suprapersonal decision making agent in its own right, but a means by which a result emerges from the decisions of many agents. A good system is one that does the job of coordination in a democratic manner. So far as possible it should simply bring about what people prefer. Normally people's preferences conflict, and then it should act as a democratic mechanism for resolving the conflict. But when there is no conflict, it should simply put into effect what everyone prefers. There is no conflict in our example. Since both people prefer J to I, if there is a choice between J and I then J should come about.

Our democrat makes no claim about the relative goodness of I and J. What she values is the nature of the social system, not its results. The system should be such that J comes about rather than I. But the occurrence of J need not be any benefit added to the existence of the system that brings it about. A democrat might sensibly think that J is worse than I but that J should come about all the same.

I offer this as a solution to Richard Wollheim's 'paradox of democracy'.[4] Suppose a choice has to be made between two alternatives. Suppose a democrat votes for the first because she believes it should come about. But suppose the democratic process comes out in favour of the second. Then the democrat will believe that the second should come about. So she believes both that the first should come about and that the second should come about. Yet these alternatives are incompatible. That is the paradox. I suggest that actually Wollheim's democrat could never have believed in the first place that the first alternative should come about. As a democrat, she should have no views about what should come about until she knows the result of the democratic process. Her reason for voting for the first alternative must have been something different: that she believed it was better. This does not contradict her belief that the second alternative should come about.

A democrat will have to expect some incoherence in what should come about. That is to say, the relation

__ should come about rather than __
if these are the only two possibilities

will not conform to expected utility theory.* In our example, a democrat may well believe that, if the only two alternatives available were (2, 2) for sure and (3, 0) for sure, then (2, 2) should come about. There is in this case a conflict of preferences: *P* prefers the second alternative and *Q* the first. In those circumstances the democrat might well believe that the best alternative should come about. And the best, I assumed, is (2, 2). Similarly she might believe that if (2, 2) for sure and (0, 3) for sure were the only two alternatives available, then (2, 2) should come about. Yet she believes that *J*, which is a gamble on (3, 0) and (0, 3), should come about rather than *I*, which is (2, 2) for sure. This is the incoherence I mean. It will not bother the democrat. The axioms of expected utility theory are intended for a rational agent. But according to a democrat the social system is not an agent at all.[5]

Coherence, defined by expected utility theory, is a part of the structure of good or 'teleological structure' as I called it in Section

---

* Strictly, the relation I mean is something like 'either __ should come about rather than __, or it does not matter which comes about, if these are the only two possibilities'. The democratic principle is incompatible with the coherence of this relation. This follows from the probability agreement theorem, reinterpreted by substituting this relation for the betterness relation. The democratic principle is clause (b) of the Pareto principle reinterpreted this way. The probability agreement theorem requires only clause (b), as the proof in Section 7.1 shows.

1.3. The democratic principle is thoroughly nonteleological. What it says should come about is not what is best and does not have teleological structure. It is the probability agreement theorem that forces us to recognize the nonteleological nature of the democratic principle.

Summary

The Pareto principle is, I think, untrue. It is an ill-begotten hybrid. It tries to link individual preferences with general good. But one should either link individual preferences with what should come about, as the democratic principle does, or individual good with general good, as the principle of personal good does. The hybrid is not viable. There is therefore no need to worry about the fact that it conflicts with coherence. It gives us no reason to doubt the coherence of the general betterness relation.

That concludes the argument of this chapter. Section 7.3 connects it with some traditional arguments in welfare economics.

7.3 Welfare economics

I expressed the Pareto principle as a condition on the general betterness relation. It is more traditionally expressed as a condition on *social preferences*:

> *Traditional Pareto principle.* (a) Two alternatives are socially indifferent if everyone is indifferent between them, and (b) if everyone either prefers the first of two alternatives to the second or is indifferent between the two, and someone definitely prefers the first, then the first is socially preferred to the second.

I have not been using the notion of social preference, because it is ambiguous. It has at least two possible interpretations.[6]

One interpretation simply identifies social preference with betterness. My way of expressing the Pareto principle adopts this interpretation and makes it explicit.

Another interpretation takes 'A is socially preferred to B' to mean that A should come about rather than B, if these are the only two possibilities. 'A is socially indifferent to B' it takes to mean that it does not matter whether A or B comes about. Under this interpretation, clause (b) of the traditional Pareto principle is my democratic principle stated on page 155. Clause (a) is this: if everyone is indifferent between two alternatives, it does not matter which of them comes about.

One consequence of the traditional Pareto principle is given by a theorem of John Harsanyi's, which I have already mentioned on page 57. Call social preferences, however interpreted, 'Paretian' if they conform to the traditional Pareto principle. The theorem is:

> *Harsanyi's theorem.* Suppose that each person has coherent preferences, and that social preferences are coherent and Paretian. Then social preferences can be represented by an expectational utility function that is the sum of expectational utility functions representing the individuals' preferences.[7]

There is a proof in Section 10.1 below.

This theorem is undoubtedly important, but not as it stands. As it stands it is useless, because two of its premises – the coherence and Paretian conditions on social preferences – are mutually inconsistent. This follows from the probability agreement theorem, which must now be written:

> *Traditional probability agreement theorem.* Suppose that each person has coherent preferences. Then social preferences cannot be both coherent and Paretian, unless everyone agrees about the probability of every state of nature.

People do not agree about the probability of every state of nature. Consequently, however social preferences are interpreted, this theorem tells us that the coherence and Paretian conditions are mutually inconsistent.

The probability agreement theorem presents welfare economics with a dilemma: it must abandon either the coherence of social preferences or else the traditional Pareto principle. Either way, it will have to repudiate Harsanyi's theorem.

The *ex-ante school* of welfare economists abandons coherence.[8] This is the best established school. It is represented, for instance, in Gérard Debreu's *Theory of Value*.[9] The ex-ante school cleaves to the traditional Pareto principle. Consequently, it has to accept incoherent social preferences. Since the general betterness relation is necessarily coherent, it must interpret social preference as something other than general betterness. The most natural interpretation available to it is the second one I mentioned above. I am not sure how successfully this interpretation can be developed, but that is a question I shall not pursue. This book is not much concerned with the ex-ante school.

The *ex-post school* abandons the traditional Pareto principle, and cleaves to coherence. This school is represented by the writings of Peter Hammond amongst others[10] (though, as I shall be explaining, Hammond's later writings are not perfectly typical of the school). It does not abandon the whole of the traditional Pareto principle, however. It retains the principle applied to outcomes without uncertainty: it accepts the principle as I stated it on page 159, if the general term 'alternative' is replaced specifically with 'outcome'. But it denies the principle applied to uncertain prospects.

What grounds does the ex-post school have for retaining the traditional Pareto principle for outcomes only? They are something like this.[11] Social preferences, the ex-post school argues, should be based on people's preferences. But it is not so clear that they should be based on people's beliefs. Beliefs are subject to standards of truth and falsity, or at least to standards of rationality and irrationality. And that means people's beliefs should not automatically be accepted as a basis for social preferences. It would be wrong, for instance, to base social preferences on a belief that was mistaken. People's preferences about prospects, though, depend partly on their probability beliefs. So we should not insist, as the traditional Pareto principle does, that social preferences should be based on these preferences. On the other hand, people's preferences about outcomes are *pure* preferences, unmixed with beliefs. So they are the proper basis of social preferences.

This reasoning, however, is mistaken. Preferences about outcomes are not always pure. Many are strongly influenced by beliefs. People's preferences amongst paintings, for instance, are influenced by their beliefs about the paintings' provenance. Even if the notion of an outcome was very much restricted – even if it was limited just to people's experiences or feelings – this would still be true. Beliefs influence the quality of experiences. Driving to work is a worse experience if you believe that other people are being deliberately aggressive than it is if you do not. So, if the aim is to draw a line between preferences that are not influenced by beliefs and those that are, the boundary between preferences about outcomes and preferences about prospects is not the right place to draw it.

I think the ex-post school really wants to draw a different line. It wants to draw a line between, on the one hand, what is actually good for a person, and, on the other, what she believes to be good for her, and the preferences that result from these beliefs. Mistakenly, the school tries to achieve its aim by starting from the traditional Pareto principle and restricting its application. Really, though, it needs to give up the Pareto principle entirely. The ex-post school is really interested in good, whereas the Pareto principle, in any form, is based on preferences. Rather than the Pareto principle, the ex-post school should adopt the principle of personal good.

To suggest that welfare economics should be founded on good, rather than preferences, draws down the wrath of many economists. But this is because of a misunderstanding. My suggestion does not deny the importance of preferences.

A person's good and her preferences are closely associated. Suppose, for a moment, they were so closely associated that the actual-preference-satisfaction theory of good (page 132) was true. Then a person's betterness relation would be the same as her preference relation. The principle of personal good would then be the same as the Pareto principle. This shows that to adopt the former is not, in itself, to deny the importance of preferences.

As it happens, the actual-preference-satisfaction theory is false. People sometimes prefer an alternative that is worse for them. In saying this, I am not implying that I, or the government, or anybody else knows better than the person herself what is good for her. To recognize that the actual-preference-satisfaction theory is false does not commit one to paternalism.

And all the same, what is good for a person coincides with her preferences to a large extent. What is good for you does not normally conflict with what you prefer. Indeed, to a large extent what is good for you is determined by your likes. If you like apples more than oranges, then that makes it the case that apples are better for you than oranges (if you are not allergic to them, not particularly in need of vitamin C, and so on). To be concerned for people's good is not to be puritan.

In a way, the principle of personal good differs from the Pareto principle simply in being more general. It allows for cases where a person's good coincides with her preferences, and it allows for cases where it does not.

The principle of personal good is formally parallel to the traditional Pareto principle. It therefore has parallel consequences. It leads to a theorem parallel to Harsanyi's:

> *Interpersonal addition theorem.* If the individual and general betterness relations are coherent, and if the principle of personal good is true, then the general betterness relation can

be represented by an expectational utility function that is the sum of expectational utility functions representing the betterness relations of individuals.

This theorem is proved and discussed in Chapter 10. Unlike Harsanyi's original theorem, it has mutually consistent premises. The premises of Harsanyi's theorem are inconsistent because different people will have preferences that reflect their differing probabilities. The interpersonal addition theorem, on the other hand, is about good rather than preferences. The good it speaks of is probability-relative. But, as I explained on page 131, a context of fixed probabilities must be implicit in statements about good such as this theorem. All the betterness relations must be understood relative to the same probabilities. So the problem of inconsistency does not arise.

The interpersonal addition theorem tells us something significant about the structure of good. Specifically, it tells us something about the way individual good is aggregated to make up general good. This is the reason I have organized this book around good and not preferences. The parallel theorem about preferences tells us nothing significant, because of its inconsistent premises. Only when we turn our attention to good is this particular feature of the ethical world revealed.

It is a feature that should very much interest welfare economists. One of the central concerns of welfare economics is aggregation across people. This generally means aggregation of good, though the term 'good' is not used.[12] I think the ex-post school, in particular, is motivated by a concern for good. But it has managed only the negative step of denying the traditional Pareto principle. It needs also to take the positive step of adopting the principle of personal good instead. Without that step, it misses the important feature of the structure of good described by the interpersonal addition theorem. In Hammond's later work, this step is taken too, though using different terms.[13]

But I have not yet argued for the principle of personal good. That is the task of Chapters 8 and 9.

Notes

1. Other proofs, within various versions of expected utility theory, appear in: my 'Bolker–Jeffrey expected utility theory', in Deschamps and Gevers, 'Separability, risk-bearing and social welfare judgements', in Hammond, 'Ex-ante and ex-post welfare optimality under uncertainty', in Hammond, 'Ex-post optimality as a dynamically consistent objective for collective choice under uncertainty', and in Seidenfeld, Kadane and Schervish, 'On the shared preferences of two Bayesian decision makers'.

2. It follows from point 7 of Theorem 3 on p. 37 of Savage's *Foundations of Statistics*.

3. *The Foundations of Statistics*, p. 31.

4. Wollheim, 'A paradox in the theory of democracy'.

5. Compare Buchanan, 'Social choice, democracy and free markets', and Sugden, 'Why be consistent?', p. 177. In 'Conflict and social agency', on the other hand, Isaac Levi argues that social institutions may indeed be taken as rational agents. Still, for reasons of his own, he would not insist they should have coherent preferences. When people's preferences conflict, institutions may have to act without being able to resolve the conflict. This will lead to incoherent preferences, but according to Levi it will nevertheless be rational. A different question is this. Even if democratic social institutions are not rational agents, their decision making is often in the hands of officials who ought to be. A democratic official ought to have coherent preferences. How is this consistent with democracy? This question is pursued further in my 'Should social preferences be consistent?'.

6. See Sen, 'Liberty and social choice'. Vilfredo Pareto himself, in his *Manuel d'Économie Politique*, may have had in mind something nearer to the principle of personal good rather than any version of the Pareto principle. The ambiguity contributes to the muddle described in Section 7.2.

7. Harsanyi, 'Cardinal welfare, individualistic ethics, and interpersonal comparisons of utility'.

8. The terms 'ex-ante' and 'ex-post' are well established, but not very apt. I shall not try to explain their origin.

9. p. 102.

10. See, for instance, his 'Utilitarianism, uncertainty and information', 'Ex-ante and ex-post welfare optimality' and 'Ex-post optimality as a dynamically consistent objective'. The latter contains a useful introduction to the ex-post approach.

11. There is a defence in Hammond, 'Ex-post optimality as a dynamically consistent objective', p. 176.

12. The term generally used is 'utility'. Economists often use this term to stand for good. See page 65 and my '"Utility"'.

13. See 'On reconciling Arrow's theory of social choice with Harsanyi's fundamental utilitarianism'. Hammond uses the terms 'social norm' and 'individual norm' for general and individual good.

Chapter 8

The Principle of Personal Good

> *The principle of personal good.* (a) Two alternatives are equally good if they are equally good for each person. And (b) if one alternative is at least as good as another for everyone and definitely better for someone, it is better.

I shall explain on page 206 that the principle of personal good is a principle of separability in the dimension of people. Together with the coherence of good, it provides a basis for applying the second separability theorem across the two dimensions of people and states of nature. That is its role in the argument of this book.

This chapter starts, in Section 8.1, by qualifying the principle of personal good in three ways. The defence of the principle begins in Section 8.2. But there is only the beginning of a defence in this chapter. The most effective objection to the principle of personal good arises from the value of equality. Chapter 9 deals with equality, and that is where the main defence of the principle takes place.

8.1 Qualifications

A clear inaccuracy in the principle as I have stated it is this. One prospect may be better than another without being better for a person, because it is better for an animal. The principle ought really to take people and animals together. For simplicity, though, I shall continue to speak of people only. The inclusion of animals is to be understood. That is one qualification.

There may be other sorts of good that are independent of the

165

good of people. Perhaps, for instance, the survival of any living species is good in itself, quite apart from any good it may do for people. I do not wish to deny the existence of goods like this. If there are any, they will not affect the arguments of this book, provided they are entirely independent of people's good. This book is simply not concerned with such goods. Of course, if they are genuine goods, people ought to promote them, even though they are not the good of people. So they compete for resources with the people's good. Eventually, therefore, they will need to be combined with people's good to arrive at an overall assessment of good. But I shall exclude the task of combination from the scope of this book too. The principle of personal good ought to be prefaced with: 'Setting aside goods that are entirely independent of the good of people, . . .' That is the second qualification. The goods that *are* at issue in this book, and that seem to conflict with the principle of personal good, are not independent of the good of people. They are involved with people's good, but they do not seem to belong to people individually. *Communal* goods, for instance, seem to belong to people together, but not to any individual. Equality is the prime example.

A third inaccuracy in the principle is shown up by this example. A couple might have a child. But suppose that, if they do, the child will have a hereditary disease that will make her life painful and unhappy. Imagine, somehow, that neither the couple nor anybody else would be made worse off by the existence of this unhappy child. It is surely obvious that it is better for the couple to refrain from having a child. But there is no one for whom that would be better. It could not be better for the child, since there would be no child if they refrained from having one. And I assumed it would not be better for anybody else. So this is a counterexample to the principle of personal good.

Counterexamples like this arise when we are comparing alternatives in one of which a person exists who does not exist in the other.[1] I do not intend the principle of personal good to apply to comparisons of this sort. It applies only when the same people exist in both of the alternatives that are being compared. This is the third qualification. It does not mean that all the people have to live all the time in both alternatives. The principle applies to alternatives that extend over a long time, during which people are born and die. Furthermore, it applies to choices that affect the time of a person's death, so that a person lives longer in one alternative than another. But the same people have to be born in each alternative.

The example of the unhappy child shows that the principle of personal good has to be limited in this way. But it casts no doubt on the principle once it is limited. The principle is a particular instance of a general idea that applies universally: that all good is people's good. The goodness of an alternative depends only on the good of the people who exist in that alternative. To put it another way: good supervenes on people's good. The example of the unhappy child is consistent with this general idea. For the couple to have a child would be bad, and its badness consists in the suffering of a person, the child. That is why it is better for them not to have a child. The example does not suggest there is any good other than people's good. When it is applied to comparisons between alternatives that contain the same people, the general idea comes down to the principle of personal good.

8.2 The beginning of a defence

How might the principle of personal good be defended?

One possible line of defence is metaphysical. It is to argue that suprapersonal entities such as nations are simply aggregates of people, and therefore cannot possess a good of their own apart from the good of the people who make them up. Since a community is made up of people, the good of a community is made up of the good of people. This sounds plausible. But can it be made into a proper argument?

Jeremy Bentham, for instance, says: 'The community is a fictitious *body*, composed of the individual persons who are considered as constituting as it were its *members*. The interest of the community then is, what? – the sum of the interests of the several members who compose it.'[2] Bentham is certainly going far too far. He is claiming that the good of a community is the *sum* of the good its members, and this is far more than he could reasonably expect to deduce from the metaphysical fact that the community is a fictitious body. But could he legitimately deduce the much weaker principle of personal good: in effect, that the good of the community is *made up* of the good of its members?

I think the answer is 'Perhaps', if he makes a number of auxiliary assumptions. But I am not going to pursue the metaphysical argument in this chapter. In Chapter 11, I shall examine a parallel metaphysical argument about aggregating good across the dimension of time, rather than across the dimension of people. I shall ask whether the good of a person is made up of the good that comes to her at times in her life. The structure of the argument would be closely similar in the two dimensions. So I shall not go through it twice.

Instead, I shall defend the principle of personal good in a more piecemeal fashion. The principle is intended to apply to probability-relative goodness – to the goodness of uncertain prospects – and not just to outcomes without uncertainty. I shall start by defending it as applied to outcomes, and then extend the argument to probability-relative goodness.

For outcomes without uncertainty, actually, I am largely going to rely on the intuitive attractiveness of the principle. To be sure, there seem to be many goods that are separate from the good of individual people, and at first these may seem to be counterexamples to the principle. But generally I, at least, find the intuitive appeal of the principle greater than the intuitive appeal of the examples.

For instance, the following example was given me by Larry Temkin. Suppose the world is populated only by sinners, who deserve punishment. Suppose some change occurs that improves the condition of these people: they remain sinners, but they become better off. Temkin suggests they might now be enjoying a better life than they deserve, and this might mean the change is bad, even though everyone benefits from it.

This example is a variant of one presented in Temkin's 'Harmful goods, harmless bads'. In the original example, the world contains saints as well as sinners. Suppose the saints are initially better off than the sinners, but then the condition of the sinners improves whilst the condition of the saints remains the same. Suppose the sinners end up better off than the saints. Temkin suggests *this* change may be bad, even though it is bad for no one. I agree the change may be bad. But if it is, I think that is because it is bad for the saints. The saints deserve better than the sinners, so if they fare worse they are suffering an injustice. To suffer an injustice is bad for you. So, although at first the saints may have seemed no worse off, they are actually worse off in this less obvious way. The harm of injustice done them may make the change worse on balance.

But in the example without saints, no one suffers an injustice. I think, therefore, that Temkin is wrong and that in this case the change cannot be bad. It depends on how retributive justice works. If it determines *absolutely* how a person ought to fare on grounds of desert, then Temkin would be right. But I think it determines how a person ought to fare *relative* to other people. It generates a relative claim of the sort I shall be discussing in Section 9.4. Sinners should be worse off than saints, but retributive justice does not determine how well off each group should be absolutely. Take a world populated only by saints. They deserve well. But suppose natural conditions are hard and their lives are not very good. Then the world is not a very good one, but I do not think it is unjust. Similarly, in a world containing only sinners, I see no injustice if the sinners fare well.

Another example of a putative nonpersonal good is the preservation of a particular culture.[3] It is a popular opinion that a culture is good for its own sake, apart from the good of the individual people whose culture it is. It seems to be a communal good.

This opinion does not necessarily conflict with the principle of personal good. The principle is compatible with the existence of communal goods of a sort. Chapter 9 describes how it is compatible with equality conceived as a communal good. The opinion that culture is a communal good would conflict with the principle only if it took a strong form: it would have to imply that it is sometimes good to preserve a culture even though doing so is not in the interests of the people whose culture it is, or in anyone else's interest either.

Is that plausible? Suppose the progress of materialism breaks up a culture. People have radios and bicycles, and think themselves better off, but they no longer speak their ancestral language and join in communal celebrations. It might be claimed that the results of this development are bad. But would that mean: they are better for the people, but bad all the same? Or would it mean: the people think themselves better off, but actually they are not, because their loss is greater than they think? If the latter, it is simply reminding us that culture is a good, for people, whose value people do not always recognize. If the former, then it is definitely denying the principle of personal good. But the former claim seems implausible to me. Would it really have been better to preserve the culture, even at the cost of denying the people the genuine benefits of material progress? I doubt it.

But I shall not dwell on these examples. Instead I am going to concentrate on the good of equality. This is, I think, the good that most threatens the principle of personal good. If equality is good, it seems like a particularly clear case of a good that must be separate from the good of people. Since equality is a relation between people, how could its goodness be the property of individual people? But I shall show it is easy to reconcile the value of equality with the principle of personal good, when the principle is applied to outcomes without uncertainty.

I shall postpone this discussion of equality to Section 9.2. I hope it will make it clear that the principle of personal good, applied to outcomes, is very undemanding.

Applied to uncertain prospects, it is a different matter. It would be unwise to rely on intuition here. Here we are dealing with probability-relative goodness, which, I explained on page 130, has to be treated with care.

Table 21 illustrates more specifically what the difficulty is. The

Table 21

		States					States	
		H	T				H	T
People	P	2	2		People	P	1	3
	Q	4	4			Q	5	3

Prospect A Prospect B

figures in the table stand for the amounts of the two people's income. Assume both people's good depends only on their own income. And let the two states be equally likely. Suppose it is good for both people to avoid risk to their income. That is to say, when two prospects give them the same expectation of income, the less risky one is better. (I shall say more about the value of risk-avoidance on page 172.) For each person, A gives her the same expectation of income as B, but A is less risky than B. Therefore, A is a better prospect for both people. The principle of personal good says A is better than B because it is better for both people. Can this be justified?

In the non-probability-relative sense – relative to what actually happens – it is not true that A is better than B for both people. We know this for sure, even though we know only the probabilities. The table shows that, whether H or T comes up, one or the other person will certainly end up worse off under A than she would have under B. We just happen not to know which person it will be. In a probability-relative sense, A is better for both people. But is this probability-relative sense really adequate grounds for saying that *A* is generally better? Can it be really be claimed that *A* is better on the grounds that it is better for both people, when it is definitely not better for both people in the end?[4] That is the difficulty.

An argument is certainly needed to justify the principle of personal good for probability-relative goodness. Fortunately, one can be found. In Section 6.3 I fixed the meaning of probability-relative goodness in terms of the balance of reasons. The argument will set out from that point.

In this argument, I shall take for granted the principle of personal good applied to outcomes. This means that the goodness of an outcome depends only on how good it is for people.

Take any two prospects. What determines which is better? The principle set out on page 139 of Section 6.3 tells us that this is a matter of the balance of teleological reasons in favour of one or the other. And the arguments of Chapter 5 tell us that each of these teleological reasons must derive from what happens in some single state of nature; there is no interaction between states. So each reason must derive from the goodness of the two prospects' outcomes in some single state. We are taking for granted that the goodness of outcomes depends only on how good they are for the people. So each teleological reason must be directed towards the good of some person. Teleological reasons are by definition directed towards good. Some of them might have been directed towards some other good besides the good of people. But the principle of personal good, applied to outcomes, tells us there are not.

Suppose it happens that the two prospects are equally good for everybody. By the principle set out on page 137 of Section 6.3, this means that, for each person, the reasons directed towards her good in favour of one prospect are equally as strong as the reasons directed towards her good in favour of the other. And teleological reasons, we have just concluded, derive only from the good of the people. Since every person's reasons are balanced, teleological reasons are balanced too. So, by the principle set out on page 139, the two prospects are equally good. This establishes clause (a) of the principle of personal good. Clause (b) can be established in the same way. That completes the argument.

But the previous paragraph conceals two presumptions, which need to be brought into the open.

The first is this. The reasons directed towards a single person's good determine which prospect is better for the person, and they also help to determine which is generally better. The presumption is that they have the same relative weights in the two applications. Is this justified?[5]

Look again at the example in Table 21. What reason directed at P's good is there in favour of A? It boils down to this: if state H comes about, P will get 2 instead of 1. The reason directed at her good in favour of B boils down to: if state T comes about, she will get 3 instead of 2. I assumed that A is actually better for her, which is to say that the former reason is stronger than the latter.

When it comes to determining which of A or B is generally better, there are four reasons to weigh up. Two of them are the ones I have mentioned, directed at P's good. And there are two similar ones directed at Q's good. How should these four reasons be weighed? We do not have to worry here about weighing against each other reasons directed at the good of the two different people. But I do claim that the two reasons directed at P's good must be given the same relative weight in determining general betterness as they have when determining betterness for P herself.

A is better for P than B because A is less risky, and I assumed it is good for P to avoid risk. In expected utility theory, the goodness of avoiding risk appears in the form of weights attached to gains and losses. Here it gives the difference between 2 and 1 more weight than the difference between 3 and 2. The goodness of avoiding risk, then, works in an anomalous way. A good normally generates a reason to prefer an alternative that possesses that good. But in expected utility theory, the goodness of avoiding risk does not generate a separate reason to prefer an alternative that is less risky. Instead it gives weights to other, previously existing reasons.

Nevertheless, the fact that it is good for P to avoid risk is something that must contribute to determining the general goodness of the alternatives. Since this goodness appears in the weighting of reasons, the weighting must be preserved in determining which alternative is generally better. This is why A is generally better than B. The benefit of risk-avoidance to the two people must appear in general good.

This is the answer to the question I asked on page 171. The fact that A is better than B for both people is a good reason for favouring A, even though the betterness is only probability-relative.

That justifies one of the presumptions hidden in the argument above. The other presumption is that, when they go to determine general good, the reasons directed towards the good of different people work independently and do not interact in any way. But one might expect them to interact. Look once more at Table 21. There is something special about the outcome that will result from prospect *B* in state *T*: both people will have the same income. If equality is valuable, it will give a special value to this outcome. But the fact of equality only appears when the two people are taken together. It will not show up in any reason directed at the good of either person individually.

So it seems that, if equality is good, it will cause an interaction between different people's reasons. It may invalidate the argument I gave for the principle of personal good, applied to prospects.[6] This thought is analogous, in the dimension of people, to Allais's objection to the sure-thing principle in the dimension of states of nature. Allais argued that interactions between different states of nature would invalidate the argument for the sure-thing principle.

There is no quick answer to this worry. The only response is to examine the value of equality in detail. Chapter 9 does that. It concludes in the end that the value of equality is indeed compatible with the principle of personal good. So the argument I have given is, indeed, sound.

Notes

1. Derek Parfit carefully examines several of them in Chapter 18 of *Reasons and Persons*.

2. *The Principles of Morals and Legislation*, p. 3.

3. See Taylor, 'Irreducibly social goods'.

4. I asked this as a rhetorical question in my paper 'Trying to value a life'. At the time I thought the answer was no. I now think there is a good reason, which I am about to describe, for giving the answer yes.

5. Thomas Nagel takes for granted that it is. He says, in *The Possibility of Altruism*, p. 134: 'When we are presented with several conflicting objective reasons stemming from the interests of another person, we must weigh them against one another by the same principles which it would be rational for that individual to employ in weighing the subjective reasons from which they originate.' But in our present context, an argument is needed.

6. In my 'Utilitarianism and expected utility', I missed this point. This part of the argument in that paper is therefore unsound.

Chapter 9

Equality

The main difficulty for the principle of personal good arises from egalitarianism. Egalitarianism is the view that equality between people is good. If that is so, it seems as though equality could not be a good that belongs to people individually. Equality is a relation between people. So it seems as though it will have to be a nonpersonal or interpersonal or suprapersonal good. It is therefore natural to expect it to be incompatible with the principle of personal good. But this chapter reconciles egalitarianism with the principle.

Section 9.1 outlines a utilitarian argument for equality. It is not a good argument, but it is the point of departure for other egalitarian theories. Sections 9.2 and 9.3 describe two broad divisions of egalitarian thinking: the communal and the individualistic. Section 9.2 ignores uncertainty, and Section 9.3 takes uncertainty into account. These sections show that individualistic egalitarianism is consistent with the principle of personal good, and that communal egalitarianism is generally not.

Sections 9.2 and 9.3 consider only the forms of the different egalitarian theories, not their grounds. Section 9.4 takes up the question of grounds: it asks why equality is good. Its answer is to ground egalitarianism in a theory of fairness. This theory supports individualistic egalitarianism against communal egalitarianism. So it supports the principle of personal good. That completes the argument of the chapter.

If equality is good, a vital question is: equality of what? Is it good that people should have the same income, or the same level of wellbeing, or what? That is one of the questions at issue in this chapter, and at the beginning I shall leave it open.

174

One other preliminary note. Throughout this chapter, I shall assume that good, both individual and general, is an arithmetic quantity. This is not required by the principle of personal good. But most of the literature on inequality assumes it, and it will make the discussion easier.

9.1 A utilitarian case for equality

Utilitarianism has an argument for equality. It aims to show that the distribution of *income* (or resources in general) between people should be equal.

The argument sets out from the utilitarian principle of distribution stated on page 16. This principle says, in effect, that general good is the total of people's good.* Let there be h people, whose good is g_1, g_2 and so on. Then general good g is given by:

$$g = g_1 + g_2 + \ldots + g_h.$$

To this add some assumptions. Assume each person's good is a function of her income only. So g_1 is $g_1(y_1)$, g_2 is $g_2(y_2)$ and so on, where y_1, y_2 and so on are the people's incomes. I shall call these 'benefit functions'. Then

(9.1.1) $$g = g_1(y_1) + g_2(y_2) + \ldots + g_h(y_h).$$

Next assume that all the benefit functions are actually the same function g, so that each person derives the same amount of good from each level of income. Then

$$g = g(y_1) + g(y_2) + \ldots + g(y_h).$$

Assume finally that g is a *strictly concave* function (see page 79). Figure 8 shows the graph of a strictly concave benefit function g. The slope of the graph is known as the 'marginal benefit' of extra income. Take a person at some level of income such as $\hat{y}$. Her marginal benefit is the extra good she would obtain from receiving an extra pound. It is the slope of the graph at $\hat{y}$. The downward curvature of the graph shows that the more money a person

---

* This is actually a slightly stronger claim than the utilitarian principle stated on page 16. The latter says only that an alternative is better than another if and only if it has a greater total of good. It allows general good to be any increasing transformation of the total of individual good. But at least until we come to take account of uncertainty (see page 187), this makes no difference.

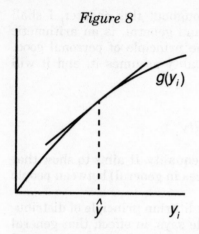

Figure 8

$g(y_i)$

$\hat{y}$ y_i

already has, the less good an extra pound will do her. That is the implication of a strictly concave benefit function. Another way of putting it is that income produces a 'diminishing marginal benefit'.

All these suppositions together imply that, for a given total of income, the more equally it is distributed the better. Because of the diminishing marginal benefit of income, if a pound is transferred from someone who has more money to someone who has less, the result will be a net increase in the total of good. The transfer will increase the good of the recipient more than it diminishes the good of the donor.

That is the standard utilitarian argument for equality. It was popular with utilitarian economists from Alfred Marshall to A. C. Pigou.[1] It is obviously consistent with the principle of personal good, because (9.1.1) is consistent with that principle.

However, this argument works only in very special circumstances: only if each person has the same benefit function g, which is a strictly concave function of her income. It is traditional and plausible wisdom that income has diminishing marginal benefit. So it is plausible that each person's benefit function will be strictly concave. But it is not at all plausible that everyone's function will be the same. One would naturally expect different people to derive different amounts of benefit from the same income.

In that case, what would utilitarianism say the distribution of income should be? Imagine you have to distribute a given total of income amongst a number of people, and you wish to maximize the total of the people's good. How should you do it? You should follow this rule: distribute it in such a way that the marginal benefit of income is the same for everyone. It is easy to see why. Suppose you happened to distribute income in some other way, so that people's marginal benefits were not all equal. Then you could increase the total of good by transferring a pound from someone with a lower marginal benefit to someone with a higher one. The loss to the former will be her marginal benefit, and the gain to the latter will be her marginal benefit. So the gain is greater than the loss. Only when everyone has the same marginal benefit will it not be possible to increase the total of good by a transfer like this.

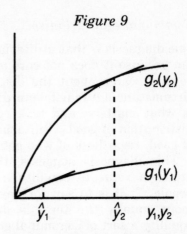

Figure 9

The rule of equalizing marginal benefits will not normally lead to equality. Figure 9 shows benefit functions for two people, both strictly concave. The distribution $(\hat{y}_1, \hat{y}_2)$ equalizes the two people's marginal benefit. So it produces the greatest possible total of good from the total of income $\hat{y}_1 + \hat{y}_2$. But it is not an equal distribution. Francis Edgeworth offered the equalizing of marginal benefits as a way to defend, not equality, but 'aristocratical privilege – the privilege of man above brute, of civilized above savage, of birth, of talent and of the male sex'. He claimed that people have different benefit functions, specifically that some classes of people have a greater capacity for pleasure than others. He quoted Tennyson:

> Woman is the lesser man, and her passions unto mine
> Are as moonlight unto sunlight and as water unto wine.[2]

Furthermore, often when people's benefit functions do genuinely seem to differ, a person with a lower function may well be one who intuition suggests deserves more income than other people. She may, for instance, have a lower function because she is handicapped.[3] Yet Figure 9 shows that equalizing marginal benefits will give her less income, not more.

As a defence of equality, then, this utilitarian argument works very poorly. It is not really an egalitarian argument at all.

9.2 Types of egalitarianism

An egalitarian might offer two alternative diagnoses of where the utilitarian argument goes wrong. Each arises from a different view about the value of equality. I shall explain these two views, and examine how far they are consistent with the principle of personal good. In this section I shall ignore uncertainty, and consider only the principle of personal good as it applies to final outcomes. I shall introduce uncertainty in Section 9.3.

Communal egalitarianism

One diagnosis is that utilitarianism is not fundamentally egalitarian because it does not care about equality in the distribution of *good*. It cares about the distribution of income, and in special circumstances it may favour distributing income equally. But good is what matters, and true egalitarianism must care about the distribution of good. Utilitarianism, though, values only the total of good, regardless of who gets it.[4]

This diagnosis suggests, then, that true egalitarianism will attach a value to equality in the distribution of good between people. That is to say, for any given total of individual good, the more equally the total is distributed the better. This makes equality a sort of communal good. I shall call this view *communal egalitarianism*. It is the view that general good can be increased without increasing the total of individual good, by distributing individual good more equally. It denies the utilitarian principle of distribution. T. M. Scanlon expresses communal egalitarianism like this: 'Fairness and equality do not represent ways in which individuals may be made *better off*. They are, rather, special morally desirable features of states of affairs and institutions.'[5]

It may seem that communal egalitarianism must be inconsistent with the principle of personal good. But actually it is not. Communal egalitarianism insists that general good can be increased without increasing the *total* of individual good. But it does not necessarily insist that general good can be increased without increasing *someone's* individual good.

Provided good is an arithmetic quantity, the principle of personal good can be put like this: good is an increasing function of people's good, and of nothing else. The principle says that

$$(9.2.1) \qquad g = f(g_1, g_2, \ldots g_h)$$

where g stands for general good and $g_1, g_2, \ldots g_h$ for the good of individuals, and that the function f is increasing in all its arguments (that is: increasing any g_i, keeping all the others constant, increases the value of f). That is all the principle of personal good requires. And so long as f has a suitable form, it will give value to equality in the way we require: for a given total of good $(g_1 + g_2 + \ldots g_h)$, the more equally it is distributed the greater is g. A function f that has this property is known as 'strictly S-concave'.

Let me define strict S-concavity more precisely. Take a distribution of good, and transfer some amount of good from a person who has more to a person who has less (but not so much that the latter ends up as well off as, or better off than, the former was originally). Unequivocally, this makes the distribution more equal. Call it an 'equalizing transfer'. Now, starting with any distribution of good, make a series of equalizing transfers, one after another. Again unequivocally, the resulting distribution will be more equal than the original one. The function *f* in (9.2.1) is *strictly S-concave* if and only if, whenever one distribution of good can be obtained from another by a series of equalizing transfers, the former has a higher value of *f* than the latter.[6]

So here is a particular communal egalitarian view: general good is an increasing strictly S-concave function of individual good. I shall call it *moderate* communal egalitarianism. It is consistent with the principle of personal good.

Even within moderate communal egalitarianism, there is lots of scope for variety, because there are many increasing strictly S-concave functions. Amongst them are *additively separable* functions, which have the form:

$$(9.2.2) \qquad g = w(g_1) + w(g_2) + \ldots + w(g_h),$$

where *w* is an increasing strictly concave function. The function *w* indicates how much a person's good counts in general good. Its strict concavity means that the better off someone is, the less does an extra unit of good coming to her count in general good. A person's good has *diminishing marginal value*, one might say. A function of this form is commonly used in economics to represent the value of equality.[7] Economists, then, are commonly additively separable communal egalitarians. 'Additively separable egalitarians', I shall sometimes call them, to make it slightly less of a mouthful.

To (9.2.2) one might add the assumption that each person's good is determined by her own income only. So $g_1 = g_1(y_1)$, $g_2 = g_2(y_2)$, and so on. Then (9.2.2) would become:

$$g = w(g_1(y_1)) + w(g_2(y_2)) + \ldots + w(g_h(y_h)),$$

or more briefly

$$g = w_1(y_1) + w_2(y_2) + \ldots + w_h(y_h).$$

This formula, too, is common in economics.[8] It is fair to say that general good in this formula is determined individualistically. Each person's income is evaluated separately from everyone else's, and then the evaluations are put together to determine general good. In calling a version of egalitarianism 'communal', I mean that it

takes the *ownership* of the good of equality to be communal: it is
not the good of any individual or individuals. The *determination* of
the good of equality may be individualistic, as it is in this example.

Individualistic egalitarianism

I said there were two alternative diagnoses of where the utilitarian
argument for equality goes wrong. The second is that it goes wrong
in taking a person's good to depend on her *own* income only. If
equality is good and inequality bad, then it is a bad thing if
someone has less income than someone else. And who is it bad for?
For the person who has less, if for no one else. The fact that
another person has more income than she does is bad for this
person. So her good depends, not only on her own income, but also
on the relation between her income and the other person's. To
assume it depends only on her own income is actually to ignore the
badness of inequality.

I shall call this view *individualistic egalitarianism*. It treats
inequality as an individual harm, and equality as an individual
good. It needs to be supported by a proper account of the harm
that inequality does to a person. I shall offer the beginnings of an
account in Section 9.4.

Individualistic egalitarianism comes in many different versions.
I shall give only a simple example, for the sake of illustrating how
the idea works formally.[9]

Suppose there are only two people, with incomes y_1 and y_2.
Suppose that, apart from the matter of equality, the good they
derive from their income is $\bar{g}_1(y_1)$ and $\bar{g}_2(y_2)$. Let us call the amount
a person is harmed by inequality her *complaint*.[10] (I do not mean
to imply that the person actually complains, or even that she feels
hard done by.) Her total good is her good apart from the matter of
equality, less her complaint. Suppose the richer person has no
complaint, but the poorer person has a complaint proportional to
the amount her income falls short of the richer person's. The first
person's complaint is nought if she happens to be richer than the
other person, or else $a(y_2 - y_1)$ if she is poorer, where the coefficient a is a constant of proportionality. So her total good is

$$(9.2.3) \qquad g_1 = \bar{g}_1(y_1) - \max\{0,\, a(y_2 - y_1)\}.$$

Similarly,

$$(9.2.4) \qquad g_2 = \bar{g}_2(y_2) - \max\{0,\, a(y_1 - y_2)\}.$$

The good of equality, then, (or the bad of inequality) has been included within the good (or bad) of the people.

What should we take general good to be? It would be possible to combine individualistic and communal egalitarianism. Having determined individuals' good by formulae like (9.2.3) and (9.2.4), which incorporate a value for equality, it would then be possible to form general good from them by a strictly S-concave function in the manner of (9.2.1). This is formally possible, though it may be pointless. It will yield a hybrid between individualistic and communal egalitarianism. I shall call a communal theory *pure* if the individuals' good is not taken to contain any component for equality. And I shall call an individualistic theory *pure* if general good is taken to be simply the total of individuals' good. For simplicity, in this book I shall deal only with pure theories, and ignore hybrids. To keep our example pure, then, let us take general good to be the total of people's good:

$$(9.2.5) \qquad\qquad g = g_1 + g_2.$$

I give individualistic egalitarianism its name because it takes the good of equality to be *owned* by individuals. The amount of this good is not *determined* individualistically, though; it depends on the relation between one person's position and other people's.

Individualistic egalitarianism may seem open to the objection that first led us to communal egalitarianism. True egalitarians, the objection goes, care about equality in the distribution of *good*. Individualistic egalitarianism may give value to equality in the distribution of income. But surely it cannot give value to equality in the distribution of good. Surely the good of individuals has to be determined before it can be determined how equally it is distributed. Consequently equality in the distribution of individual good cannot itself be a part of individual good.

Communal egalitarians may or may not be right that true egalitarianism is concerned with equality in the distribution of good. Later in this chapter and the next, I shall be giving reasons to suggest they are wrong. But in any case, individualistic egalitarianism can accommodate their opinion if it needs to. Surprisingly perhaps, there is actually no difficulty about making equality of individual good itself an individual good. It is only a matter of setting up some simultaneous equations. Take two people again and suppose, for the sake of illustration, that the better-off person has no complaint, and the worse-off person has a complaint proportional to the amount her good falls short of the other person's. Then, instead of (9.2.3) and (9.2.4), we shall have:

(9.2.6) $g_1 = \bar{g}_1 - \max\{0,\, a(g_2 - g_1)\}$

and

(9.2.7) $g_2 = \bar{g}_2 - \max\{0,\, a(g_1 - g_2)\}$.

Given $\bar{g}_1$ and $\bar{g}_2$, the people's good apart from the matter of
equality (these might be functions of y_1 and y_2 as before), (9.2.6)
and (9.2.7) will determine g_1 and g_2. To keep the egalitarianism
purely individualistic, general good might be taken simply as the
total $(g_1 + g_2)$. Even so – even though for a given total of good an
equal distribution is no better than an unequal one – this formula
will still recognize the value of equality in the distribution of good.
The value is embedded in the individuals' own good.

Pure individualistic egalitarianism is not only consistent with
the principle of personal good; it actually implies it. Indeed, it
implies the stronger utilitarian principle of distribution: that
general good is the total of individual good. The utilitarian
principle of distribution is not anti-egalitarian, then. It is consistent with individualistic egalitarianism; it is only anti-communal-
egalitarian.

Pure individualistic egalitarianism is not committed to any
further utilitarian view, though. A pure individualistic egalitarian
need not believe, for instance, that a person's good consists in her
pleasure. In Section 9.4, I shall argue that a person's good consists
partly in how fairly she is treated; unfairness is bad for a person,
whatever she may feel about it. This leads to a version of individualistic egalitarianism. On the other hand, individualistic egalitarianism is *consistent* with all sorts of utilitarian theories. It is even
consistent with the theory that a person's good consists in her
pleasure. A utilitarian might believe that general good is the total
of people's good, that each person's good is her pleasure, and that
a person's pleasure is diminished if the person finds herself
enjoying less pleasure than other people. This utilitarian would be
a pure individualistic egalitarian. In the example, she would accept
(9.2.5), (9.2.6) and (9.2.7), or equations like them. We have here a
second utilitarian argument for equality, an alternative to the one
in Section 9.1.[11]

Temkin's argument

This is the best place to reply to an argument of Larry Temkin's
against the principle of personal good, presented in his 'Harmful
goods, harmless bads'.

In this article, Temkin chiefly argues, not against the principle of personal good, but against another principle, which he calls 'the slogan':

One situation cannot be worse (or better) than another *in any respect* if there is no one for whom it is worse (or better) *in any respect*.

The slogan is not implied by the principle of personal good. But in arguing against it, Temkin is indirectly attacking the principle, because he claims that, in refuting the slogan, he thereby removes support from the principle.

The basis of this claim is the following argument. Suppose the slogan is false. Then there could be two situations A and B such that A is not worse than B for anyone in any respect, and yet in some respect A is worse than B. According to the principle of personal good, since A is not worse for anyone than B, A is not worse than B. Since it is worse than B in some respect, there must be some other respect in which it is better than B, and this must be enough to outweigh the respect in which it is worse. So the fact that A is not worse than B depends on the fortunate presence of a sufficiently important respect in which it is better than B. And how could we always rely on such a fortunate coincidence? If there can be cases where one alternative is worse than another in some respect, despite being not worse for anybody in any respect, then surely there can also be cases where one alternative is worse than another *tout court*, despite not being worse for anybody in any respect. These would be cases in which the fortunate balancing respect did not appear. If the slogan is false, then, the truth of the principle of personal good depends on a fortunate coincidence, which is surely undependable.

Now consider the views of a communal egalitarian. Let her be a pure communal egalitarian, who does not believe inequality is an individual harm. And let her be a moderate communal egalitarian, who believes general good is an increasing function of individual good. Let A and B be two distributions that are identical, except that a person who is already well off in B is even better off in A. A is less equal than B. But our communal egalitarian would say that A is in no respect worse for anybody than B, because she does not take inequality to be a personal harm. On the other hand, I presume she would be willing to say that A is worse than B in one respect. It is less equal than B, and she takes that to be a bad thing. So this communal egalitarian disagrees with the slogan.

She does, however, accept the principle of personal good; she believes general good to be an increasing function of individual good. And just because she rejects the slogan, she will not feel any the less secure in this principle. She believes, as a matter of principle, that general good depends only, and positively, on the good of individuals. In comparing A and B, she does not think that fortunately there is some respect in which A is better than B, which cancels out the respect in which it worse. She does think inequality is a bad thing, and she thinks it a communal bad in the sense I have spelled out. So she does think A is worse than B in one respect, though it is worse for nobody. But this respect is not one that has an independent force in determining the general goodness of the alternatives. General good depends only on the good of individuals.

I think Temkin's notion of a 'respect' is too equivocal to hang his argument on. Taking it one way, I should, like the communal egalitarian, be happy to give up the slogan. But a respect taken that way is not necessarily an independent consideration that separately helps to determine the goodness of the alternatives. Temkin's argument, though, implicitly assumes it is. So I see no strength in his case against the principle of personal good.

Conclusion

Applied to outcomes without uncertainty, the principle of personal good is compatible with a wide variety of egalitarian views, both communal and individualistic. To speak roughly, if you favour equality, you will favour redistribution from the better off to the less well off. This will increase general good. It will also increase the good of the less well off. So it is not a way of making the distribution better without making it better for somebody. Your belief is therefore consistent with the principle of personal good.

Only if your egalitarianism is extreme, will it conflict with the principle. If you believe it is better, for the sake of equality, to take good from better-off people without giving any to the less well off, then that is not consistent with the principle. Such a view is possible within communal egalitarianism. Only *moderate* communal egalitarianism, which takes general good to be an increasing function of individuals' good, is consistent with the principle of personal good. On the other hand, pure individualistic egalitarianism cannot conflict with the principle of personal good. A pure individualistic egalitarian would say that you might, perhaps, *try* to increase general good by taking good from the better off without giving it to the worse off. You might, say, take money away from the rich and burn it. But if you *succeed* in increasing general good as a result, that will be because you have actually benefited the less well off. The reduction in inequality itself will have benefited them, even though they receive no money.

9.3 Equality under uncertainty

Now I shall introduce uncertainty. So once more we shall be dealing with two dimensions at once: people and states of nature. In this context, the principle of personal good is more demanding.

In this section, I shall not be concerned with the idea that it is good to equalize the goodness of the prospects people are faced with: that it is good to equalize people's probability-relative good, in other words. Peter Diamond's example, which I examined in Section 5.7, can be used to illustrate this idea. In Table 16 on page 111, we may assume that alternative A gives each person an equally good prospect, whereas alternative B makes the people's prospects unequal. Like Diamond, one might think A better than B on that account. In Section 5.7, I explained that this thought poses a threat to the sure-thing principle; it suggests that general good might not be coherent. I tried to ward off this threat in that section. Now I am coming to a quite different threat, not to coherence, but to the principle of personal good. The example I shall use here is designed so that, in either alternative, both people face equally good prospects. So the value of equalizing the goodness of prospects is not at issue.

Look at Table 22. The two states of nature in the table are equally probable. For the moment, interpret the numbers as the

Table 22

		States of nature				States of nature	
		H	T			H	T
People	P	2	1	People	P	2	1
	Q	2	1		Q	1	2

Prospect A   Prospect B

people's incomes. And suppose – an auxiliary assumption – that each person's good depends only on her own income.

Prospect *A* is equally as good for *P* as prospect *B*, because, in either, *P* has an equal chance of 1 or 2 units of income. The two prospects are equally good for *Q* too, for the same reason. The principle of personal good implies, therefore, that the two are equally good generally. An egalitarian, though, will think differently. The two prospects may be equally good for the two people individually. But *A* is sure to lead to equality, and *B* to inequality. An egalitarian will therefore think *A* better.

Here is a conflict between egalitarianism and the principle of personal good. Does it mean the principle will have to go?

An egalitarian thinks *A* better. But what is better about it? It leads to equality, but what is good about that? One answer is that life is better in a more equal society: people enjoy better relationships with each other, feel less jealousy or guilt, and so on. Equality, in fact, improves the welfare of the people. In the example, this means that a person's good depends, not just on her own income, but also on the other person's, and on how close it is to hers. That draws the sting of the example. The example only threatened the principle of personal good because of the auxiliary assumption that a person's good depends only on her own income. Now I have removed the threat by denying the assumption.

But the conflict can be recreated. Reinterpret the figures in Table 22 to stand for the people's good, not their income. Then *A* and *B* are equally good for both people, for the same reason as before, and this conclusion does not now depend on any auxiliary assumption. So the principle of personal good says the two prospects are equally good. But an egalitarian might think that actually *A* is better, because it equalizes the people's good.

This second version of the example gives us only two options: deny that *A* is better than *B*, or give up the principle of personal good. Which should we do?

Individualistic egalitarianism

The answer of a pure individualistic egalitarian is plain: the principle of personal good is right, and *A* is no better than *B*. What possible case is there for saying *A* is better than *B*? I have already mentioned the point that a more equal society is better to live in. It is therefore better for the people. But in the present version of the example, Table 22 shows the whole of the people's good. The individual benefits of living in an equal society, whatever they may be, have already been taken into account. So they give us no further reason to think A better than B.

It may also be true that, quite apart from benefits like those I mentioned, equality is good in a further way. It may be good in itself, not because of the good effects it has on people's lives, but intrinsically. Whether or not it gives people better relationships and happier lives, a more equal society may simply be better.

Individualistic egalitarians can agree about that too. In Section 9.4, I shall develop the idea in terms of fairness. Inequality may well be unfair, whether or not anyone feels bad about it. This is consistent with individualistic egalitarianism. But individualistic egalitarians will insist that the intrinsic good of equality is a personal good. It belongs to people individually. If inequality is bad, then it is bad for somebody. It may be bad for the people at the top, and it is certainly bad for the people at the bottom. The badness they suffer is, specifically, unfairness, and the unfairness is being suffered by particular people. Therefore, it, too, has already been taken into account in the figures in Table 22. So it gives us no further reason for thinking A better than B. A is no better than B, and the principle of personal good is undamaged.

Communal egalitarianism

What is the response of a communal egalitarian to the example of Table 22?

There is an annoying complication to deal with first. Communal egalitarianism is not committed to any particular view about the goodness or badness of risk. It is not committed to risk neutrality, for instance. So, whatever it says about the goodness of outcomes, it need not favour maximizing the *expectation* of goodness when faced with alternative prospects like A and B. So far as general good is concerned, A is more risky than B. So different views about the goodness or badness of risk could lead to different conclusions about the relative goodness of A and B, even given a constant view about the goodness of equality.

As it happens, I can see no grounds in this case for anything other than risk neutrality about general good. So far as each individual is concerned, both prospects are equally risky. And I can see no reason to be bothered by risk to general good, over and above the risk to individuals. I shall say more about this on page 230. Nevertheless, some other attitude to risk is an available option for a communal egalitarian. So I need to allow for it.

Since general good is coherent, the general goodness of a

prospect can be represented by an expectational utility function (a function having the expected utility form of (5.1.1) on page 91). Of two prospects, the better one has the greater expected utility. (This is general utility, of course, representing general good.) The expectation of utility, then, determines the relative goodness of prospects. And utility must be an increasing transform of good, because the better of two outcomes must have the greater utility. This means that, from now on in this discussion of communal egalitarianism, I can simply work with general utility rather than general good. That will cut through the annoying complication. Utility will stand as a proxy for good. It is what a communal egalitarian values the expectation of. If she is risk neutral about good, she values the expectation of good; for her, utility is then a linear transform of good, and may as well be taken as good itself. If she is not risk neutral, utility will be some nonlinear transform of good.

This leads me to revise a definition. From now on in this book, what I mean by the *additively separable* version of communal egalitarianism is the version that says *general utility* – that which the communal egalitarian values the expectation of – has the additively separable form

$$(9.3.1) \qquad u = w(g_1) + w(g_2) + \ldots + w(g_h),$$

where w is an increasing strictly concave function. This formula is (9.2.2) from page 179, with general utility replacing general good.

The distinction between additively separable communal egalitarians and others will soon turn out to be important. So this new definition needs emphasizing. Think of a communal egalitarian who believes that general good has the form

$$g = (g_1 g_2 \ldots g_h)^{1/h},$$

which is *not* additively separable. But suppose she does not believe in risk neutrality about general good. She believes in maximizing, not the expectation of general good, but instead the expectation of the logarithm of general good. For her, general utility is

$$\begin{aligned} \log(g) &= \log(g_1 g_2 \ldots g_h)^{1/h} \\ &= (1/h)\log(g_1) + (1/h)\log(g_2) + \ldots + (1/h)\log(g_h). \end{aligned}$$

And this *is* an additively separable function of the people's good, g_1, g_2 and so on. So according to my revised definition, this person is an additively separable egalitarian. An additively separable egalitarian, then, can only be distinguished from any other sort of communal egalitarian by reference to her attitude to risk. The distinction is a subtle one, therefore.

That is the complication out of the way. Now let us return to the question of what communal egalitarianism has to say about the example of Table 22.

Start with the additively separable version. The expected utility of A according to the additively separable formula (9.3.1) is

$$\tfrac{1}{2}\{w(2) + w(2)\} + \tfrac{1}{2}\{w(1) + w(1)\}.$$

The expected utility of B is

$$\tfrac{1}{2}\{w(1) + w(2)\} + \tfrac{1}{2}\{w(2) + w(1)\}.$$

And these are the same. Additively separable egalitarianism therefore takes A and B to be equally good. This makes it consistent with the principle of personal good.

However, it also reveals something else about the additively separable version. I assume it is *pure* communal egalitarianism we are dealing with. So I assume the individuals' good contains no component for equality. Given that, one might well think that a true egalitarian *should* believe A to be better than B. An *individualist* egalitarian denies A is better than B, I explained, because for her the good of equality is already taken account of in the people's good. But for a pure communal egalitarian, that is not so. And the fact is that A definitely leads to equality, whereas B definitely leads to inequality. Surely, then, an egalitarian should think A better. Yet additively separable egalitarianism implies it is not. This strongly suggests this is not really an egalitarian view. I shall take up this point again on page 198.

We have found that the additively separable version of communal egalitarianism is consistent with the principle of personal good. But no other version is. Any other version will deny that A and B are equally good. The proof of this point will appear in Chapter 10. It is, in fact, a consequence of the interpersonal addition theorem proved in that chapter; the example of Table 22 shows this addition theorem at work. The principle of personal good, the theorem proves, together with the coherence of individual and general good, requires general utility to be an additively separable function of individual good. Any function that is not additively separable will conflict with the principle.

A well-chosen version of communal egalitarianism can make pretty good sense of the example.[12] For instance, take utility to be:

(9.3.2) $$u = \sqrt{(g_1 g_2)}.$$

It is easy to check that this formula will make A better than B, as seems to be right. And the formula is reasonable in other respects too. So it constitutes a good challenge to the principle of personal good.

However, even such a reasonable communal egalitarianism as the sort given by (9.3.2) has at least one difficulty to face. Look at Table 23. The numbers in this table stand for the people's good, and the states of nature in the table are equally likely. A communal egalitarian has to take general good to be a strictly S-concave function of individual good. Strict S-concavity implies that the function is symmetrical. That is to say, permuting the distribution of good between people makes no difference to general good.* The alternatives C and D in Table 23 are symmetrical and must therefore be equally good according to a strictly S-concave function. Now suppose that risk is bad for P: of two alternatives with the same expectation of good for her, the safer one is better for her. Then D is better for the first person. Next suppose risk is *good* for Q. Then D is better for Q too. So D is better for both people. Given that, it is hard to doubt that D must be generally better. We are questioning the principle of personal good in general. But in this particular application, it is hard to doubt. The source of our

Table 23

		States of nature				States of nature	
		H	T			H	T
People	P	2	1	People	P	1.5	1.5
	Q	1.5	1.5		Q	2	1

Prospect C Prospect D

---

* *Proof.* A permutation can be done two people at a time. Permuting the good of two people can be thought of as a transfer of good from the better-off of the two to the less well-off. If just a tiny bit less good were transferred, it would be an equalizing transfer (defined on page 179). And an equalizing transfer has to increase general good, if good is an S-concave function of individual good. Consequently (provided the function is continuous), permuting good between two people cannot reduce general good. Nor can permuting it back again, once it has been permuted. It follows that a permutation must leave general good unchanged.

general doubt is a concern for equality, but in respect of equality there is nothing to choose between the alternatives C and D. The argument I presented in Section 8.2 is consequently enough to show that D is better than C. Yet communal egalitarianism has to rate C and D equally good. Whenever the badness or goodness of risk differs for different people, communal egalitarianism will run into trouble of this sort.

It may not be insuperable trouble, though. Bernoulli's hypothesis about good (page 142) insists on risk neutrality about good. It says that risk to good is neither good nor bad for a person. If this is so, the problem I have just described cannot arise. And Section 6.5 suggests that Bernoulli's hypothesis is defensible. So I do not offer this problem as a conclusive objection to communal egalitarianism.

Nor do I offer as an objection to non-additively-separable communal egalitarianism the mere fact that it conflicts with the principle of person good. I could have done that: the principle has an intuitive appeal, which might be used against any egalitarian theory that denies it. But that move would be a mistake. As I explained on page 130, it would be a mistake to rely on the intuitive appeal of the principle of personal good when it is applied to probability-relative good. Nor can I use the argument of Section 8.2. In that section, I presented an argument for the principle of personal good. But that argument is not able to support the principle against communal egalitarianism. It assumed away interactions between the good of different people, and non-additively-separable communal egalitarianism claims precisely that there are such interactions.

To defend the principle of personal good, therefore, I need to argue independently against non-additively-separable communal egalitarianism. I shall argue that, if any sort of egalitarianism is true, it is the individualistic sort. This is the task of Section 9.4.

Dispersion

Adopting individualistic egalitarianism is a second instance of a strategy I have used before. In Chapter 5, the sure-thing principle was threatened by counterexamples like Maurice Allais's. The sure-thing principle is a principle of separability. It claims that what happens in one state of nature can be evaluated independently of what happens in other states. But the counterexamples point to apparent interactions between states, which seem to prevent such a state-by-state evaluation. I dealt with the problem, as I put it in Section 5.7, by *dispersing* to the states themselves the values that apparently arise from interactions between states. More precisely, I claimed that the values are in fact dispersed, despite appearances.

The principle of personal good is another principle of separability. It claims that what happens to one person can be evaluated independently of what happens to other people. The value of equality threatens this claim. It suggests that one person's position can only be evaluated in its relation to other people's. An evaluation of general good, therefore, must involve some interaction between the situations of different people. Individualistic egalitarianism, though, takes the value of equality to be dispersed amongst individuals. That is how it averts the threat to the principle of personal good.

In the argument about the sure-thing principle, my strategy of dispersion raised worries about emptiness. It seemed that it might save the sure-thing principle only at the expense of destroying the principle's content. A similar worry comes up now. The principle of personal good, if defended by the dispersion argument, might end up without content. The point of egalitarianism may particularly seem to be that there is a good, equality, that does not belong to people individually. It seems particularly opposed to the principle of personal good. If the principle turns out not to deny egalitarianism, then perhaps it will deny nothing.

Dispersion is a general strategy of argument that can be used to support separability in different dimensions. And it may raise similar doubts in different dimensions. I would not try to defend the strategy in general. I am sure that some ways of using it would be genuinely pointless, because they would render separability empty. The strategy needs a particular defence on each occasion.

On the present occasion, the strategy appears in the form of individualistic egalitarianism. My defence will be that, truly, the good of equality is an individual good. The harm done by inequality is truly a harm done to people. Individualistic egalitarianism is no artificial device designed to preserve separability, but the best way of understanding the actual value that equality has. The argument of Section 9.4 is intended to make this point.

9.4 Fairness and equality

In Section 9.1, I gave a utilitarian argument for equality, but since then I have not tried to offer grounds for egalitarianism. I have taken it for granted that equality is good, and discussed the different forms its goodness might take. But to discover the true form of its goodness, we must ask why equality is good in the first place. I am going to ground the value of equality in a theory of fairness. I shall first propound the theory, and then argue that this theory gives support to individualistic egalitarianism. Communal egalitarianism, or at least the non-additively-separable sort, does not seem to me well grounded.

Fairness

The principal evidence I have to offer in support of my theory of fairness is that, so far as I can see, it is the only adequate way of explaining the fairness of lotteries. It often happens that there are several candidates to receive some indivisible commodity, but not enough is available to go round them all. ('Commodity' in this section refers to any good thing; 'good' would be a more natural term, but would cause confusion.) This happens, for instance, when a parent has too few sweets to go round all the children. A more important example: there are not enough kidneys available as transplants for everyone who needs one. Diamond's example discussed on pages 111–115 is a formalized version of the problem. On some occasions like this, it seems that the best way to choose between the candidates is by a random lottery. The advantage of a lottery is that it is fair. My account of fairness explains why this is so, and I can find no other adequate explanation. So I think that understanding the fairness of a lottery is a useful way of coming to understand fairness in general. I have set out my argument about fairness and lotteries elsewhere.[13] Here I shall simply outline the account of fairness without much argument. I hope it will seem plausible anyway.

Suppose some commodity, divisible or not, is to be distributed amongst a number of candidates. It might, for instance, be income to be distributed amongst a population, or kidneys amongst people with kidney disease. For each candidate there will be reasons why she should have the commodity, or some of it. One reason why a person should have some income, for instance, might be that she would derive some benefit from it. This is a straightforward utilitarian reason: for a utilitarian, the fact that a person would benefit from income is a reason why she should have some (a reason that may be overridden by conflicting reasons, of course). This reason would need to be spelt out more fully by specifying her good as a function of the income she gets. Another reason might be that the person is entitled to income because she has worked for

it. A reason why a particular person should receive a kidney might
be that she has children to bring up, or that she enjoys life. All
these reasons will have some part to play in determining who
should have the commodity, and how much.

But what part? One might simply weigh the reasons against
each other, and allocate the commodity to the people for whom the
reasons are strongest. I must make this more precise. Take the
commodity one unit at a time. (If it is divisible, take very small
units; if not, take its natural units.) For each unit, weigh each
person's reasons why she should have the unit against other
people's. Award the unit to the person for whom the reasons are
strongest on balance. Then do the same for the next unit. A
utilitarian, for instance, would award each small unit to the person
who would derive most benefit from it. A communal egalitarian
would weigh the reasons differently. She believes general good is
some other function of individual good, not the total. So she would
award the unit to the person whose getting it would most increase
general good according to this function. But whichever formula for
general good is used, the result of distributing the commodity one
unit at a time this way will normally be to maximize general good
according to the formula. Weighing leads to maximizing.

The weighing of reasons, however, is not all there is to determining who should get the commodity. It ignores the question of
fairness between the people.

Take this example. Someone has to be sent on an unpleasant
and very dangerous – probably fatal – mission. One person out of
a group must be chosen to go. And one of the people has special
talents that make her more likely than the others to accomplish
the mission well. So there are stronger reasons why she, rather
than one of the others, should go. The commodity to be distributed
here is the good of being left behind. There are stronger reasons
for giving this commodity to the untalented candidates. So if the
weighing of reasons completely determined what should be done,
the talented candidate should simply be sent. But it is plausible to
think that this would be unfair to her; it would be fairer to hold a
lottery amongst all the candidates. If it is very important to have
the mission performed well, it may be that fairness should give
way to expediency, and the talented person should be sent. But
even if sending her without a lottery would, on balance, be right,
it would nevertheless be unfair to her.

How can this be? How can the weighing of reasons fail to
determine completely what should be done? To understand fairness
we must start by dividing the reasons why a person should get a

commodity into two classes: *claims* and other reasons. By a claim to the commodity, I mean a duty owed to the candidate herself that she should have it. Many reasons are not claims. In the case of the dangerous mission, there are reasons for giving the commodity of staying behind to the untalented candidates, rather than the talented one. But their lack of talent does not give the untalented candidates a stronger *claim* to this commodity. It is not owed to *them* that they should be left behind.

Claims, and not other reasons, are the object of fairness. Fairness is concerned only with mediating between the claims of different people. If there are reasons why a person should have a commodity, but she does not get it, no unfairness is done her unless she has a claim to it.

But when it mediates between people's claims, what exactly does fairness require? Does it require simply that claims should be given their proper weight when they come to be weighed against other reasons and the claims of other people? This cannot be enough because all reasons should be given their proper weight, and weighing reasons does not capture the requirements of fairness, as I have explained. Weighing up is the treatment we would naturally give conflicting duties owed to a single person. But conflicting claims are duties owed to different people. Weighing them up, like duties owed to a single person, does not give proper recognition to the people's separateness.[14]

So does fairness require, perhaps, that claims should be given extra heavy weight? This would not be enough either. In the example of the dangerous mission, suppose everybody has the same claim to the commodity of being left behind. So claims are exactly matched. But there is a separate reason why the talented person should not get this commodity: she would accomplish the mission better if she was sent. So if claims are simply weighed up, however much weight they are given, the result will be that the talented person gets sent. But it is unfair that she should be required to endanger her life just because of her special talents. She might make this plausible complaint. She has as strong a claim to be left behind as anybody else. But because of her talents, the weighing up of reasons simply amounts to overriding her claim. It never even puts it on the cards that she might get what she has a claim to. This is not giving her claim the recognition it deserves.

When claims conflict, I suggest that what fairness requires is not that they be weighed against each other and other reasons, but that they actually be *satisfied in proportion to their strength*.

In this formula, I do not mean 'proportion' to be taken too precisely. The essential point is that fairness prescribes how far each person's claim should be satisfied *relative to* the satisfaction of other people's claims. Stronger claims require more satisfaction and equal claims require equal satisfaction. Also, weaker claims cannot simply be overridden by stronger ones: if a stronger claim is satisfied to some extent, then so should a weaker one be to a lesser extent.

My suggestion merely extends and tightens up a principle that is often taken for granted: that people equally situated should be equally treated. Economists call this the principle of 'horizontal equity'.[15] My suggestion tightens it up by applying it only to people with equal *claims*, and not to people equally situated in other respects. And my suggestion extends the principle by adding the proportionality rule to the equality rule. The extension is very natural. If claims of equal strength should receive equal treatment, it is implausible that a slightly stronger claim should totally override a slightly weaker one.

The essential point of my account of fairness is that it makes fairness a relative matter. It is not at all concerned with the absolute level of satisfaction of claims. If several people have equal claims to some commodity, they are all treated perfectly fairly so long as they each get the same amount of it, even if the amount is small or even none at all. Of course, the more they get the *better*. There is at least one reason for each of them to have the commodity, namely the reason that constitutes a claim. It is therefore better if they each get more rather than less. But it is no fairer. It is not fairness that makes it better.

In the example of the dangerous mission, claims are equal. Fairness therefore requires that either everyone goes or no one. Assume that neither of these alternatives is possible. Then the requirement of fairness cannot be satisfied. Some unfairness cannot be avoided, because someone has to go whilst others, who have no stronger claim to be excused, stay behind.

Unfairness is almost inevitable when there is not enough of an indivisible commodity to go round everyone who has a claim. But I believe a lottery can mitigate the unfairness. People cannot all get the commodity in proportion to their claims, but they can at least have a chance at getting it in proportion to their claims. Having a chance, I believe, is a sort of surrogate satisfaction of the claim. This explains the fairness of a lottery. But it is an argument I cannot make here.[16]

Equality

That completes my summary of the theory of fairness. Whenever people have equal claims to something, then fairness requires they should have equal shares of it. It is in one respect bad if they do not: it is unfair. So this account of fairness provides a basis for explaining the badness of inequality and the goodness of equality. But what I have said so far about fairness leaves a great deal open. The theory can be developed in many different ways, to produce different views about the value of equality. I shall not develop it far.[17] I have only three points to make.

One of the things I have so far left open is which reasons are claims and which are not. Suppose we are interested in the distribution of income between people. For each person, there are reasons why she should have some income. I mentioned some on page 193. If the person would derive some benefit from income, that is a reason why she should have some. If she has earned some income, that is another reason. Some of these reasons may be claims, and others not. There is scope for a great deal of disagreement about this. One view is that claims can only arise historically, through the process of trading and contracting. Another is that everyone has an equal claim to good. And there are many other possible views.

Each one will imply something about what an egalitarian should be concerned for the equality *of*. For the sake of an example, suppose that claims arise from need. Suppose that people have claims to have their needs satisfied, and that these claims are all equal.[18] If this is so, a distribution of income will only be fair if people's needs are equally satisfied. We should therefore be concerned for equality in the satisfaction of needs.

If we suppose, on the other hand, that people have equal claims to good, then fairness will require the distribution of good across people to be equal. We should be concerned for equality in the distribution of good. The first point I want to make is that it is easy to doubt this is the right view to take. The fact that a person will benefit from income is a reason why she should have income. But unless it is a claim, it is no concern of fairness. And it is easy to doubt that people have claims to good rather than, say, to the satisfaction of their needs, or to the resources they require to build a life for themselves, or to what Amartya Sen calls 'capabilities'.[19] The view that true egalitarianism is concerned with equality in the distribution of good is the guiding principle of communal egalitarianism. Seen from the perspective of fairness, it is by no means as obvious as it may have seemed when I introduced it on page 178. I showed on page 181 that individualistic egalitarianism can accommodate this view. But on the other hand, it can also easily accommodate different views about the nature of claims. It can accommodate the view that what we have claims to, and what we should aim to equalize, are resources, or capabilities, or something else.

My second point is brief, but the most important. Unfairness, as I have described it, is plainly an individual harm. There is unfairness if someone's claim is satisfied less than in proportion to its strength. Since a claim is a duty owed particularly to the person, the unfairness is plainly suffered by that person. If, say, people have equal claims to the satisfaction of needs, and some people have their needs less well satisfied than others do, then those people are suffering unfairness. This is exactly how individualistic egalitarians see the badness of inequality, and not how communal egalitarians see it. So individualistic egalitarianism fits the theory of fairness, and communal egalitarianism does not.

My third point concerns only the additively separable version of communal egalitarianism. Unfairness is a matter of how well each person does compared with other people. It is a relative matter. The amount of unfairness cannot be determined by looking at each person's position separately. Therefore, if the value of equality is a matter of fairness, an additively separable formula is quite unsuited to measuring it. An additively separable function of people's good takes each person's good separately, assigns a value to it and then adds up the separate values for each person. The value assigned to one person's good is independent of anyone else's. Larry Temkin says: 'The problem with this view is clear. It is not concerned with equality. Equality describes a relation obtaining between people that is essentially comparative. People are more or less equal relative to one another. The view in question is concerned with how people fare, but not with how they fare relative to each other.'[20] I agree. And the example of Table 22 on page 185 makes it clearer. As I explained on page 189, the additively separable formula does not adequately capture what egalitarianism requires in that example.

This does not mean that additively separable egalitarianism is silly. It turns out not to be a truly egalitarian view, and it does not properly represent what fairness demands, but nevertheless it represents very well what Derek Parfit calls 'the priority view'.[21] Suppose some benefit comes to a person. This adds to general good.

The priority view is the view that the contribution to general good is greater the less well off the person is. Benefits to worse off people count for more than benefits to better off people. The essential feature of the priority view is that the contribution of a benefit to general good depends only on how well off is the person it comes to; the contribution is not affected by the person's position relative to other people. The additively separable formula captures this view very well, just because it is additively separable.

As Parfit points out, the practical consequences of the priority view are hard to distinguish from the practical consequences of egalitarianism. The priority view has the consequence that, for any given total of good, the more equally it is distributed the better. This seems like a hallmark of egalitarianism. Indeed, it is the way I originally defined communal egalitarianism in Section 9.2. (And for convenience I shall continue to use this definition, so that the priority view – not perfectly correctly – comes under the heading of communal egalitarianism.) Conversely, any egalitarian will think it better to benefit worse off people than better off, because that promotes equality. However, the example of Table 22 is able to separate the two viewpoints. The priority view, represented by the additively separable formula, takes the alternatives *A* and *B* to be equally good. True egalitarianism takes *A* to be better, unless the figures in the table already incorporate an individualist value for equality.

I must add one cautious note. I have suggested that the distinction between additively separable egalitarianism and other communal egalitarian views captures the intuitive distinction between the priority view and true egalitarianism. I can see no other satisfactory way of making the intuitive distinction precise. But I explained on page 189 that the former distinction depends in a subtle way on attitudes to risk. Perhaps one should be cautious about capturing an intuitive distinction in such a subtle manner.

Conclusion

From all this, I conclude that, if equality is valuable, individualistic egalitarianism captures its value properly, and communal egalitarianism does not. Unlike communal egalitarianism, individualistic egalitarianism is not committed to the view that what matters is equality of *good*, rather than, say, of resources. And, since what is bad about inequality is its unfairness, inequality is clearly a harm suffered by individuals.

Additively separable egalitarianism remains a credible viewpoint. It is not strictly egalitarian, but represents the priority view. And that, for now at least, seems plausible. I shall have more to say about it in Chapter 10.

But I can find little to be said for non-additively-separable communal egalitarianism. And this is the only egalitarian position that conflicts with the principle of personal good. So I conclude in favour of the principle of personal good.

Notes

1. Marshall, *Principles of Economics*, pp. 471–2, and (more unequivocally stated) Pigou, *The Economics of Welfare*, p. 89. There is a thorough working-out of the egalitarian implications of the utilitarianism in Mirrlees, 'An exploration in the theory of optimal income taxation'.

2. Edgeworth, *Mathematical Psychics*, pp. 78–9. The couplet is from Tennyson's *Locksley Hall*, stanza 76.

3. This point comes from Sen, *On Economic Inequality*, pp. 15–18. Note that the person with a lower benefit function does not *necessarily* deserve more income in compensation. She might simply have expensive tastes, for instance; see Dworkin 'What is equality?'. Richard Brandt, in *A Theory of the Right and the Good*, pp. 316–19, defends utilitarianism against Sen's example by claiming that handicapped people will probably not have a benefit function that is lower than other people's in the way shown in Figure 9. But this is a weak defence. It is certainly possible that a person might have such a lower function because of a handicap. And in such a case utilitarianism will lead to an antiegalitarian conclusion.

4. In *A Theory of Justice*, p. 26, John Rawls makes this complaint about utilitarianism.

5. 'Rights, goals and fairness', p. 81.

6. Sen, *On Economic Inequality*, pp. 54–6, especially the note on p. 56.

7. For instance, in Atkinson and Stiglitz, *Public Economics*, p. 340. Support for this view can be found in Hurley, *Natural Reasons*, pp. 368–82.

8. For instance, Atkinson, 'On the measurement of inequality'. I have criticized this version of egalitarianism in my 'What's the good of equality?'

9. There are more detailed examples in 'What's the good of equality?'

10. This term comes from Temkin, *Inequality*.

11. Compare Mirrlees, 'The economic uses of utilitarianism'.

12. In 'Incentives, compensation, and social welfare', Margaret Meyer and Dilip Mookherjee consider an example like the one in Table 22. Their response is to favour a non-additively-separable formula.

13. In 'Fairness'.

14. Compare Rawls, *A Theory of Justice*, pp. 22–7.

15. See, for instance, Atkinson and Stiglitz, *Lectures on Public Economics*, pp. 353–5. David Wiggins takes it for granted in 'Claims of need'.

16. It is developed in my 'Fairness'.

17. It is pursued further in my 'What's the good of equality?'

18. David Wiggins examines this idea in 'Claims of need'. He asks what sort of claim can arise from need. It cannot, he thinks, be an absolute right: no one can have an absolute right to have her needs satisfied. I think my theory of fairness answers Wiggins's question satisfactorily. Claims are relative, not absolute; they require satisfaction only in proportion to the satisfaction of the claims of other people. See my 'Fairness'.

19. Many authors have argued for views of this sort. See, for instance, Dworkin, 'What is equality?', Sen, *The Standard of Living*, and Scanlon, 'Preference and urgency'. I should mention that Scanlon's conclusion is slightly different from the suggestion I am making, a fact that may be concealed by a difference of terminology. For Scanlon, a 'claim' includes any aspect of a person's well-being that others should take into account when deciding what to do. So it includes all the 'reasons', as I have called them, that stem from the person's interest. I, on the other hand, have allowed the possibility of reasons that are not claims. In 'Preference and urgency', Scanlon argues that a person's claims are determined by the urgency or objective importance of what she requires, rather than by her own preferences. Given his notion of claims, this seems a much stronger conclusion than the suggestion I am making. It means, not only that our concern for *equality* should be directed towards urgency, but that *all* our moral concerns should be. However, Scanlon also argues in 'Preference and urgency' that urgency should determine our notion of *good* or wellbeing: what is good for a person is to have her urgent requirements, rather than her preferences, satisfied. To be more exact, Scanlon allows that we may have more than one conception of wellbeing, but that this should be one. ('The moral basis of interpersonal comparisons' makes this clearer.) This means that Scanlon, if he is an egalitarian at all, is a communal egalitarian; he believes in equality in the distribution of good, at least in one sense of good. I quoted him as a representative of communal egalitarianism on page 178 above.

20. *Inequality*.

21. *On Giving Priority to the Worse Off*.

Chapter 10

The Interpersonal
Addition Theorem

In Chapters 6 and 7, I argued that the individual and general betterness relations are coherent. In Chapters 8 and 9, I argued for the principle of personal good. Putting these conclusions together gives us:

> *The interpersonal addition theorem.* If the individual and general betterness relations are coherent, and if the principle of personal good is true, then the general betterness relation can be represented by an expectational utility function that is the sum of expectational utility functions representing the betterness relations of individuals.

This is John Harsanyi's theorem from page 160, reinterpreted in terms of betterness rather than preferences. I explained in Section 7.3 that a reinterpretation is necessary because the original theorem has inconsistent premises. The reinterpreted theorem escapes the inconsistency by implicitly assuming a context of fixed probabilities. All the betterness relations mentioned in the theorem must be understood relative to the same probabilities.

Section 10.1 proves the theorem. If you are not interested in proofs, skip that section.

The theorem leads to two remarkable conclusions. Firstly, it links the aggregation of good across the dimension of people with its aggregation across the dimension of states of nature. The result is that, in favourable circumstances, it links the value of equality in the distribution of good with the value of avoiding risk to good. Section 10.2 explains this link.

The second conclusion is even more remarkable. The theorem tells us that general utility is the sum of individual utilities. Since these utilities represent the general and individual betterness relations, this may seem, at first glance, to say that general good is the total of individual good. It may seem like the utilitarian principle of distribution. But actually this is not so; the theorem does not by itself imply the utilitarian principle.[1] Nevertheless, it does imply it if we add as an extra premise Bernoulli's hypothesis from page 142: that it is always best for a person to maximize the expectation of her good. Bernoulli's hypothesis says there is no value in avoiding risk to good. Joined with the addition theorem it implies the utilitarian principle of distribution, which implies in turn that there is no value in avoiding inequality in the distribution of good between people. All this is explained in Section 10.3. That section also takes up again the assessment of Bernoulli's hypothesis that I began in Section 6.5.

10.1 Proof

This section proves the interpersonal addition theorem.[2] In this section, I shall take for granted the theorem's premises: the principle of personal good and the coherence of the individual and general betterness relations.

Step 1

Suppose there are h people and s states of nature. We shall be interested in the goodness of prospects like $(x_1, x_2, \ldots x_s)$, which leads to outcomes x_1, x_2, and so on in the different states. Each outcome may affect the interests of many different people.

Between these prospects, there will be a betterness relation for the ith person:

__ is at least as good for person i as __.

This relation is coherent. Expected utility theory (Section 5.1) tells us that it can therefore be represented by an expectational utility function V_i. (I use the letter 'V' instead of 'U' for a reason that will appear.) V_i will be a function of the prospects, and it will have the expected utility form (5.1.1) on page 91. That is:

(10.1.1) $V_i(x_1, x_2, \ldots x_s) = p_1 v_i(x_1) + p_2 v_i(x_2) + \ldots + p_s v_i(x_s).$

The ps are probabilities and v_i is a subutility function. The probability agreement theorem on page 152, read with the individual betterness relations taking the place of preference relations, ensures that the ps will be the same for each person.

Each prospect will determine a value of i's subutility in each state of nature: $v_i(x_1)$ in the first state, $v_i(x_2)$ in the second state, and so on. Write these values v_{i1}, v_{i2}, and so on. This is true for each person. So a prospect will actually determine a whole long vector of subutilities, one for each person in each state of nature:

$$(v_{11}, v_{12}, \ldots v_{1s}, v_{21}, v_{22}, \ldots v_{2s}, \ldots v_{h1}, v_{h2}, \ldots v_{hs}).$$

The component v_{21} in this vector, for instance, is the subutility that the prospect brings to the second person in the first state of nature.

Different prospects will generally determine different vectors of subutilities. But sometimes two prospects may happen to determine the same vector: they may happen to make all the subutilities the same, for every person in every state of nature. If they do, that means these prospects are equally good for everybody in every state. So they are equally good for everybody. It follows by the principle of personal good that they are equally good. The goodness of a prospect, therefore, is fully determined by the subutilities it leads to. Prospects are ordered by the general betterness relation

__ is at least as good as __.

To each prospect there corresponds a vector of subutilities. And we now see that if the same vector corresponds to two prospects, those prospects have the same place in the ordering. The betterness relation therefore orders the vectors. (Indeed, so long as we are interested only in goodness, we may as well think of a prospect as just its vector of subutilities.) Each place in the vector is a *location* and the subutility in that place is the *occurrence* at that location, as I defined locations and occurrences on page 66. And the vectors are ordered by betterness.

It may seem odd to take occurrences to be subutilities, since on page 69 I took subutilities to be functions *of* occurrences. But the subutilities I am taking as occurrences are defined by the expected utility functions of *individuals*, quite independently of the general betterness relation. It is therefore legitimate for the *general* betterness relation to be defined over vectors of these previously determined subutilities. Later (in (10.1.3)), it will turn out that the general betterness relation can be represented by a utility function that is the sum of functions of each of the individual subutilities. Technically these functions are themselves subutility functions, but to avoid confusion I shall not give them that name.

Step 2

So the general betterness relation orders the vectors of subutilities. I shall next show that this ordering has crosscutting separability (which is defined on page 69). The locations can be arranged on a two-dimensional grid, with the rows standing for people and the columns for states of nature. The definition of crosscutting separability requires there to be at least two people and at least two states of nature. I take that for granted. The vector of subutilities can be arranged like this:

$$
\begin{array}{cccc}
v_{11} & v_{12} & \cdots & v_{1s} \\
v_{21} & v_{22} & \cdots & v_{2s} \\
\vdots & \vdots & & \vdots \\
v_{h1} & v_{h2} & \cdots & v_{hs}
\end{array}
$$

I shall show that each column and each row of the grid is separable in the ordering.

The columns are separable because the general betterness relation is coherent, specifically because it conforms to the sure-thing principle. The subutilities in each column depend only on the outcome in the corresponding state of nature. But the sure-thing principle says that the states are strongly separable. So each column is separable. Indeed, the separability of the columns would follow just from the *weak* separability of the states of nature, which is much less than the sure-thing principle.

The rows are separable because of the principle of personal good. Take two prospects that, for each person i, both give that person the same value of utility V_i. Since V_i represents goodness for i, these prospects are equally good for each person. Consequently the principle of personal good says they are equally good. Therefore, when general good is represented by a utility function U, they will both give the same value for U. The value of U must consequently be fully determined by the values of all the V_is. U, that is to say, is a *function* of the V_is:

$$(10.1.2) \qquad U = W(V_1, V_2, \ldots V_h).$$

Equation (10.1.1) shows that, in turn, each V_i is a function of v_{i1}, v_{i2}, and so on. So

$$V = W(V_1(v_{11}, v_{12}, \ldots v_{1s}), V_2(v_{21}, v_{22}, \ldots v_{2s}),$$
$$\ldots V_h(v_{h1}, v_{h2}, \ldots v_{hs})).$$

Each of the subvectors $(v_{11}, v_{12}, \ldots v_{1s})$, $(v_{21}, v_{22}, \ldots v_{2s})$ and so on is separable, that is to say. (See page 68.) And these are just the rows of the table of subutilities. So the rows are separable. In effect, the principle of personal good implies weak separability between people.

The principle of personal good also says that increasing one person's good, whilst the good of everyone else remains constant, increases general good. The function W must therefore be increasing in all its arguments.

I have shown, then, that the general betterness ordering, defined over the vector of subutilities, has crosscutting separability. By the second separability theorem on page 70, it is therefore additively separable. This means it can be represented by an additively separable utility function:

(10.1.3) $$U = f_{11}(v_{11}) + f_{12}(v_{12}) + \ldots + f_{1s}(v_{1s}) +$$
$$f_{21}(v_{21}) + f_{22}(v_{22}) + \ldots + f_{2s}(v_{2s}) +$$
$$\ldots +$$
$$f_{h1}(v_{h1}) + f_{h2}(v_{h2}) + \ldots + f_{hs}(v_{hs}).$$

Step 3

Putting this fact of additive separability together with what we already know about the function U tells us more. Unfortunately, the argument here requires some slightly complicated algebra. I shall go through it first, and then explain afterwards what the algebra is really doing.

We already know that, since U represents the general betterness relation, it has to be a function of the V_is, which represent the individual betterness relations. Equation (10.1.2) tells us that. Furthermore, we know that each V_i has the expected utility form shown in (10.1.1). So, from (10.1.2) and (10.1.1):

(10.1.4) $$U = W((p_1 v_{11} + p_2 v_{12} + \ldots + p_s v_{1s}),$$
$$(p_1 v_{21} + p_2 v_{22} + \ldots + p_s v_{2s}),$$
$$\ldots$$
$$(p_1 v_{h1} + p_2 v_{h2} + \ldots + p_s v_{hs})).$$

Our conclusions will come from putting (10.1.3) and (10.1.4) together.

Suppose v_{11}, starting from some value $\bar{v}$, changes to some value $\hat{v}$, whilst all the other subutilities stay constant. What effect does this have on U? Equation (10.1.3) shows that it changes U by $f_{11}(\hat{v}) - f_{11}(\bar{v})$. The crucial point is that this amount is independent of the value of any of the subutilities apart from v_{11}.

Equation (10.1.4) also says how much U is affected when v_{11} changes. U changes from

$$W((p_1\bar{v} + V_1'), V_2, V_3, \ldots V_h)$$

to $\qquad W((p_1\hat{v} + V_1'), V_2, V_3, \ldots V_h)$

where V_1' is $(p_2v_{12} + p_3v_{13} + \ldots + p_sv_{1s})$. That is, V_1' is V_1 less p_1v_{11}, the part of V_1 that changes. When v_{11} changes, V_1' and all of V_2, V_3, $\ldots V_h$ stay constant. Now we know that the size of this change in U must be independent of all the subutilities apart from v_{11}. So it must be independent of V_1' and V_2, V_3, $\ldots V_h$. For most forms of the function W, the change in U will certainly not be independent of these things. But suppose W has the special form

$$W(V_1, V_2, \ldots V_h) = a_1V_1 + W_-(V_2, V_3, \ldots V_h),$$

where a_1 is a constant and W_- is any function. Then U will change from

$$a_1(p_1\bar{v} + V_1') + W_-(V_2, V_3, \ldots V_h)$$

to $\qquad a_1(p_1\hat{v} + V_1') + W_-(V_2, V_3, \ldots V_h).$

The size of this change is $a_1p_1(\hat{v} - \bar{v})$, which is independent of V_1' and V_2, V_3, $\ldots V_h$. Furthermore, it should be obvious that this form of the function W is the only one that will make sure the change is independent of these things. Therefore, W has to have this form: the argument V_1 in the function has to be separated out from the other arguments, and multiplied by just a constant.

Next consider the effect on U of a change in v_{21}. Equation (10.1.3) shows that this effect, too, will have to be independent of all the other subutilities. Consequently, the same argument will show that, in the function W, the argument V_2 too, like V_1, has to be separated out from the other arguments and multiplied by just a constant. Indeed, the same will be true of all the arguments. That brings us to the conclusion that W has the linear form

(10.1.5) $\qquad W(V_1, V_2, \ldots V_h) = a_1V_1 + a_2V_2 + \ldots + a_hV_h + b,$

where b and all the a_is are constants. Each a_i will have to be positive because W has to be an increasing function of each V_i.

That is the end of the complicated algebra, so let us now review what it has achieved. From the beginning we knew that, when a person's subutilities are aggregated across states of nature to arrive at her overall utility, they are aggregated in a linear fashion: they are multiplied by probabilities and added up. This is because the person's utilities conform to expected utility theory. We then found that general utility is additively separable, a fact expressed in equation (10.1.3). This additive separability forces some symmetry on aggregation across the dimensions of people and states of nature. It implies that, because subutilities are aggregated linearly across states of nature, then they also have to be aggregated linearly across people. That is what (10.1.5) says.

Step 4

Equation (10.1.1) defined a utility function V_i and a subutility function v_i for the ith person. Take a_i and b from (10.1.5), and use them to define transforms (see page 70) of V_i and v_i:

$$U_i = a_i V_i + b/h,$$
$$u_i = a_i v_i + b/h.$$

These transforms are increasing because a_i is positive. Because U_i is an increasing transform of V_i, it represents the same ordering as V_i (see page 71). Furthermore, the following manipulation (which uses (10.1.1) and the fact that probabilities must add up to one) shows that U_i has the expected utility form.

$$(10.1.6) \qquad U_i = a_i V_i + b/h$$
$$= a_i\{p_1 v_i(x_1) + p_2 v_i(x_2) + \ldots + p_s v_i(x_s)\} + \{p_1 + p_2 + \ldots + p_s\}b/h$$
$$= p_1\{a_i v_i(x_1) + b/h\} + p_2\{a_i v_i(x_2) + b/h\} + \ldots + p_s\{a_i v_i(x_s) + b/h\}$$
$$= p_1 u_i(x_1) + p_2 u_i(x_2) + \ldots + p_s u_i(x_s).$$

U_i, then, is another expectational utility function, besides V_i, that represents i's betterness relation.

Now, U, which represents the general betterness relation, is given by the function $W(V_1, V_2, \ldots V_h)$. By (10.1.5), then,

$$(10.1.7) \quad U = a_1 V_1 + a_2 V_2 + \ldots + a_h V_h + b$$
$$= \{a_1 V_1 + b/h\} + \{a_2 V_2 + b/h\} + \ldots + \{a_h V_h + b/h\}$$
$$= U_1 + U_2 + \ldots + U_h.$$

The general betterness relation, that is to say, is represented by a function U that is the sum of expectational utility functions representing the individual betterness relations.

This is almost the addition theorem. Only one thing more is needed: to show that U is expectational. From (10.1.6) and (10.1.7),

$$
\begin{aligned}
U &= p_1u_1(x_1) + p_2u_1(x_2) + \ldots + p_su_1(x_s) + \\
&\quad p_1u_2(x_1) + p_2u_2(x_2) + \ldots + p_su_2(x_s) + \ldots + \\
&\quad p_1u_h(x_1) + p_2u_h(x_2) + \ldots + p_su_h(x_s) \\
&= p_1\{u_1(x_1) + u_2(x_1) + \ldots + u_h(x_1)\} + \\
&\quad p_2\{u_1(x_2) + u_2(x_2) + \ldots + u_h(x_2)\} + \ldots + \\
&\quad p_s\{u_1(x_s) + u_2(x_s) + \ldots + u_h(x_s)\} \\
&= p_1u(x_1) + p_2u(x_2) + \ldots + p_su(x_s),
\end{aligned}
$$

where the function u is the sum $(u_1 + u_2 + \ldots + u_h)$. And this is the expected utility form (5.1.1) on page 91; the function u is general subutility. So U is expectational. Notice that this is so only because the probabilities, p_1, p_2 and so on, are the same in everybody's utility functions.

That concludes the proof of the interpersonal addition theorem.

10.2 Connecting dimensions

The rest of this chapter asks what can be learnt from the theorem. The answer depends on what construction we can place on the people's utilities U_i and their subutilities u_i.

A preliminary remark. We know from Section 6.4 that each person's betterness relation will be represented by a whole family of expectational utility functions, not just one. So will the general betterness relation. The utilities are cardinal, which means that each member of a family is an increasing linear transform of every other member. Now look again at the statement of the interpersonal addition theorem on page 202. The theorem does not say you can take *any* function from each person's family, and have it turn out that adding these functions together, one for each person, will produce an expectational function representing general betterness. It says you can select *one* function from each person's family in such a way that these functions will add up to make an expectational function representing general betterness.

The theorem tells us that there is one function for each person that will work this trick. But it gives us no guidance about which one. That will have to come from elsewhere. We shall be in a better position to know where when we have a better understanding of what the utility functions mean.

The first thing the interpersonal addition theorem does is connect together the aggregation of good across the two dimensions of people and states of nature. The same utility functions are added together in both types of aggregation. The functions are defined to represent what is good for the people in the face of uncertainty, but the theorem shows that they also determine what is good in aggregation across people.

To see the point more sharply, remember one thing first from page 140. Just as the utility functions U and U_i represent the general and individual betterness relations for prospects, the subutility functions u and u_i represent these relations for outcomes. Since utility and subutility therefore play such closely parallel roles, I shall now revert to my practice of calling both 'utility' and leaving the context to distinguish.

The addition theorem says that the general utility of a prospect is the sum of its individual utilities. It follows that the general utility of an outcome is the sum of its individual utilities:

$$u(x) = u_1(x) + u_2(x) + \ldots u_h(x).$$

An outcome has no uncertainty in it. It might, for instance, be a particular distribution of income amongst people. The goodness of an outcome is a matter of weighing the good of different people against each other. This formula tells us what will result from this weighing across the dimension of people. It is determined by people's utility functions.

But these functions *also* determine the goodness of risky prospects for each person. For the ith person, the goodness of the prospect $(x_1, x_2, \ldots x_s)$ is:

$$U_i(x_1, x_2, \ldots x_s) = p_1 u_i(x_1) + p_2 u_i(x_2) + \ldots + p_s u_i(x_s).$$

This is a matter of weighing the good of the ith person across the dimension of states of nature. So the very same cardinal utility functions determine how good is weighed across the two dimensions. (Compare Section 4.3, which reached a parallel conclusion for a much simpler example.)

That is the first consequence of the addition theorem. It is one of the principal conclusions that Harsanyi wished to draw from his original version of the theorem.[3] It is similar to the conclusion he drew from his earlier argument discussed in Section 3.3. But the earlier argument is vulnerable to the objections I raised in that section. It deduces its conclusion about the weighing of good across people from the decisions people would make on their own behalf if placed behind a veil of ignorance. And that deduction is not adequately justified. The new argument from the addition theorem, on the other hand, has nothing to do with a veil of ignorance. It deduces its conclusion simply from the complex interconnections of actual betterness relations.

The conclusion is certainly a remarkable one. By adopting a simplifying assumption, I can make it more concrete. I shall assume for the moment that people's good is an arithmetic quantity. I made this assumption in Chapter 9, and a comparison with that chapter will be useful.

I shall write the ith person's good as g_i. One outcome is at least as good for i as another if and only if it has at least as great a utility u_i. So increasing g_i means increasing u_i: u_i is an increasing function of g_i. We may write it $u_i(g_i)$. Figure 10 is a graph of this function. I have drawn it curving downwards: the function is strictly concave. Section 4.3 explains that strict concavity implies risk aversion about good. More accurately, now we are dealing with betterness relations, it implies that risk is bad for the ith person. In general, the form of the function $u_i(g_i)$ is a matter of the goodness or badness for i of risk to i's good.

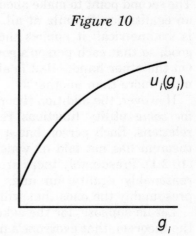

Figure 10

The addition theorem says that, for any outcome

(10.2.1) $$u = u_1(g_1) + u_2(g_2) + \ldots + u_h(g_h).$$

Let us compare this with the egalitarian formulae given in Chapter 9, particularly with (9.3.1) on page 188 and (9.3.2) on page 189.

Equation (10.2.1) makes general utility an additively separable function of individual good. So, first of all, it rules out communal egalitarianism, apart from the additively separable sort. It rules out (9.3.2), for instance. This should not be a surprise. The example discussed in Section 9.3 showed that non-additively-separable communal egalitarianism is incompatible with the principle of personal good. I said on page 189 that this example showed the interpersonal addition theorem at work. The theorem assumes the principle of personal good, and it derives the conclusion that non-additively-separable communal egalitarianism is false.

I think this conclusion is correct. However, the addition theorem cannot claim the credit for it. The theorem shows that non-additively-separable communal egalitarianism is inconsistent with the principle of personal good. But, at the point in Chapter 9 where the two came into conflict, the only defence I had to offer for the latter was to argue independently against the former. I established the principle of personal good, a premise of the addition theorem, only by independently showing that non-additively-separable communal egalitarianism is false. The argument against non-additively-separable communal egalitarianism is therefore in Chapter 9, and not in the addition theorem.

The second point to make about (10.2.1) is that it is not necessarily an egalitarian formula at all. Compare it with (9.3.1). The latter is symmetrical: it applies the same function w to each person's good, so that each person's good counts the same in general good. On the other hand, (10.2.1) allows one person's good to count for much more than another's.

However, the addition theorem tells us that (10.2.1) is true only for *some* utility functions representing the people's betterness relations. Each person has a family of utility functions, and the theorem has not told us which member of the family appears in (10.2.1). Presumably there are functions that would make (10.2.1) reasonably egalitarian and, if equality is valuable, these are presumably the ones that will appear.

Let us suppose, for the sake of drawing out the implications of the theorem, that everyone's utility function u_i in (10.2.1) happens to be the same, say $\bar{u}$. Then (10.2.1) becomes

$$(10.2.2) \qquad u = \bar{u}(g_1) + \bar{u}(g_2) + \ldots + \bar{u}(g_h).$$

In this case, general utility is a symmetrical function of people's good. Remember that $\bar{u}$ is an expectational utility function for each person. So its form is determined by what is good for each person in the face of uncertainty. Suppose risk to good happens to be a bad thing. Then $\bar{u}$ will be strictly concave. We shall end up with a function for general utility that is the same in form as (9.3.1). It is a communal egalitarian function. It implies that, of two outcomes that have the same total of people's good, the one in which the good is more equally distributed is the better.

This egalitarian consequence results from the strict concavity of the people's utility functions. And that is the result of the badness of risk. Suppose alternatively that risk is neither good nor bad: two prospects that offer the same expectation of good for a person are always equally good for her. Then the function $\bar{u}$ will be linear. In that case, (10.2.2) tells us that two outcomes are equally good if the total of people's good is the same in each. It supports the utilitarian principle of distribution. If the utility functions were strictly convex, a positively inegalitarian conclusion would emerge from (10.2.2).

Equation (10.2.2), then, associates the value of equality and the value of avoiding risk. It says that equality in the distribution of good between people is good if and only if it is good for a person to avoid risk to her good.

Equation (10.2.2) assumes, though, that everyone has the same utility function. Since the form of a person's utility function represents the goodness or badness of risk to her, this is only possible if risk is good or bad for everyone to the same degree. If it is not, then people's utility functions – indeed their entire families of utility functions – will differ. Then no very clearly egalitarian conclusion will emerge from (10.2.1).

Speaking vaguely, one might still perhaps say that strictly concave functions have a tendency to favour equality. If everyone's function is strictly concave but the functions are not all the same, it is not generally true that, for a given total of good, it is better to have it more equally distributed. Nevertheless, the better off a person is, the less does an increase in her good contribute to general good. Certainly the converse is true: linear and strictly convex functions have no tendency to favour equality. And the form of these functions is a matter of the goodness or badness of risk. So there remains some association between the value of avoiding risk and the value of equality.

This is the concrete result of the conclusion we drew on page 210 that the same utility functions determine how good is aggregated both across the dimension of states and across the dimension of people.

10.3 The utilitarian principle of distribution

Recall from page 142:

> *Bernoulli's hypothesis about good.* One alternative is at least as good for a person as another if and only if it gives the person at least as great an expectation of her good.

Section 6.5 explains that Bernoulli's hypothesis is equivalent to the hypothesis that utility represents good cardinally, and that it implies risk neutrality about good.

If Bernoulli's hypothesis is true, it will greatly expand the significance of the interpersonal addition theorem. The theorem says we can pick one out of each person's family of expectational utility functions in such a way that general utility is the sum of the functions we have picked. It does not tell us which to pick, however. But if Bernoulli's hypothesis is true, one member of each person's family of functions is none other than her good itself, g_i. If that is so, it is hard to doubt this is the one to pick. (An argument on page 217 below enforces this conclusion, and also states it more accurately. What I have just said is a little imprecise.) General utility will then simply be the sum of people's good. One alternative will be at least as good as another if and only if it has at least as great a total of people's good. And this is just the utilitarian principle of distribution.

Bernoulli's hypothesis, then, promises to take us through the addition theorem to the utilitarian principle of distribution. This would imply, for one thing, the defeat of communal egalitarianism. Communal egalitarianism, as I explained on page 178, denies the utilitarian principle. That is the significance of Bernoulli's hypothesis in this chapter. The utilitarian principle of distribution is a second implication that Harsanyi wished to draw from his original version of the addition theorem.[4] This implication, we now see, requires Bernoulli's hypothesis as well as the theorem.

Section 10.2 made a connection between the badness of risk and the goodness of equality. To this, Bernoulli's hypothesis adds the claim that risk is actually not bad but neutral. It consequently implies that equality (in the distribution of good) is also neutral. Neutrality about equality is the hallmark of the utilitarian principle of distribution. This is how Bernoulli's hypothesis comes to support the utilitarian principle.

The question remains: is Bernoulli's hypothesis true? On this now hangs the more vital question: is the utilitarian principle of distribution true?

At the end of Section 6.5, I left the truth of Bernoulli's hypothesis unsettled. I did describe one way of defending it, though. When we compare the goodness or badness of uncertain prospects, we have to weigh possible gains of good in some states of nature against possible losses in others. Utility is defined to embody the results of this sort of weighing across states of nature. And it is plausible that this sort of weighing also determines our quantitative notion of good. If so, utility will represent good cardinally. Quantities of good will be determined in such a way that Bernoulli's hypothesis comes out true.

I am sure that a good part of this defence is correct. I cannot see what use we can have for the notion of quantities of good except when we weigh differences in good in comparing alternatives. So it is in weighing up differences that we can expect the notion to get its meaning. However, we do not weigh goods across the dimension of states of nature only. We sometimes also weigh them across people and across time. Either of these dimensions might be the meaning-giving one, where the metric of good is determined. If so, quantities of good might be determined in a way that conflicts with utility, and Bernoulli's hypothesis might turn out false.

So let us now consider weighing in these other dimensions, starting with weighing across people.

Weighing across people

Take the example shown in Table 24, which is exactly parallel to Table 19 on page 146. To determine which of the distributions in Table 24 is better, one person's good has to be weighed against the other's. The consideration in favour of distribution A is that it gives P £100 instead of £20. In favour of B is that it gives Q £320 instead of £200. How should these conflicting considerations be weighed?

Here we can turn to the interpersonal addition theorem. This theorem says we can find the right weights from the people's utility functions. To do so, we have to make sure that for each person we have picked the appropriate one of her utility functions.

Table 24

People		People	
P	Q	P	Q
£100	£200	£20	£320

Distribution A Distribution B

Each person has a family of functions, and the theorem does not say which is the right one to pick. But it does say there is a right one. And once we have it, differences in utility determine the weights that should be given to the opposing considerations. Once we have the appropriate functions u_P and u_Q, we know from the theorem that the better distribution is the one that gives the greater total of utility. So we compare the totals:

$$\{u_P(100) + u_Q(200)\} \text{ with } \{u_P(20) + u_Q(320)\}.$$

This is equivalent to comparing the utility differences:

$$\{u_P(100) - u_P(20)\} \text{ with } \{u_Q(320) - u_Q(200)\}.$$

So these utility differences tell us the weights that the people's good has in determining the overall goodness of the distribution. Suppose, for instance, that the two utility differences are equal. Then the difference in P's good between £100 and £20 counts for exactly as much as the difference in Q's good between £320 and £200, in the weighing-up of good across the dimension of people.

If this is the dimension in which the notion of the quantity of good is determined, then the fact that the two differences in good *count* the same will imply that they actually *are* the very same difference in good: the difference in P's good between £100 and £20 is the same as the difference in Q's good between £320 and £200.

But consider what a communal egalitarian would say about this. I have already dealt with non-additively-separable communal egalitarianism in Section 10.2. So take an additively separable egalitarian. She believes that the goodness of alternatives such as A and B is determined from people's good by the formula (9.3.1) on page 188. For our two people, the formula is:

$$u = w(g_P) + w(g_Q),$$

where w is a strictly concave function. In this formula, g_P and g_Q are the people's good, and the function w determines how their good g_P and g_Q counts in determining overall good. Since w is strictly concave, a given increase in a person's good counts for less, the more good she already has. The quantity of good and how much good counts are clearly different things, this communal egalitarian would say. Indeed, as I explained on page 198, additively separable egalitarianism is really the priority view, and the whole point of the priority view is that the same amount of good received by different people counts differently towards general good. To suppose that good and how much good counts are the same is simply to take for granted the utilitarian principle of distribution

$$u = g_P + g_Q,$$

which does not distinguish between quantities of good and how much those quantities count.

The addition theorem, however, gives a special strength to the opposing argument, which the communal egalitarian has missed. The theorem tells us that it is people's utility functions that determine how much the people's good counts in weighing across the dimension of people. These are expectational utility functions. So, as I explained in Section 6.5, they *also* tell us how much the people's good counts in weighing across the dimension of states of nature, when evaluating uncertain prospects. The very same functions give the weights in weighing across two different dimensions. This very much strengthens the claim that they determine the meaning of quantities of good. The same quantities are what *count* in two different dimensions, and this strongly suggests that they actually *are* quantities of good. A distinction between quantities of good and how much those quantities count now seems very empty. If I understand him, this is Harsanyi's argument in his two papers entitled 'Nonlinear social welfare functions'.

The priority view depends on this distinction. It must, therefore, supply a way of giving meaning to quantities of good, independently of how much they count. And, up to this point in the argument, it has not done so.

So the addition theorem helps to support Bernoulli's hypothesis. And then, having supported it, it derives from it the utilitarian principle of distribution. So the theorem has a double role in defending the utilitarian principle.

Furthermore, weighing across people provides another buttress for this principle. Bernoulli's hypothesis and the addition theorem together imply the utilitarian principle, but they need one extra assumption to do so. That emerged on page 214. Bernoulli's hypothesis tells us that utility represents good cardinally. That is to say, within each person's family of utility functions there is one that is actually the person's good itself. The interpersonal addition theorem tells us that *some* function out of each person's family, when added to some function out of each other person's, goes to determine general good. The extra assumption is that this particular function is the one that is the person's good. I said on page 214 that this seems almost inevitable. But the argument I have since gone through puts it beyond doubt. According to the argument, the utility that the theorem tells us goes to make up general good is the very utility that determines the meaning of quantities of good. So it cannot fail to be the one, out of the person's family, that is actually her good.

However, this remark is oversimplified. On page 146, I explained that, if weighing across states of nature determines our quantitative notion of good, any of a person's expectational utility functions can measure her good equally well. There is no single one of them that is actually the person's good. But the previous paragraph assumed there is.

So here is a more accurate statement of the point. The interpersonal addition theorem tells us that the general betterness relation is represented by a general utility function with the form

$$U = (u_1 + u_2 + \ldots + u_h).$$

U is an additively separable function. Consequently, we know from the uniqueness theorem on page 74 that another additively separable function

$$V = (v_1 + v_2 + \ldots + v_h)$$

will represent the same general betterness relation if and only if v_1, v_2 and so on are increasing linear transforms of u_1, u_2 and so on, with the same scaling factor. Suppose we select a set of utility functions, one for each person, by the condition that the functions fit the addition theorem: that they add up to make a function representing the general betterness relation. This condition does not pick out just one set of functions, but many sets, each related to the others by increasing linear transformations with the same scaling factor. We may say that the addition theorem determines people's utilities *cocardinally*. (See page 75.)

Now, our idea is that utilities given by the theorem determine the quantitative notion of good for people. So good will be determined cocardinally. Any of the sets of utility functions picked out by the theorem can equally well measure people's good. Let us select one set arbitrarily. The individual utilities in this set will measure individual good, so the total of people's utilities will measure the total of people's good. The addition theorem tells us that the total utility represents general betterness. The total of good therefore represents general betterness. That is to say: one alternative is better than another if and only if it has a greater total of people's good. And this is the utilitarian principle of distribution.

Weighing across times

There is a good case, then, for thinking that the addition theorem brings the utilitarian principle of distribution in its train. Still, we have not yet reached the end of the argument. A communal egalitarian has a rejoinder up her sleeve. She may concede that the metric of good has to be fixed by the weighing-up of goods. But there is one more dimension of weighing to consider: the dimension of time. Perhaps this is where quantities of good get their meaning. When the goods that come to a person at different times are weighed to determine the person's overall good, how is that done? It might yet turn out to give good a metric that defeats Bernoulli's hypothesis. On the other hand, if it should turn out that expectational utility determines how good is weighed in the dimension of time too, as well as in the other two dimensions, that would make Bernoulli's hypothesis almost irresistible. And the utilitarian principle of distribution would follow.

We need next, therefore, to look at the weighing of goods across the dimension of time. That is the subject of Chapter 11. But I have some other things to say first.

Interpersonal comparisons of good

Just suppose, for the moment, that the argument was complete, and the utilitarian principle of distribution could, indeed, be derived from the addition theorem. What would that tell us?

First, it might tell us something about the vexed question of interpersonal comparisons of good. Many people believe that one person's good cannot be compared in quantity with another's.[5] Yet I have been suggesting that the addition theorem will provide a basis of comparison. It will determine whether a difference in one person's good is more or less than a difference in another person's. In the example of Table 24, whether distribution A is better or worse than B will determine whether the difference in P's good between £100 and £20 is more or less than the difference in Q's good between £320 and £200. Does this provide an argument against the view that interpersonal comparisons of good are impossible? John Harsanyi seems to suggest as much in *Rational Behavior and Bargaining Equilibrium*?[6] But the answer is no. The possibility of interpersonal comparisons of good is an assumption of the theorem, not a conclusion. The theorem assumes that the general betterness relation is coherent, and that includes an assumption that it is complete. If one person's good cannot be compared with another's, then the general betterness relation will simply not be complete. Distribution *A* in Table 24 may be neither better nor worse than *B*, nor equally as good as *B* either. If so, the comparison of *A* and *B* evidently gives no basis for an interpersonal comparison of the people's good.

However, *if* one person's good can be compared with another's, the argument I have gone through does say something about the nature of the comparison. I said that the weighing up of goods across people helps to determine the metric of people's good. As we form a judgement about whether a particular benefit to one person *counts* for more or less than some other particular benefit to someone else, we are at the same time determining whether it *is* a greater or lesser benefit. To say one benefit 'counts for more' than another means it is better to bring about this benefit rather than the other. So this is an ethical judgement. Ethical judgements help to determine our metric of good, then. In 'The moral basis of interpersonal comparisons', T. M. Scanlon argues that interpersonal comparisons of good cannot be independent of value judgements. This is an example of that point. But I do not want to suggest that the determination must all go in one direction. It is not as though, when we make ethical comparisons of distributions across people, the betterness ordering of the distributions must be given in advance, so that we simply find out from this ordering the quantitative scales of good for individuals. To some extent we may already have an idea of how one person's good compares with another's, which we can use to form judgements about the goodness of alternative distributions, and to some extent we may already have an idea of what distributions are better than others. These two ideas need to be brought into line. Together they will determine a betterness ordering for distributions, and a metric of good for people.[7]

The value of equality

The question of whether the addition theorem supports the utilitarian principle of distribution has been hotly disputed. Amartya Sen, for one, has gone to some trouble to argue it does not.[8] But although I shall pursue this question further in Chapter 11, it is time to recognize that, by this point in the discussion, not very much is still at stake.

Why should anyone need to deny that the addition theorem implies the utilitarian principle? The utilitarian principle seems to repudiate the value of equality. But there are some decent egalitarian positions open even to someone who concedes that the addition theorem implies the utilitarian principle.

For one thing, she could be a non-additively-separable communal egalitarian. She could adopt some sensible-seeming formula, such as (9.3.2) on page 189. This position requires her to deny the utilitarian principle, as does any communal egalitarian view. But it also requires her to deny a premise of the addition theorem: the principle of personal good. Non-additively-separable communal egalitarianism is inconsistent with this principle, as I explained in Section 9.3. It therefore has no need to deny that the addition theorem implies the utilitarian principle. Because I believe in the principle of personal good, I think this position is unsatisfactory, and I argued against it in Section 9.4. But it is not ruled out by the addition theorem.

Alternatively, she could be a pure individualistic egalitarian, as I defined this view on page 181. This is the position I recommend. Individualistic egalitarianism is, I have argued, the most successful sort of egalitarianism anyway; it captures the value of equality better than communal egalitarianism. It is pure if it accepts the utilitarian principle, and it loses nothing by doing so.

The one position that is ruled out, if the addition theorem implies the utilitarian principle, is additively separable egalitarianism. An additively separable egalitarian accepts the premises of the addition theorem, but she denies the utilitarian principle of distribution. So if the addition theorem implies the utilitarian principle, her position is untenable. The only question now at issue in our discussion, then, is whether additively separable egalitarianism is tenable. This is not a pointless question. Additively separable egalitarianism represents the priority view. It is the view that, in distributing good amongst people, priority should be given to the worse off. So the question is whether the priority view is tenable.

Still, the argument of this section shows how little there is at stake even in this. To someone who adopts the priority view, the truth of the utilitarian principle seems the central issue of equality. For her, the distributions of income, resources or other material things are all peripheral issues. She is concerned with the distribution of the thing that ultimately matters: people's good. And the utilitarian principle denies that the worse off should be given priority in the distribution of this thing. So it seems to her vital to refute the utilitarian principle. But the argument about the utilitarian principle in this section has been about mere meaning.

If it should turn out in the end to confirm the principle, that will be simply because the quantity of people's good acquires its meaning in such a way that the total of people's good is equal to general good. It is only possible to give extra weight to the good of worse-off people if we have a metric of good that is independent of the weight we give it. But the argument of this section denies that good has such a metric. If the priority view should turn out to be untenable, that would not be the failure of a substantive view that the good of worse-off people deserves priority. It would simply be because we have no metric for a person's good that is independent of the priority we assign it.

If the argument succeeds, therefore, it will not be a blow against equality. It will merely show that the important issues about equality lie elsewhere. They are not to do with the distribution of good, but with the distribution of those other things that at first seemed peripheral, like income. These things have a natural metric of their own.

Nevertheless, the utilitarian principle of distribution still deserves investigation. I shall pursue the question of its truth, from a new angle, in Chapter 11.

Notes

1. Scanlon, in 'Contractualism and utilitarianism', p. 110, suggests that the utilitarian principle of distribution might follow from the principle of personal good alone, but this is not so.

2. Other proofs, conducted within various different versions of expected utility theory, appear in Border, 'More on Harsanyi's cardinal welfare theorem', in my 'Bolker–Jeffrey expected utility theory', in Deschamps and Gevers, 'Separability, risk-bearing and social welfare judgements', in Fishburn, 'On Harsanyi's utilitarian cardinal welfare theorem', in Hammond, 'Ex-ante and ex-post welfare optimality under uncertainty', in Hammond, 'Ex-post optimality as a dynamically consistent objective for collective choice under uncertainty', and in Harsanyi, 'Cardinal welfare, individualistic ethics, and interpersonal comparisons of utility'. The proof in this section is Hammond's, from the second of his papers listed above.

3. 'Cardinal welfare, individualistic ethics, and interpersonal comparisons'.

4. In 'Morality and the theory of rational behaviour', Harsanyi offers his theorem as direct support for the utilitarian principle.

5. A view like this is expressed by W. S. Jevons in *The Theory of Political Economy*, p. 85.

6. pp. 81–2.

7. If I understand it, this is Richard Jeffrey's suggestion in 'On interpersonal utility theory'.

8. For instance, in 'Welfare inequalities and Rawlsian axiomatics', 'Non-linear social welfare functions', and 'Utilitarianism and welfarism'. See also Harsanyi's response: 'Nonlinear social welfare functions: a rejoinder to Professor Sen'.

Chapter 11

Utilitarian Metaphysics?

In Section 10.3, I was exploring the grounds of the utilitarian principle of distribution. I was asking whether, in particular, the principle could be derived from the interpersonal addition theorem. I had reached the point where I needed to examine the aggregation of good across the dimension of time. That is the object of this chapter.

Section 11.1 sets out an intertemporal addition theorem, the exact analog, across the dimension of time, of the interpersonal addition theorem. A premise of the new theorem is the 'principle of temporal good', the exact analog of the principle of personal good. It turns out that the principle of temporal good would, if true, give crucial support to the utilitarian principle. But Section 11.2 explains that the principle of temporal good is, on the face of it, dubious. Section 11.3, on the other hand, describes how this principle might nevertheless be defended. The defence is metaphysical. It is founded on a disuniting metaphysics of personhood, which I first introduced in Chapter 3. Section 11.3 completes a chain of argument extending from a disuniting metaphysics to the utilitarian principle of distribution. Section 11.4 draws conclusions.

11.1 The intertemporal addition theorem

Take a person, and divide her life into a number of 'times'. I shall discuss on page 227 the principles that should guide the division. Each time may last for a while; it may be a period rather than a moment. And now, for some particular time, consider the person's 'dated betterness relation' for that time, the relation

224

___ is at least as good as ___ for the person at the time.

Each blank is to be filled in with a prospect, as before.

One might doubt the existence of dated betterness relations. But we do often speak of how good things are for a person at one time or another. For instance, we might say that a vaccination is bad for you at the time it is done, because it makes you ill for a while, but it is good for you in the long run. To be sure, we might be a little reluctant to say it is bad for you at the time it is done. If we think it is actually good for *you*, that may make us reluctant to say it is bad for you at any time. But I think this reluctance is easily overcome. There is really no difficulty in recognizing that the vaccination may be bad for you at one time, even though the badness may be outweighed by a greater benefit later. So I think there is no real difficulty in recognizing the existence of dated betterness relations.

My expression 'at least as good for the person at the time' may be misleading. A dated betterness relation relates uncertain prospects; it is probability-relative. I explained on page 131 that we must maintain a context of fixed probabilities. As time passes, new information will become available, and no doubt probabilities will change. But my dated betterness relations, whatever date they are attached to, are always to be understood relative to the same constant probabilities. The natural probabilities to use are those prevailing at the time the assessment of betterness is made. Vaccinating a child against measles is better for the child five years afterwards than not vaccinating her, because she is less likely to catch measles at that time. Certainly, if the vaccination damages the child's brain, it may turn out worse for her five years afterwards, relative to the probabilities then prevailing. But that is another matter.

The real worry about dated betterness relations is not, I think, whether they exist, but whether they capture all that is good or bad for a person. The claim that they do is expressed in this

> *Principle of Temporal Good.* (a) If two alternatives are equally good for a person at every time, they are equally good for her, and (b) if one alternative is at least as good as another for the person at every time and definitely better for her at some time, it is better for her.

Roughly: all good is dated. This principle is the main subject of this chapter. I shall consider arguments for and against it. But first, in the rest of this section, I shall explain its importance.

Each of a person's dated betterness relations conforms to the sure-thing principle. This follows from a simple extension of the arguments of Section 6.3. In that section, I showed the coherence of a person's undated betterness relation. I took the arguments about rationality from Chapter 5 and applied them to a particular class of reasons: reasons directed at the good of the person. Now I can take the same arguments and apply them to an even narrower class: reasons directed at the good of a particular person at a particular time. I assume this principle

A prospect *A* is at least as good as another *B* for a person at a time if and only if the reasons directed towards the good of the person at the time for preferring *A* to *B* are at least as strong as the reasons directed towards the good of the person at the time for preferring *B* to *A*.

The argument of Section 6.3 then quickly establishes the sure-thing principle for dated betterness relations.

It is, as usual, a matter of logic that each dated betterness relation is transitive. But, as usual (see page 136), I have to mention a doubt that dated betterness relations are necessarily complete. Subject to that qualification, though, these relations are coherent.

This is a true theorem:

The intertemporal addition theorem. If a person's betterness relation is coherent, and so are all her dated betterness relations, and if the principle of temporal good is true, then the person's betterness relation can be represented by an expectational utility function that is the sum of expectational utility functions representing her dated betterness relations.

The intertemporal addition theorem is exactly parallel to the interpersonal addition theorem on page 202. The proof is exactly the one given in Section 10.1, with the appropriate reinterpretation. The two addition theorems together give us:

The combined addition theorem. Suppose the general betterness relation is coherent, and so is each person's betterness relation, and so are all of each person's dated betterness relations. And suppose that the principle of personal good is true, and so is the principle of temporal good for each person. Then the general betterness relation can be represented by a utility function that is the sum of utility functions representing each person's betterness relation. And each of these in turn is the sum of utility functions representing the person's dated betterness relations.

Now is the moment to discuss the division of a person's life into times. Times, as I call them, can be periods of any length, and together they must constitute a partition of the whole life. The division can be done in any number of different ways, and we are free to choose one that suits our argument. We may choose a way that is most likely to make the premises of the intertemporal addition theorem come out true. The most contentious premise is the principle of temporal good. This principle may or may not be credible in the end, but the freedom to slice up times as we choose gives it some help. Presumably it will be most plausible if we take each time to be a long period of life. The longer the periods, the more likely are the goods that come to a person to show up within one or another individual period. Unfortunately, however, we are not free to take the whole of life as just one period. The proof of the intertemporal addition theorem requires there to be at least two times, just as the interpersonal addition theorem requires at least two people (see page 205). A partition into just a few times is likely to be the most successful.

The continuity of time is a disanalogy between the dimension of time and the dimension of people. But it makes no difference to the formal analysis. To apply the theorems, time is anyway chopped into a discrete number of times. A continuous dimension is not a novelty at this stage of the argument; we have been dealing with one all along. The dimension of states of nature is continuous. For instance, the possible temperatures on Mount Washington at three o'clock tomorrow form a continuous range. For convenience I have always dealt with a finite number of discrete states of nature. In effect, I have partitioned the complete set of states into a finite partition, and then treated each member of the partition as a state on its own. Now I am doing the same with time.

The intertemporal and combined addition theorems take as their premises the coherence of the various betterness relations, and the principles of personal and temporal good. I have claimed (setting aside doubts about completeness), that the betterness relations are coherent. And I have claimed that the principle of personal good is true. So the truth of the conclusions of these addition theorems turns on the principle of temporal good.

Suppose the conclusions *are* true; what would that tell us? Look back to Section 10.3, and particularly to page 217. There I explained that the same utility functions supply the weights when good is aggregated across both the dimensions of people and states of nature. That was the consequence of the interpersonal addition theorem. Our new theorems tell us that the same utility functions supply the weights in aggregation across the *three* dimensions of time, people and states of nature. This follows from a simple extension of the arguments in Section 10.3. If it is true, it will make it very hard to resist the conclusion that these functions represent quantities of good. I can think of no other context where the notion of quantities of good could get its meaning. Whenever there is weighing up to be done, according to the theorems, the total of utility always determines what is best. The same utilities always determine how much good counts in every context. In these circumstance, it would surely be impossible to maintain a distinction between good and how much good counts. Utility, which says how much good counts, would represent actual quantities of good. And, given that, the utilitarian principle of distribution will follow.

If the principle of temporal good is true, then, it will make the utilitarian principle of distribution irresistible. That is the significance of the principle.

11.2 The principle of temporal good

The prima-facie evidence is against the principle of temporal good. It is easy to think of things that seem to be good for a person without being good for her at any particular time. One example is success. Suppose someone works to achieve a particular aim, and succeeds. Her success seems, prima facie, to be good for her. But it is often hard to know at what date it can be good for her. Derek Parfit[1] mentions the example of a person who works for much of her life to save Venice from the sea. If Venice really is saved, this will make her work worthwhile, whereas if Venice is eventually swamped her work will have been pointless. That her work is worthwhile seems good for her, but it is hard to know when she receives this good. Whether or not Venice is saved may not even be determined until after her death.

But examples like this are inconclusive. Someone who believes in the principle of temporal good can deal with them in either of two ways. She can deny that there really are goods of this sort. For instance, she might deny that success – as opposed to feeling successful or believing you are successful – is really a good. Or else she can assign some date to the good. For instance, she might date the good of success to all the dates when a person is working for it.

I have a different sort of example, which links the dimensions of time and uncertainty. Suppose there are only two times, and compare the pair of prospects for a person shown in Table 25. The

Table 25

| | States of nature | | | | States of nature | |
	H	*T*			*H*	*T*
Times				Times		
S	2	1		*S*	2	1
T	2	1		*T*	1	2

Prospect *A*   Prospect *B*

numbers show the quantities of good that come to the person at the times.* Prospects *A* and *B* are equally good for the person at both times, since at both times they each give her an equal chance of 1 or 2 units of good. The principle of temporal good therefore implies that prospects *A* and *B* are equally good for the person. But it is plausible that actually *B* is better for her. *B* gives her, for sure, 3 units of good altogether, whereas *A* gives her either 2 or 4 units. From the point of view of the person's lifetime total of good, *A* is risky and *B* safe. So if there is any value in avoiding risk to the person's good, *B* is better. Its superior value appears from the standpoint of the person as a whole, and does not show up in either of the times in the person's life taken separately. The principle of temporal good, though, says that all good must show up at some particular time. This example suggests that may be wrong.

Compare the example of Table 22 on page 185, which is the

---

* I have shown the amounts of good as numbers, for the sake of analogy with Table 22 on page 185. But this example does not depend on good's being an arithmetic quantity. (Nor, indeed, does the example of Table 22.) All that is required is that '1' and '2' should stand for outcomes that are not equally good for the person at the time.

interpersonal analog of this intertemporal example. In the interpersonal example, prospects *A* and *B* are equally good for each person. So the principle of personal good implies they are equally good. And in that case there is no analogous reason for doubting this conclusion. In the interpersonal example, there is no standpoint analogous to the standpoint of the person as a whole. There is no plausible reason why it should be good to avoid risk to the total good of the two people taken together. The principle of personal good is not threatened by the example in the same way as the principle of temporal good.

The interpersonal example did pose an opposite threat to the principle of personal good. Although it showed no reason to prefer *B* to *A* on grounds of safety, there may seem to be a reason to prefer *A* to *B* on grounds of equality. I considered that possibility at length in Chapter 9, and concluded against it. I concluded in favour of the principle of personal good.

This pair of examples shows up a major disanalogy between the principle of personal good and the principle of temporal good. The latter is on especially shaky ground because prospects can be judged from a standpoint of a person as a whole, a standpoint that links different times together. There is no analogous standpoint that links different people together in the same way.

11.3 The metaphysical argument

Section 11.2 presents a prima-facie case against the principle of temporal good. This section examines whether, nevertheless, the principle can be defended.

One strategy of defence would be to rely on some particular theory of what a person's good consists in. Take, for instance, the theory that a person's good consists in good feelings such as pleasure. All good of this sort occurs at a particular time; a feeling must occur at some time or other. So it may look as though the principle of temporal good would follow from this theory. But actually that is not so. This feeling theory of good says only what the goodness of an *outcome* consists in; it says nothing about the goodness or badness of *risk*. Look again at the example of Table 25. The feeling theory would say that the quantities of good shown in the table must be quantities of good feelings. But it is perfectly consistent with the theory to think that prospect *B* is better than *A*, because from the standpoint of the person as a whole it is less risky. The feeling theory of good is consistent with recognizing the standpoint of the person as a whole. So this theory, at least, cannot support the principle of temporal good. There may be some other theory of good that will do so, but I cannot think of one.

Instead, I am going to examine a different line of defence. On page 167 I declined to pursue a metaphysical defence of the principle of personal good. But in this section I shall examine a metaphysical defence of the principle of temporal good.

This defence sets out from a view that I called on page 42 a *disuniting* metaphysics of personhood. A disuniting metaphysics denies the full unity of a person over time, and instead assimilates the relationships between different times in a person's life to the relationships between different people. 'We regard the rough subdivisions within lives as, in certain ways, like the divisions between lives', says Derek Parfit.[2] It seems plausible that a disuniting theory might be able to give support to the principle of temporal good. It might assimilate the principle of temporal good to the principle of personal good. Since I have argued that the latter is true, this might support the former. Specifically, a disuniting metaphysics might deny the standpoint of the person as a whole. And that standpoint is what first led to doubts about the principle of temporal good in Section 11.2.

On the face of it, the principles of personal good and of temporal good are metaphysically not closely analogous. The principle of personal good is about putting together the good of different things – people. The principle of temporal good is about putting together the good of a single thing – a person – that comes to her at different times. At all times in her life, a person is the same person, one thing. This is what makes available the standpoint of the person as a whole. It is the source of reasonable doubts about the principle of temporal good. Across people, there is nothing analogous to this fact that a person is the same person at all times. There is nothing that is the same at all people.

But a disuniting metaphysical theory makes an analogy where, on the face of it, there is not one. It supposes a person is in some way made up of temporal stages. Each stage is a thing on its own. According to the theory, that a person is the same person at different times means simply that person-stages existing at different times make up a single person. This fact, then, is analogous to the fact that different people make up a single society. And the theory supposes that the good of a person at a time is the good of the person-stage that exists at that time. The principle of temporal good, therefore, is about putting together the good of different things, just like the principle of personal good. With this analogy in place, the reasons that support the latter principle may be able to support the former too.

This, then, is how a metaphysical argument might go. The rest of this section lays out an argument along these lines. It is not, however, a complete argument; it leaves some gaps.

The beginning of the argument must be to establish that people are made up of temporal stages in the first place. In this paper, though, I am not concerned with the merits of the disuniting theory itself; only with its implications.[3] So I shall take this much for granted.

The notion of being made up of is vague. Societies are made up of people and water is made up of molecules, but the relation between a society and its people is not very similar to the relation between water and its constituent molecules. So different disuniting theories are possible, each with its own account of the relation between a person's stages and the person. One view is that this relation is membership, a relation formalized in set theory. Another is that it is the relation of part to whole, a relation formalized in mereology.[4] All the theories, though, must share this implication: the properties of a person must supervene on the properties of her stages.* That is to say: a person could not have been different in any way without any of her stages being different. If she could have, then she could not be said to be made up of her stages.

The principle of temporal good says the good of a person supervenes on her dated goods: her good could not have been different without one of her dated goods being different. (It also

---

* In a trivial sense, this must be so. Suppose the person has the property F. If, instead, she had not had this property, then all of her stages would have been different in at least this respect: they would have had the property of being stages of a person who does not have property F. But I am speaking of supervenience in a nontrivial sense. To define it adequately I would need to rule out in some way such trivial properties of stages. Lewis's way ('New work for a theory of universals', p. 359) would be to define supervenience in terms of the *intrinsic* or nonrelational properties of the stages. But this will not do, at least for my purposes. Whether or not a person has the property of leading a worthwhile life may depend on whether or not she is in love at some time, and we would want this to be consistent with supervenience. Being in love, though, is not an intrinsic property, at least as Lewis understands 'intrinsic'. (See also Lewis, 'Extrinsic properties'.)

says the direction of supervenience is positive: more good for the person implies more good for her at some time. But I shall leave aside the question of direction. This is one of the gaps in the argument that I mentioned.) The disuniting metaphysics treats the person's good at a time as the good of one of her stages. So, granted the metaphysics, the principle of temporal good says the good of a person supervenes on the good of her stages.

The disuniting metaphysics implies, as I say, that the good of a person (being one of her properties) supervenes on the properties of her stages. But that it supervenes on the *good* of her stages is a big further step. Compare a different example. I am made up of my spatial parts. My properties supervene on the properties of my parts. But my good does not supervene on the good of my parts. It is even true that my parts have their own goods: exercise is good for my muscles and fish is said to be good for my brain.[5] But things can be good for me without being good for any of my parts.

The theory that a person is made up of temporal stages, then, is not enough. Something needs to be added to it. Another example shows the sort of thing it needs to be. A society is made up of people. And it is natural to think that the good of the society *does* supervene on the good of its members; nothing can be good for the society without being good for one of its members. This, at any rate, is an implication of the principle of personal good. So what is the difference between the example of me and my spatial parts and the example of a society and its members? It must be something to do with the *way* in which the parts and the members go to make up me and the society. And this must be something to do with the relations amongst them. It must be that my parts are related together in such a way that they make up an aggregate, me, whose good does not supervene on the good of the parts. On the other hand, this must not be true of the members of a society.

So we need to examine the relations between a person's temporal stages. Are they such that the stages form an aggregate, the person, whose good does not supervene on the good of the stages? Could one argue that they do not?

Here is a way. Suppose we add to the disuniting metaphysics a further premise: that the relations between a person's stages in virtue of which the stages make up a person are not significant in respect of good. I shall discuss later whether this premise is defensible. But first I shall show it is enough to give us the argument we are looking for. An outline of the argument is this. If these relations between stages are not significant in respect of good, then it makes no difference to good whether or not a particular collection of stages makes up a person. And this implies that, when a collection does happen to make up a person, this person cannot have a good of her own apart from the good of the stages. What follows fills out this outline.

Some terminology will be useful. I shall call a person's good *autonomous* if it does not supervene on the good of the person's stages. I shall call those relations between a person's stages in virtue of which the stages make up a person the *unifying* relations. And if a relation is significant in respect of good, I shall call it *axiologically* significant.

I need next to define more precisely the notion of axiological significance. What, exactly, is meant by the premise that the unifying relations are not significant in respect of good? Clearly it should be understood counterfactually. A first approach is: if the unifying relations between a person's stages did not hold, then the good and bad in the world would be just as it actually is. This formula, however, picks up causal factors that I do not mean to be picked up. If these relations did not hold, that is likely, for causal reasons, to make a difference to the good of individual stages. Suppose, for instance (as Parfit believes) that amongst the unifying relations are relations of memory. If some wizened person-stage remembers the achievements of some youthful person-stage, that is part of what makes these two stages components of the same person; it is one of the unifying relations. Now, if *this* relation did not hold, so the wizened stage did not have this memory, that stage would probably be less content than it actually is. There would therefore be less good in the world than there actually is. One could say, then, that this relation of memory is axiologically significant in a causal way. But when I say that the unifying relations are not axiologically significant, I do not mean to deny their causal significance. I mean they have no axiological significance *apart* from a causal one.

What I mean by the premise is this: if the unifying relations between a person's stages did not hold, but the good and bad of each stage was just as it actually is, then the good and bad in the world would be just as it actually is. Granted that, we can argue as follows that a person can have no autonomous good.

Take a person, and imagine what it would be like if the unifying relations between her stages did not hold, but the good and bad of each stage remained the same. Imagine, say, that half way through her life, the person was magically swept out of existence, and in her place appeared a new person similar in all respects, who then lived out the rest of her life. The details of the magic required to work this trick will depend on what the unifying relations are, and there are different theories about that. There might have to be an infinitesimal gap in spatio-temporal continuity, say. Or the new person might have to be made out of new matter. Or something else. But, whatever it is, imagine the magic done in such a way that it leaves unaltered the good and bad of every stage. For one thing, all the stages' experiences, including memory-experiences, will have to be the same as the experiences of the actual person.

Now, suppose that the person had an autonomous good independent of the good of her stages. According to our premise, if the magic I described was done, the good or bad in the world would be just as it actually is. So the person's autonomous good would still exist. But there would be no one it could belong to. There would be no one taking the place of this person. Instead there would be a conflation of two people. A conflation is not a person, and it is not the sort of thing that could possibly have an autonomous good. So the person could not have had an autonomous good after all. QED.

This argument leaves something to worry about. The magic it requires may seem to be impossible. It may seem that magic could not possibly sever the unifying relations without altering the good or bad of stages. To put it another way: the premise from which I am arguing is a counterfactual conditional that may seem to have an impossible antecedent. It may seem to be impossible for the unifying relations between the stages of a person not to hold, whilst at the same time the good and bad of each stage remains exactly as it is actually is. We already know this is *causally* impossible, because severing the unifying relations would cause the good or bad of stages to alter. But it may also seem *metaphysically* impossible. Whether or not one takes this view will depend on one's theory of what the good or bad of stages consists in. But here is a plausible example. It might plausibly be claimed that it is bad for a stage to be deceived about its past by its memory-experiences. And the magic will surely cause bads of this sort. After the magic has happened, later stages will have memory-experiences of actions that will lead them to believe these actions were done by earlier stages of the same person. But actually they were not. Because the magic has severed the unifying relations, the person who performed these actions was someone different. So the later stages are deceived by their memory-experiences.

I think, however, that this worry can be overcome. The antecedent of the conditional is not impossible, though it may be a more remote possibility than I have described so far. To explain it, in this paragraph and the next I shall adopt without question David Lewis's modal semantics.[6] If necessary, we can envision the possibility as follows. Take a possible world in which there are *two* perfect duplicates of our person, living duplicate lives on duplicate planets. Call them P and Q. Now consider the collection of stages in this possible world that consists of all the stages from the first half of P's life and all the stages from the second half of Q's life. All of the stages in this collection are counterparts of the corresponding stages in the actual person's life. And I cannot see how the good and bad of each stage in the collection could fail to be just the same as the good and bad of its counterpart. Certainly, no stage in the collection is deceived by its memory-experiences; each will have genuine memories of the actions of earlier stages of the same person. But this collection of counterpart stages in the possible world is not linked by the unifying relations. So the actual stages have counterparts possessing just the same good and bad as themselves, but not linked by the unifying relations. That is what we needed.

Taking the counterfactual in this more elaborate way also makes the final step of my argument particularly clear. If the person had an autonomous good, then so would the collection of counterpart stages in the possible world. But it is particularly clear that this collection is not the sort of thing that can have a good of its own. It is a collection of stages living on different planets.

I conclude, then, that the argument is successful. The premise that the unifying relations are not axiologically significant, taken together with a disuniting metaphysics, implies that a person does not have an autonomous good. Her good supervenes on the good of her stages. This is (apart from the direction of supervenience, which I mentioned on page 233) the principle of temporal good. So it only remains to ask whether the premise can be defended.

I shall not pursue this question far. I shall only mention that Derek Parfit's work[7] provides one model for a defence. It contains extensive arguments about what 'matters' (as Parfit puts it) in the relations between person-stages. Parfit argues for a disuniting metaphysics, and he argues that the unifying relations between a person's stages, in virtue of which they make up a person, are certain psychological connections. He includes connections of memory, intention and so on: one stage of a person remembers what another did, one carries out intentions formed by another, and so on. Normally (excluding science-fictional cases such as the fission of a person), a chain of stages will make up a person if and only if each stage in the chain is connected psychologically in the appropriate way to another.

On Parfit's account, then, our premise amounts to the claim that these psychological connections are not axiologically significant. Parfit calls a view like this 'extreme,' but says it is defensible on the basis of his arguments about what matters.[8] So here is one way the premise might be defended.

Parfit's work also offers another way. Parfit believes that, speaking roughly, a person's life may be divided into periods that are not very closely connected psychologically. An old person is not very closely connected with the young person she once was. These are the 'rough subdivisions within lives' mentioned in the remark I quoted on page 231. Suppose we treat each of these periods as a stage. They are connected psychologically, and they therefore make up a person. But the connections may be weak enough to be axiologically insignificant or at least unimportant. Parfit does not consider this view extreme; it seems to be his own.[9] It is a defence of our premise, if an imprecise one.

I started this section by asking whether the principle of temporal good could be defended on a metaphysical basis. I described a possible defence that sets out from a disuniting metaphysics of personhood. But it turned out that an extra premise would certainly be needed before the principle could be derived: the premise that the unifying relations between a person's stages are not axiologically significant. Now we have found in Parfit's arguments a possible foundation for this premise. If it is a metaphysical foundation, then the whole defence of the principle of temporal good will be metaphysical. But is it? There are two steps to the argument I took from Parfit: first, that the unifying relations are psychological connections; and second, that psychological connections are not axiologically significant. Parfit's case for the first step is purely metaphysical; it is about the nature of a person. But he does not really argue for the second step. It seems likely to me that it will require an ethical argument, not a purely metaphysical one.

11.4 Conclusion

Section 11.3 does not contain a complete argument. But suppose a complete argument *was* made out deducing the principle of temporal good from a disuniting metaphysics. Section 11.1 shows that the principle of temporal good, if true, lends very strong support to the utilitarian principle of distribution. So a chain of argument would have been completed, linking the disuniting metaphysics to the utilitarian principle.

In Sections 3.1 and 3.2, I discussed Parfit's attempt to make this same link. But I argued that it is unsuccessful. The new argument I have developed contains an essential ingredient that is missing from Parfit's: the addition theorems.

The theorems make two essential contributions. Firstly, they make a logical connection between the dimensions of time and people. A disuniting metaphysics is a view about the dimension of time. The utilitarian principle is a view about the dimension of people. The theorems link the two. So they open the way for a tight argument to be made from one to the other. They offer a precise target for the metaphysics to shoot at. It needs to establish the principle of temporal good – nothing more and nothing less. If it can do that, the addition theorems will do the rest.

Without the theorems, the dimensions can only be linked by analogy. I described on page 47 the very heavy demands that an analogical argument makes. There are inevitably disanalogies between the dimensions, but an analogical argument has to show that not one of the disanalogies is distributionally significant. This effectively forces it to show that not one of the relations between the stages that make up a person – including the contingent relations – is axiologically significant. My argument has a corresponding requirement, which emerged in Section 11.3. It has to show that the *unifying* relations are not axiologically significant. The unifying relations are those relations between stages in virtue of which the stages make up a person. They are only a few out of all the relations between stages. So this requirement is much less demanding.

The second contribution of the theorems is simply the additivity. The utilitarian principle says the goodness of an alternative is given by the *total* of people's good. The theorems make sure of that. I explained in Section 3.2 that I can find nothing in Parfit's argument to establish additivity.

Still, my argument is not complete. There are two major gaps in it. There is, first of all, the one I have repeatedly drawn attention to in this book. The addition theorems require the various betterness relations to be coherent. One part of coherence is completeness. And one might easily doubt that betterness relations are complete, because there may be incommensurable goods. This is, I think, much the most serious gap.

The other big gap has only just appeared in Section 11.3. It is the extra premise that needs to be added to the disuniting metaphysics in order to derive the principle of temporal good. The unifying relations must not be axiologically significant. Taking a lead from Parfit, I mentioned some ways this premise might be defended, but I did nothing more than that. A proper defence would be a major task.

I have one point to make about it. I asked on page 237 whether the defence of the premise would be purely metaphysical. I concluded that it probably would not be; it might well require some specifically ethical argument. If so, then my argument does not provide a purely metaphysical basis for the utilitarian principle of distribution. This means it will give some support to a claim of John Rawls's. In 'The independence of moral theory', Rawls argues that moral theory is independent of metaphysical arguments about personhood. He is willing to grant that a particular moral theory, utilitarianism, may be supported by a particular, disuniting, theory of personhood. But he claims that one's theory of personhood will be determined by one's moral theory, and not by independent nonmoral considerations. Now, certainly, a disuniting metaphysics has been defended on nonmoral grounds by Parfit and also by David Lewis.[10] But I am suggesting that the utilitarian moral theory may require the injection of an ethical argument as well as the metaphysics. So moral theory may well retain its independence in this different way.

It is time I revealed my own inclinations. I have been testing out the derivation of the utilitarian principle from a disuniting metaphysics. But I hope no one will assume I am looking for a firm foundation for the utilitarian principle, and hoping that a disuniting metaphysics might provide one. If the utilitarian principle could really be derived from a disuniting metaphysics, that discovery could count either in favour of the principle or against the metaphysics. I am inclined against the metaphysics myself, despite Lewis's and Parfit's arguments, though I have not tried to offer opposing arguments in this book. But I am fascinated by the connection between this metaphysical view and utilitarianism. A disuniting metaphysics of personhood is the commonest, indeed almost the universal, view of economists. Robert Strotz says: 'The individual over time is an infinity of individuals, and the familiar problems of interpersonal utility comparisons are there to plague us.'[11] In speaking of successive selves occupying one body, Thomas Schelling confesses: 'It is only in talking with economists that I feel at all secure in using the terminology of "selves".'[12] In economics, the disuniting metaphysics is closely associated with utilitarianism. The association is clearest in J. A. Mirrlees's 'The economic uses of utilitarianism'. Mirrlees's paper makes use of the addition theorems in its argument, and provided much of the stimulus for this book.

Perhaps the main conclusion I should draw from my argument about the utilitarian principle is that it is a less important argument than appears at first sight. I said this at the end of Chapter 10. The utilitarian principle seems to deny the value of equality. And certainly, it does, in a way, deny the value of equality in the distribution of good. But the most satisfactory sort of egalitarianism embeds the value of equality within the good of individuals. Consequently, an egalitarian need not repudiate the utilitarian principle. The truth of the utilitarian principle becomes, in the end, merely a matter of meaning. It is a matter of choosing a metric for good.

Notes

1. *Reasons and Persons*, p. 151.
2. *Reasons and Persons*, pp. 333–4.
3. For references see note 3 on page 58.
4. Mereology, or 'the calculus of individuals', is described in Goodman, *The Structure of Appearance*, pp. 33–44.
5. This is Jeeves's opinion. Thomas Schelling has a similar view about poultry: 'We probably believe, if we bother to think about it, that ultimately the roast duck that I order is enjoyed in my brain.' ('The mind as a consuming organ', p. 192.)
6. See particularly his 'Counterpart theory'.
7. *Reasons and Persons*, Part III.
8. p. 343.
9. For instance, p. 333.
10. Parfit, *Reasons and Persons*, Part III; Lewis, *Philosophical Papers: Volume 1*, pp. 76–7.
11. 'Myopia and inconsistency', p. 179.
12. 'Self-command', p. 8.

Bibliography

Allais, Maurice, 'The foundations of a positive theory of choice involving risk and a criticism of the postulates and axioms of the American school', in Maurice Allais and Ole Hagen (eds), *Expected Utility Hypothesis and the Allais Paradox*, Reidel, 1979, pp. 27–145. First published in French in 1952.

Allais, Maurice, 'La psychologie de l'homme rationnel devant le risque: la théorie et l'experience', *Journal de la Société de Statistique de Paris*, (1953), pp. 47–73.

Arrow, Kenneth J., *Essays in the Theory of Risk-Bearing*, North-Holland, 1970.

Arrow, Kenneth J., *Social Choice and Individual Values*, Second Edition, Yale University Press, 1963.

Atkinson, Anthony B., 'On the measurement of inequality', *Journal of Economic Theory*, 2 (1970), pp. 244–63.

Atkinson, Anthony B., and Stiglitz, Joseph E., *Lectures on Public Economics*, McGraw–Hill, 1980.

Barry, Brian, *Theories of Justice*, Harvester–Wheatsheaf, 1989.

Bell, Daniel E., 'Disappointment in decision making under uncertainty', *Operations Research*, 33 (1985), pp. 1–27.

Bell, Daniel E., 'Regret in decision making under uncertainty', *Operations Research*, 30 (1982), pp. 961–81.

Bennett, Jonathan, 'Two departures from consequentialism', *Ethics*, 100 (1989), pp. 54–66.

Bentham, Jeremy, *An Introduction to the Principles of Morals and Legislation*, Oxford, 1823. Reprinted by Hafner, 1948.

Bernoulli, Daniel, 'Exposition of a new theory on the measurement of risk', *Commentarii Academiae Scientiarum Imperialis Petropolitanae*, 5 (1738). Translation by Louise Sommer in *Econometrica*, 22 (1954), pp. 23–36. Reprinted in Alfred N. Page (ed.), *Utility Theory: a Book of Readings*, Wiley, 1968, pp. 199–214.

Blackorby, Charles, and Donaldson, David, 'Social criteria for evaluating population change', *Journal of Public Economics*, 25 (1984), pp. 13–33.

Bolker, Ethan D., 'Functions resembling quotients of measures', *Transactions of the American Mathematical Society*, 124 (1966), pp. 292–312.

Bolker, Ethan D., 'A simultaneous axiomatization of utility and subjective probability', *Philosophy of Science*, 34 (1967), pp. 333–40.

Border, K. C., 'More on Harsanyi's cardinal welfare theorem', *Social Choice and Welfare*, 2 (1985), pp. 279–81.

Brandt, Richard, *A Theory of the Good and the Right*, Oxford University Press, 1979.

Broome, John, 'Bolker–Jeffrey expected utility theory and axiomatic utilitarianism', *Review of Economic Studies*, 57 (1990), pp. 477–502.

Broome, John, 'Can a Humean be moderate?', in R. G. Frey and Christopher Morris (eds), *Value, Welfare and Morality*.

Broome, John, 'Choice and value in economics', *Oxford Economic Papers*, 30 (1978), pp. 313–33.

Broome, John, 'The economic value of life', *Economica*, 52 (1985), pp. 281–94.

Broome, John, 'Fairness', *Proceedings of the Aristotelian Society*, 91 (1990–91), pp. 87–102.

Broome, John, 'Rationality and the sure-thing principle', in Gay Meeks (ed.), *Thoughtful Economic Man*, Cambridge University Press, 1991.

Broome, John, 'Should social preferences be consistent?', *Economics and Philosophy*, 5 (1989), pp. 7–17.

Broome, John, 'Some principles of population', in David Collard, David Pearce and David Ulph (eds), *Economics, Growth and Sustainable Environments*, Macmillan, 1988, pp. 85–96.

Broome, John, 'Trying to value a life', *Journal of Public Economics*, 9 (1978), pp. 91–100.

Broome, John, 'Uncertainty and fairness', *Economic Journal*, 94 (1984), pp. 624–32.

Broome, John, 'Utilitarianism and expected utility', *Journal of Philosophy*, 84 (1987), pp. 405–22.

Broome, John, '"Utility"', *Economics and Philosophy*, 7 (1991).

Broome, John, 'What's the good of equality?', in John D. Hey, *Current Issues in Microeconomics*, Macmillan, 1989, pp. 236–62.

Buchanan, J. M., 'Social choice, democracy and free markets', *Journal of Political Economy*, 62 (1954), pp. 114–23.

Clark, M. J., Fleishman, A. B., and Webb, G. A. M., 'Optimisation of the radiological protection of the public', National Radiological Protection Board, paper NRPB-R120.

Dancy, Jonathan, *Moral Reasons*, Blackwell, forthcoming.

Davidson, Donald, *Inquiries Into Truth and Interpretation*, Oxford University Press, 1984.

Debreu, Gérard, 'Representation of a preference ordering by a numerical function', in R. M. Thrall, C. H. Coombs and R. L. Davis (eds), *Decision Processes*, Wiley, 1954, pp. 159–65.

Debreu, Gérard, *Theory of Value*, Wiley, 1959.

Debreu, Gérard, 'Topological methods in cardinal utility theory', in Kenneth J. Arrow, Samuel Karlin and Patrick Suppes (eds), *Mathematical Methods in the Social Sciences, 1959*, Stanford University Press, 1960, pp. 16–26.

Deschamps, Robert, and Gevers, Louis, 'Separability, risk-bearing and social welfare judgements', in Jean-Jacques Laffont (ed.), *Aggregation and Revelation of Preferences*, North-Holland, 1979, pp. 145–60.

Diamond, Peter A., 'Cardinal welfare, individualistic ethics and interpersonal comparisons of utility: comment', *Journal of Political Economy*, 75 (1967), pp. 765–6.

Drèze, Jacques H., 'Axiomatic theories of choice, cardinal utility and subjective probability: a review', in Jacques H. Drèze (ed.), *Allocation Under Uncertainty*, Macmillan, 1974, pp. 3–23.

Dworkin, Ronald, 'What is equality?', *Philosophy and Public Affairs*, 10 (1981), pp. 185–246 and 283–345.

Edgeworth, Francis Y., *Mathematical Psychics*, Kegan Paul, 1881.

Eells, Ellery, *Rational Decision and Causality*, Cambridge University Press, 1982.

Ellingsen, Tore, 'Cardinal utility: a history of hedinometry', typescript, 1990.

Ellsberg, Daniel, 'Classic and current notions of "measurable utility"', *Economic Journal*, 64 (1954), pp. 528–56. Reprinted in Alfred N. Page (ed.), *Utility Theory: a Book of Readings*, Wiley, 1968, pp. 269–96.

Ellsberg, Daniel, 'Risk, ambiguity, and the Savage axioms', *Quarterly Journal of Economics*, 75 (1961), pp. 643–69.

Findlay, J., *Values and Intentions*, Allen and Unwin, 1961.

Fishburn, Peter C., *The Foundations of Expected Utility*, Reidel, 1982.

Fishburn, Peter C., 'On Harsanyi's utilitarian cardinal welfare theorem', *Theory and Decision*, 17 (1984), pp. 21–8.

Fishburn, Peter C., 'On the foundations of decision making under uncertainty', in Michael Balch, Daniel McFadden and S. Wu (eds), *Essays on Economic Behavior Under Uncertainty*, North-Holland, 1974, pp. 25–44.

Fishburn, Peter C., 'Subjective expected utility theory: a review of normative theories', *Theory and Decision*, 13 (1981), pp. 139–99.

Foot, Philippa, 'Utilitarianism and the virtues', *Mind*, 94 (1985), pp. 196–209. Reprinted in Samuel Scheffler (ed.), *Consequentialism and Its Critics*, Oxford University Press, 1988, pp. 224–42. Page references to the reprinted version.

Friedman, Milton, *Capitalism and Freedom*, University of Chicago Press, 1962.

Goodman, Nelson, *The Structure of Appearance*, Third Edition, Reidel, 1977.

Gorman, W. M., 'The structure of utility functions', *Review of Economic Studies*, 35 (1968), pp. 367–90.

Griffin, James, *Well-Being: Its Meaning, Measurement and Moral Importance*, Oxford University Press, 1986.

Haksar, Vinit, *Equality, Liberty and Perfectionism*, Oxford University Press, 1979.

Hammond, Peter J., 'Consequentialist demographic norms and parenting rights', *Social Choice and Welfare*, 5 (1988), pp. 127–45.

Hammond, Peter J., 'Consequentialist foundations for expected utility', *Theory and Decision*, 25 (1988), pp. 25–78.

Hammond, Peter J., 'Ex-ante and ex-post welfare optimality under uncertainty', *Economica*, 48 (1981), pp. 235–50.

Hammond, Peter J., 'Ex-post optimality as a dynamically consistent objective for collective choice under uncertainty', in P. K. Pattanaik and Maurice Salles (eds), *Social Choice and Welfare*, North-Holland, 1983, pp. 175–205.

Hammond, Peter J., 'On reconciling Arrow's theory of social choice with Harsanyi's fundamental utilitarianism', in George R. Feiwel (ed.), *Arrow and the Foundations of the Theory of Economic Policy*, New York University Press, 1987, pp. 179–221.

Hammond, Peter J., 'Utilitarianism, uncertainty and information', in Amartya Sen and Bernard Williams (eds), *Utilitarianism and Beyond*, Cambridge University Press, 1982, pp. 85–102.

Hare, R. M., 'Rights, utility, and universalization: Reply to J. L. Mackie', in R. G. Frey (ed.), *Utility and Rights*, Blackwell, 1984, pp. 106–20.

Harrison, Ross, 'Discounting the future', *Proceedings of the Aristotelian Society*, 82 (1981–2), pp. 45–57.

Harsanyi, John C., 'Cardinal utility in welfare economics and in the theory of risk-taking', *Journal of Political Economy*, 61 (1953), pp. 434–5. Reprinted in his *Essays on Ethics, Social Behavior and Scientific Explanation*, Reidel, 1976, pp. 3–5.

Harsanyi, John C., 'Cardinal welfare, individualistic ethics, and interpersonal comparisons of utility', *Journal of Political Economy*, 63 (1955), pp. 309–21. Reprinted in his *Essays on Ethics, Social Behavior and Scientific Explanation*, Reidel, 1976, pp. 6–23. Page references to the reprinted version.

Harsanyi, John C., 'Morality and the theory of rational behavior', *Social Research*, 44 (1977), pp. 623–56. Reprinted in Amartya Sen and Bernard Williams (eds), *Utilitarianism and Beyond*, Cambridge University Press, 1982, pp. 39–62.

Harsanyi, John C., 'Nonlinear social welfare functions: a rejoinder to Professor Sen', in R. Butts and J. Hintikka (eds), *Foundational Problems in the Special Sciences*, Reidel, 1977, pp. 293–6.

Harsanyi, John C., 'Nonlinear social welfare functions: do welfare economists have a special exemption from Bayesian rationality?', *Theory and Decision*, 6 (1975), pp. 311–32. Reprinted in his *Essays on Ethics, Social Behavior and Scientific Explanation*, Reidel, 1976, pp. 64–85. Page references to the reprinted version.

Harsanyi, John C., *Rational Behavior and Bargaining Equilibrium in Games and Social Situations*, Cambridge University Press, 1977.

Harsanyi, John C., 'Von Neumann–Morgenstern utilities, risk taking, and welfare', in George R. Feiwel (ed.), *Arrow and the Ascent of Modern Economic Theory*, New York University Press, 1987, pp. 545–58.

Haslanger, Sally, 'Persistence, change and explanation', *Philosophical Studies*, 56 (1989), pp. 1–28.

Hurley, S. L., *Natural Reasons*, Oxford University Press, 1989.

Jackson, Frank, 'Decision theoretic consequentialism and the nearest and dearest objection', *Ethics*, forthcoming.

Jackson, Frank, 'A probabilistic approach to moral responsibility', in Ruth Barcan Marcus, Georg J. W. Dorn and Paul Weingartner (eds), *Logic, Methodology and Philosophy of Science VII*, Elsevier, 1986, pp. 351–65.

Jeffrey, Richard C., *The Logic of Decision*, Second Edition, Chicago University Press, 1983.

Jeffrey, Richard C., 'On interpersonal utility theory', *Journal of Philosophy*, 68 (1971), pp. 647–56.

Jeffrey, Richard C., 'Risk and human rationality', *The Monist*, 70 (1987), pp. 223–36.

Jevons, William Stanley, *The Theory of Political Economy*, Penguin, 1970. First edition: Macmillan, 1871.

Kagan, Shelly, 'The additive fallacy', *Ethics*, 99 (1988), pp. 5–31.

Kahneman, Daniel, and Tversky, Amos, 'Prospect theory: an analysis of decision under risk', *Econometrica*, 47 (1979), pp. 263–91.

Kanbur, Ravi, 'The standard of living: uncertainty, inequality and opportunity', in Amartya Sen with others, *The Standard of Living*, edited by Geoffrey Hawthorne, Cambridge University Press, 1987, pp. 59–69.

Kranz, David H., Luce, R. Duncan, Suppes, Patrick, and Tversky, Amos, *Foundations of Measurement: Volume I, Additive and Polynomial Representations*, Academic Press, 1971.

Kymlicka, Will, 'Rawls on teleology and deontology' *Philosophy and Public Affairs*, 17 (1988), pp. 173–90.

Levi, Isaac, 'Conflict and social agency', *Journal of Philosophy*, 79 (1982), pp. 231–47.

Lewis, David, 'Counterpart theory and quantified modal logic', *Journal of Philosophy*, 65 (1968), pp. 113–26. Reprinted with additions in his *Philosophical Papers: Volume 1*, Oxford University Press, 1983, pp. 26–46.

Lewis, David, 'Extrinsic properties', *Philosophical Studies*, 44 (1983), pp. 197–200.

Lewis, David, 'New work for a theory of universals', *Australasian Journal of Philosophy*, 61 (1983), pp. 343–77.

Lewis, David, *On the Plurality of Worlds*, Blackwell, 1986.

Lewis, David, 'Radical interpretation', *Synthese*, 23 (1974), pp. 331–44.

Lewis, David, 'Survival and identity', in Amelie O. Rorty (ed.), *The Identities of Persons*, University of California Press, 1976, pp. 17–40. Reprinted with an addition in his *Philosophical Papers, Volume 1*, Oxford University Press, 1983, pp. 55–77.

Loomes, Graham, and Sugden, Robert, 'Disappointment and dynamic consistency in choice under uncertainty', *Review of Economic Studies*, 53 (1984), pp. 271–82.

Loomes, Graham, and Sugden, Robert, 'The importance of what might have been', in O. Hagen, and F. Wenstøp (eds), *Progress in Utility and Risk Theory*, Reidel, 1984, pp. 219–35.

Loomes, Graham, and Sugden, Robert, 'Regret theory: an alternative theory of rational choice under uncertainty', *Economic Journal*, 92 (1984), pp. 805–24.

McClennen, Edward F., *Rationality and Dynamic Choice*, Cambridge University Press, 1990.

McClennen, Edward F., 'Sure-thing doubts', in B. P. Stigum, and F. Wenstøp (eds), *Foundations of Utility and Risk Theory with Applications*, Reidel, 1983, pp. 117–36.

Machina, Mark J., 'Dynamic consistency and non-expected utility models of choice under uncertainty', in Michael Bacharach and Susan Hurley (eds), *Foundations of Decision Theory: Issues and Advances*, Blackwell, 1991.

Machina, Mark J., '"Expected utility" analysis without the independence axiom', *Econometrica*, 50 (1982), pp. 277–323.

Machina, Mark J., '"Rational" decision making versus "rational" decision modelling', *Journal of Mathematical Psychology*, 24 (1981), pp. 163–75.

Mackie, J. L., *Ethics: Inventing Right and Wrong*, Penguin, 1977.

MacLean, Douglas, 'Rationality and equivalent redescriptions', typescript, 1988.

MacLean, Douglas, 'Social values and the distribution of risk', in Douglas MacLean (ed.), *Values at Risk*, Rowman and Allanheld, 1986, pp. 75–93.

Macrimmon, Kenneth R., and Larsson, Stig, 'Utility theory: axioms versus "paradoxes"', in Maurice Allais and Ole Hagen (eds), *Expected Utility Hypothesis and the Allais Paradox*, Reidel, 1979, pp. 333–409.

Manne, Alan S., 'The strong independence assumption – gasoline blends and probability mixtures', *Econometrica*, 20 (1952), pp. 665–8.

Marshall, Alfred, *Principles of Economics*, Eighth Edition, Macmillan, 1920.

Meyer, Margaret A., and Mookherjee, Dilip, 'Incentives, compensation, and social welfare', *Review of Economic Studies*, 54 (1987), pp. 209–26.

Mirrlees, J. A., 'The economic uses of utilitarianism', in Amartya Sen and Bernard Williams (eds), *Utilitarianism and Beyond*, Cambridge University Press, 1982, pp. 63–84.

Mirrlees, J. A., 'An exploration in the theory of optimum income taxation', *Review of Economic Studies*, 38 (1971), pp. 175–208.

Moore, G. E., *Ethics*, Second Edition, Oxford University Press, 1966.

Moore, G. E., *Principia Ethica*, Cambridge University Press, 1903.

Morton, Adam, *Disasters and Dilemmas*, Blackwell, 1991.

Morton, Adam, 'Hypercomparatives', typescript, 1987.

Myerson, Roger B., 'Utilitarianism, egalitarianism, and the timing effect in social choice problems', *Econometrica*, 49 (1981), pp. 883–97.

Nagel, Thomas, 'Equality' *Critica* (1978). Reprinted in his *Mortal Questions*, Cambridge University Press, 1979, pp. 106–27. Page references to the reprinted version.

Nagel, Thomas, *The Possibility of Altruism*, Oxford University Press, 1970.

Neumann, John von, and Morgenstern, Oskar, *Theory of Games and Economic Behavior*, Second Edition, Princeton University Press, 1944.

Nozick, Robert, *Anarchy, State and Utopia*, Basic Books, 1974. Extract reprinted in Samuel Scheffler (ed.), *Consequentialism and Its Critics*, Oxford University Press, 1988, pp. 134–41.

Pareto, Vilfredo, *Manuel D'Économie Politique*, Second Edition, 1927. Parts translated by Ann Stranquist Schwier in Alfred N. Page (ed.), *Utility Theory: a Book of Readings*, Wiley, 1968, pp. 168–81 and 375–83.

Parfit, Derek, 'Comments', *Ethics*, 96 (1986), pp. 832–72.

Parfit, Derek, *On Giving Priority to the Worse Off*, Oxford University Press, forthcoming.

Parfit, Derek, *Reasons and Persons*, Oxford University Press, 1984.

Pettit, Philip, 'Consequentialism', in Peter Singer (ed.), *A Companion to Ethics*, Blackwell, 1991, pp. 230–40.

Pettit, Philip, 'Decision theory and folk psychology', in Michael Bacharach and Susan Hurley (eds), *Foundations of Decision Theory: Issues and Advances*, Blackwell, 1991.

Pigou, A. C., *The Economics of Welfare*, Fourth Edition, Macmillan, 1932.

Rawls, John, 'The independence of moral theory', *Proceedings and Addresses of the American Philosophical Association*, 48 (1974–5), pp. 5–22.

Rawls, John, *A Theory of Justice*, Harvard University Press, 1971.

Regan, Donald H., 'Against evaluator relativity: a response to Sen', *Philosophy and Public Affairs*, 12 (1983), pp. 93–112.

Samuelson, Paul A., 'Probability, utility and the independence axiom', *Econometrica*, 20 (1952), pp. 670–8. Reprinted in his *Collected Scientific Papers, Volume 1* (edited by Joseph E. Stiglitz), Massachusetts Institute of Technology Press, 1966.

Samuelson, Paul A., 'Utility, preference and probability', in his *Collected Scientific Papers, Volume 1* (edited by Joseph E. Stiglitz), pp. 127–36.

Savage, Leonard J., *The Foundations of Statistics*, Second Edition, Dover, 1972.

Scanlon, T. M., 'Contractualism and utilitarianism', in Amartya Sen and Bernard Williams (eds), *Utilitarianism and Beyond*, Cambridge University Press, 1982, pp. 103–28.

Scanlon, T. M., 'The moral basis of interpersonal comparisons', in Jon Elster and John Roemer (eds), *Interpersonal Comparisons of Well–Being*, Cambridge University Press, 1991.

Scanlon, T. M., 'Rights, goals and fairness', in Stuart Hampshire (ed.), *Public and Private Morality*, Cambridge University Press, 1978, pp. 93–111. Reprinted in Samuel Scheffler (ed.), *Consequentialism and*

Its Critics, Oxford University Press, 1988, pp. 74–92. Page references to the reprinted version.

Scanlon, T. M., 'Preference and urgency', *Journal of Philosophy*, 72 (1975), pp. 655–69.

Scheffler, Samuel (ed.), *Consequentialism and Its Critics*, Oxford University Press, 1988.

Scheffler, Samuel, *The Rejection of Consequentialism: A Philosophical Investigation of the Considerations Underlying Rival Moral Conceptions*, Oxford University Press, 1982.

Schelling, Thomas C., 'The mind as a consuming organ', in Jon Elster (ed.), *The Multiple Self*, Cambridge University Press, 1986, pp. 177–96.

Schelling, Thomas C., 'Self-command in practice, in policy, and in a theory of rational choice', *American Economic Review Papers and Proceedings*, 74 (1984), pp. 1–11.

Schultz, Bart, 'Persons, selves and utilitarianism', *Ethics*, 96 (1986), pp. 721–45.

Schumm, George F., 'Transitivity, preference and indifference', *Philosophical Studies*, 52 (1986), pp. 435–7.

Seidenfeld, Teddy, Kadane, Joseph B., and Schervish, Mark J., 'On the shared preferences of two Bayesian decision makers', *Journal of Philosophy*, 86 (1989), pp. 225–44.

Sen, Amartya, 'Liberty and social choice', *Journal of Philosophy*, 80 (1983), pp. 5–28.

Sen, Amartya, 'Non-linear social welfare functions: a reply to Professor Harsanyi', in R. Butts and J. Hintikka (eds), *Foundational Problems in the Special Sciences*, Reidel, 1977, pp. 297–302.

Sen, Amartya, 'Rationality and uncertainty', *Theory and Decision*, 18 (1985) pp. 109–27.

Sen, Amartya, 'Rights and agency', *Philosophy and Public Affairs*, 11 (1982), pp. 3–38. Reprinted in Samuel Scheffler (ed.), *Consequentialism and Its Critics*, Oxford University Press, 1988, pp. 187–223.

Sen, Amartya, with others, *The Standard of Living*, edited by Geoffrey Hawthorne, Cambridge University Press, 1987.

Sen, Amartya, 'Utilitarianism and welfarism', *Journal of Philosophy*, 76 (1979), pp. 463–89.

Sen, Amartya, 'Welfare inequalities and Rawlsian axiomatics', *Theory and Decision*, 7 (1976), pp. 243–62. Reprinted in R. Butts and J. Hintikka (eds), *Foundational Problems in the Special Sciences*, Reidel, 1977, pp. 271–92.

Skyrms, Brian, *The Dynamics of Rational Deliberation*, Harvard University Press, 1990.

Slote, Michael, *Beyond Optimizing: A Study of Rational Choice*, Harvard University Press, 1989.

Slote, Michael, 'Satisficing consequentialism', *Aristotelian Society Supplementary Volume*, 58 (1984), pp. 139–63.

Stocker, Michael, *Plural and conflicting values*, Oxford University Press, 1989.

Strotz, R. H., 'Myopia and inconsistency in dynamic utility maximization', *Review of Economic Studies*, 23 (1955–6), pp. 165–80.

Sugden, R., 'Why be consistent? A critical analysis of consistency requirements in choice theory', *Economica*, 52 (1985), pp. 167–83.

Suppes, Patrick, *Axiomatic Set Theory*, Van Nostrand Reinholt, 1960.

Taylor, Charles, 'Irreducibly social goods', in Geoffrey Brennan and Cliff Walsh (eds), *Rationality, Individualism and Public Policy*, Centre for Research on Federal Financial Relations, Canberra, 1989, pp. 45–63.

Temkin, Larry S., 'Harmful goods, harmless bads', in R. G. Frey and Christopher Morris (eds), *Value, Welfare and Morality*.

Temkin, Larry S., *Inequality*, Oxford University Press, forthcoming.

Temkin, Larry S., 'Intransitivity and the mere addition paradox', *Philosophy and Public Affairs*, 16 (1987), pp. 138–87.

Thomson, Judith Jarvis, 'Imposing risks', in Mary Gibson (ed.), *To Breathe Freely*, Rowman and Allanheld, 1985, pp. 124–40.

Thomson, Judith Jarvis, 'Parthood and identity across time', *Journal of Philosophy*, 80 (1983), pp. 201–20.

Tversky, Amos, 'Additivity, utility and subjective probability', *Journal of Mathematical Psychology*, 4 (1967), pp. 175–201.

Tversky, Amos, 'A critique of expected utility theory: descriptive and normative considerations', *Erkenntnis*, 9 (1975), pp. 163–73.

Tversky, Amos, and Kahneman, Daniel, 'Rational choice and the framing of decisions', *Journal of Business*, 59 (1986), pp. 250–78.

Vallentyne, Peter, 'Utilitarianism and the outcome of actions', *Pacific Philosophical Quarterly*, 68 (1987), pp. 57–70.

Vickrey, William S., 'Measuring marginal utility by reaction to risk', *Econometrica*, 13 (1945), pp. 319–33.

Vickrey, William S., 'Risk, utility and social policy', *Social Research* (1961). Reprinted in Edmund S. Phelps (ed.), *Economic Justice*, Penguin, 1973 pp. 286–97.

Weirich, Paul, 'Expected utility and risk', *British Journal for the Philosophy of Science*, 37 (1986), pp. 419–42.

Wiggins, David, 'Claims of need', in Ted Honderich (ed.), *Morality and Objectivity*, Routledge and Kegan Paul, 1985, pp. 149–202.

Wiggins, David, *Sameness and Substance*, Blackwell, 1980.

Williams, Bernard, 'A critique of utilitarianism', in J. J. C. Smart and Bernard Williams *Utilitarianism: For and Against*, Cambridge University Press, 1973, pp. 77–150. Part reprinted in Samuel Scheffler (ed.), *Consequentialism and Its Critics*, Oxford University Press, 1988, pp. 20–50. Page references to the reprinted version.

Wollheim, Richard, 'A paradox in the theory of democracy', in Laslett, Peter, and Runciman, W. G., (eds), *Philosophy, Politics and Society*, Second Series, Blackwell, 1962, pp. 71–87.

Index